STIR Futures

Trading Euribor and Eurodollar futures

By Stephen Aikin

Hh

HARRIMAN HOUSE LTD

3A Penns Road
Petersfield
Hampshire
GU32 2EW
GREAT BRITAIN

Tel: +44 (0)1730 233870
Fax: +44 (0)1730 233880
Email: enquiries@harriman-house.com
Website: www.harriman-house.com

First edition published in Great Britain in 2006 by Harriman House.
This second edition published 2012.
Copyright © Harriman House Ltd

The right of Stephen Aikin to be identified as Author has been asserted in accordance
with the Copyright, Designs and Patents Act 1988.

ISBN: 978-0857192-19-6

British Library Cataloguing in Publication Data
A CIP catalogue record for this book can be obtained from the British Library.

Printed and bound by Lightning Source.

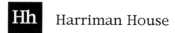 Harriman House

Contents

eBook edition

As a buyer of the print edition of *STIR Futures* you can now download the eBook edition free of charge to read on an eBook reader, your smartphone or your computer. Simply go to:

http://ebooks.harriman-house.com/stirfutures2

or point your smartphone at the QRC below.

You can then register and download your eBook copy of the book.

www.harriman-house.com

About the Author

Stephen Aikin has been a derivatives trader for over 20 years and has worked as a professional training consultant for the last five, delivering finance and derivatives courses to leading institutions in London, Zurich and New York.

He started his career working for several investment banks. In 1988 he became a member of the London International Financial Futures Exchange (Liffe), where he started trading STIR futures on German interest rates. Stephen has specialised in relative value trading – both intra- and inter-contract – and has experienced consistent profitability over 20 years.

He is educated to MSc (Finance) level and holds several professional qualifications in the finance sector.

Preface

Who this book is for

This book is written for the aspiring trader but will also appeal to the experienced trader looking for a new market or trading strategy. Even those traders already experienced in trading STIR futures might find new inspiration and trading ideas from the sophisticated strategies presented in the trading section.

The learning curve is steep and constant, but all the information and concepts needed by the aspiring trader are presented simply and should be easily understood. Some prior knowledge of buying and selling securities might be helpful. The websites of the futures exchanges listed in the Appendices are useful sources of introductory information.

What this book covers

This book does not pretend to be a guide to making a trading fortune, and neither is it selling a trading system. Instead, it is a comprehensive guide to STIR futures markets, showing how professional traders can profit from their unique characteristics, particularly by using spreads and similar trading strategies. It details all the necessary tools and methodologies for these sophisticated trading strategies, appealing to the experienced STIR futures trader, whilst also providing guidance for the aspiring trader.

The majority of trading examples used in the book can be calculated by the use of pre-built functions that are standard within Microsoft Excel, rather than assuming that everyone has access to expensive subscription-based quantitative software.

How this book is structured

The book consists of four parts, designed to be read sequentially. Readers can dip into various sections but might find references to methodologies described earlier.

1. STIR Futures

Part 1 is a broad introduction to STIR futures, describing what they are, where they are traded, how they are priced, and how they can be used to hedge borrowing or lending exposures. This is followed by a comprehensive review of the drivers of STIR futures, which describes the underlying influences that create price movement and how this should be interpreted by traders.

2. The Mechanics of STIR Futures

Part 2 is concerned with the mechanics of the STIR futures markets, including clearing and settlement procedures, how the markets are accessed, the software options available, and what influences the choice of STIR futures contracts to trade.

3. Trading STIR Futures

Part 3 is the trading section, with the majority comprising a thorough analysis of the spread relationships that exist both within STIR futures and against other interest rate products. STIR futures are often described as the 'building blocks of finance', which makes them perfect for spread trading, providing many more trading permutations with lower risk profiles than traditional directional trading instruments.

4. Trading Considerations of STIR Futures

Part 4 covers trading considerations and provides insights into the marketplace and its population, characteristics and the trading decision-making process.

The Appendices supply extra detail, including contact information, for those interested in taking matters further.

Supporting website

A website supporting this book can be found at **www.stirfutures.co.uk**.

Introduction

Most people are only aware of interest rate changes when they make the newspaper or television headlines, but interest rates are moving all the time. They are driven by the supply and demand of money being borrowed and lent in the money markets. STIR futures are one of the key financial derivatives in this market.

STIR futures first appeared in the 1980s as the Eurodollar contract, based on US interest rate deposits traded on the Chicago Mercantile Exchange (CME). CME's success encouraged European emulation, resulting in the formation of the London International Financial Futures Exchange (now NYSE Liffe but referred to as Liffe in the text) in the early eighties and the creation of the Short Sterling (UK rates), Euromark (German rates), Euroswiss (Swiss rates) and Eurolira (Italian rates) STIR futures.

All futures were then traded by a method called *open outcry*. This involved the shouting out of order flow into a circular pit populated by traders wearing the colourful jackets of their company's livery. Nowadays, almost all trading is computerised, creating a global virtual trading pit with no restriction on the number of participants it can hold. Consequently, STIR futures volumes have exploded in recent years. Arguably they are now the largest financial market in the world. It is not unusual for the leading STIR futures contracts, the Eurodollar and Euribor, to each trade over two trillion dollars' or euros' worth of interest rate transactions every day. Compare that with the $150 billion traded on a good day at the New York Stock Exchange, or even with the entire foreign exchange market, which trades approximately $3-trillion-worth per day, and it gives a clear idea of just how large the STIR futures markets are.

However, STIR futures are unique amongst financial markets in that individual traders can compete and trade on equal terms with other participants such as banks and large funds. It is a completely level playing field – unlike other markets, remaining free from domination by middlemen and market makers. Today's fully computerised STIR futures markets support a global network of professional individual traders who benefit from the unique characteristics of these markets. Traders are not restricted to using a broker's service or trading platform but can directly buy and sell into the central marketplace with similar technology and market information as the largest players.

Futures are often perceived as being highly risky trading instruments. This is not helped by the rogue trader scandals of the likes of Leeson, Kerviel and Adoboli, who between them lost $10 billion fraudulently trading futures. Futures have also made it to the silver screen; Hollywood has glamorised futures trading in films like *Trading Places* and *Rogue Trader*. On celluloid, futures trading is highly speculative and an easy route to bankruptcy.

Admittedly, futures can be extremely risky instruments, especially if over-leveraged, but they are a broad class. It is unfair to categorise all futures as having the same risk profile. STIR futures are lower risk than most other types of futures contract and they can provide a lower trading risk profile than shares, currencies or spread betting. They do this by providing consistent returns from a diverse range of low-risk strategies not available in any other financial market.

Recent years have seen a growing number of individuals trading STIR futures for their own account, attracted by the professional direct market access and level terms of competition. Some traders have been very successful. Many more are content with an attractive and flexible lifestyle. Of course, some aspiring traders have discovered that a life in the markets is not for them. But the vast majority of people who leave it behind do so as a personal decision and not because of outlandish losses to be read about in the media.

Hopefully, this book will provide you with the knowledge to trade STIR futures intelligently, allowing you to make your own informed decision about this unique market and financial instrument.

STIR Futures – Quick Summary

1. STIR futures comprise one of the largest financial markets in the world. The two largest STIR futures contracts, the Eurodollar and Euribor, regularly trade in excess of one trillion dollars and euros each day.

2. The STIR futures markets are fully computerised, allowing easy global access.

3. Professional STIR future traders need a minimum capital of approximately £25,000 to start trading their own account, though sometimes nothing is required to join a trading arcade's proprietary trading scheme.

4. STIR futures are one of the lowest-risk financial futures contracts and trading spreads or similar strategies provides an even lower risk profile. Trading STIR futures can provide more frequent and consistent returns with lower risk than most other kinds of financial product.

5. STIR futures are essentially financial building blocks. This makes them very suitable for trading against each other or other interest-rate contracts. The sheer number of trading permutations offered by their range of contracts and spreads allow traders to find their own professional niche.

STIR Futures

1

Introduction to STIR Futures

What are futures?

Futures are derivatives, meaning that they derive their value from an underlying asset like a commodity such as oil or a financial asset such as a bond, stock index or interest rate.

Futures are traded on regulated futures exchanges such as Liffe in London or CME in the United States and are structured as legally binding contracts. This means a counterparty to a trade undertakes to physically or notionally make or take delivery of a given quantity and quality of a commodity at an agreed price on a specific date or dates in the future.

What are STIR futures?

STIR futures are a variety of future contract where the underlying asset is a Short Term Interest Rate.

A short-term interest rate (STIR) futures contract can be defined as:

- a legally binding contract
- notionally to deposit or borrow
- a given amount of a specified currency
- at an agreed interest rate
- on a specific date in the future
- for a specified period.

For example, the three-month Euribor futures contract traded on Liffe is:

- a legally binding contract
- notionally to deposit or borrow €1m
- at an agreed interest rate
- on the delivery date
- for a nominal 90-day period.

This effectively means that a Euribor future provides a mechanism for locking in a forward borrowing or lending rate for a specified amount of euros on a given date for a nominal 90-day period.

This contrasts with a spot borrowing or lending for 90 days, which would be fully funded and unsecured, starting today for 90 days.

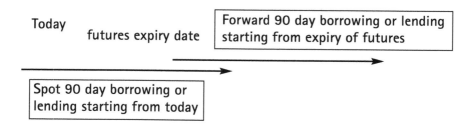

Similarities with other futures contracts

STIR futures are similar to other futures contracts in that they are:

- traded on regulated futures exchanges that provide the legal framework, contract specifications and the trading mechanism

- settled via a central counterparty to remove credit risk between market participants

- characterised by a unit of trading, tick size and settlement procedures.

Differences with other futures contracts

STIR futures differ from other futures in that they:

- have multiple delivery cycles, sequential to several years, covering a broad spectrum of the near-dated yield curve; this means that STIR futures have many different expiries trading simultaneously within the same contract, which allows a unique trading perspective

- have highly similar risk characteristics between delivery cycles

- include spread trading and other trading strategies, allowing many different trade permutations and ideas, with different risk profiles

- are arguably the most liquid class of futures by nominal value.

Derived from interest rates

Futures are broadly classed as derivatives since they are derived from another product; and are called futures since they are not for immediate purchase or sale but at a future date.

STIR futures are derived from interest rates covering a deposit period of three months, extending forward from three months up to ten years. These interest rates refer to near-term money market interest rates which are comprised of the unsecured inter-bank deposits markets (also known as the depo market). From these money markets comes the daily fixing of London Inter-Bank Offered Rate (LIBOR), or its European equivalent: European Inter-Bank Offered Rate (EURIBOR). These are the reference rates that are used to settle STIR futures on expiry.

LIBOR

The London Inter-Bank Offered Rate is defined as the rate of interest at which banks borrow funds from other banks in reasonable market size (e.g. $5m) in the London inter-bank market just prior to 11am London time. It is considered a key benchmark rate in the financial markets, having been in widespread use since 1984. LIBOR covers ten currencies with 15 maturities up to 12 months and is used as the basis for pricing a variety of interest rate products such as floating-rate notes, interest rate swaps, interest rate caps and floors and exchange-traded STIR futures and options.

Reuters acts as official fixing agent on behalf of the British Bankers Association. It determines LIBOR fixings by obtaining rates from contributor banks prior to 11am and these contributed rates are ranked in order, with the top and bottom quartiles removed and the remaining rates arithmetically averaged.

EURIBOR

EURIBOR is very similar to LIBOR but is the market standard for the euro. It was established by the European Banking Federation and ACI with the first EURIBOR rates quoted on 4 January 1999.

The fixing process is similar to LIBOR, with the following differences:

- panel of around 44 of the most active banks in the euro zone area
- this leads to a greater ratio of smaller banks to larger banks in comparison to LIBOR
- computed as an average of quotes for 15 maturities with the top and bottom 15% rejected (rather than top and bottom 25% as with LIBOR)
- published at 11am (CET) daily.

> The LIBOR fixing scandal (2012) will lead to a regulatory reform of the LIBOR and EURIBOR fixing processes. It is highly likely that responsibility for LIBOR will be removed from the British Bankers Association and there will be changes to the fixing methodology.

Movement of interest rates

The following chart shows how these LIBOR rates for UK, USA, Swiss and EURIBOR rates have moved over time and how they have been influenced by major events.

It can be seen that country interest rates are influenced by the state of their economies and market expectations for interest rate levels in the future. Sharp movements are often caused by economic or political events. UK interest rates fell sharply in 1992 when sterling withdrew from the European Exchange Rate Mechanism (ERM) and global rates were cut sharply after 9/11 in 2001, after the tech market collapse in 2002 and the credit crunch in late 2008.

Fig. 1.1 – Three-month LIBOR rates for GBP, USD, CHF and three-month Euribor for EUR

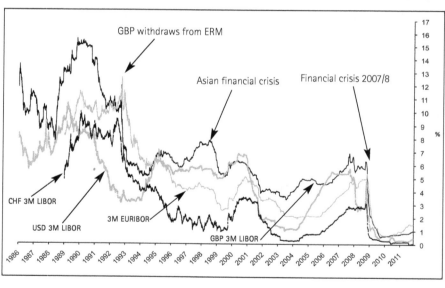

Traded on exchanges

STIR futures are traded on regulated futures exchanges, such as London International Financial Futures Exchange (Liffe) in the UK or the Chicago Mercantile Exchange (CME) in the USA. Nowadays virtually all contracts are transacted electronically via computerised trading. These exchanges provide the mechanism and legal framework for access to their particular markets.

Different exchanges have different STIR products, usually determined by their geographical origins. Euribor futures (based on European interest rates) are traded on Liffe and the Eurodollar futures (based on US interest rates) are mainly traded on CME. However, competition between exchanges can mean that popular contracts are sometimes quoted on several exchanges.

Buyers and sellers of STIR futures connect to these exchanges, either directly as members of the exchange or indirectly using a member as an agent. These buyers and sellers can be banks, corporate treasurers or speculative traders such as hedge funds, proprietary groups or individuals, formerly called locals but now known as liquidity providers (LP). These speculative traders attempt to make money from price action, whereas banks and treasurers tend to use the markets as hedging tools to risk-manage other interest rate exposures.

Exchange-traded futures are often portrayed as having no inherent counterparty risk. Generally this is true for exchange members, since credit risk between the counterparties to a trade is removed by the intermediation of a highly capitalised clearing house, which effectively guarantees each side of the deal, meaning that a buyer of a futures contract need not worry about the creditworthiness of the seller and vice-versa.

However, traders who are not exchange members but use the services of one to access the markets can be at risk of default by the exchange member.

Where and how are they traded

Futures on short-term interest rates are traded by exchanges all over the world, including Europe, the United States, South America, Australia, Asia and Japan. A list of some of these futures is included in the Appendices.

Focus on the big two contracts

Not all contracts are of equal trading stature. Some are a lot larger and more liquid than others and some, although being large and liquid, are not readily accessible or are of different contract design. Examples of the former include Euroyen, and of the latter Australian 90-day bank bills.

Consequently, this book will focus on the two biggest contracts, namely the Euribor future traded on the UK-based Liffe and the Eurodollar future traded on the US-based CME. Other notable STIR futures are Short Sterling on UK rates and Euroswiss on Swiss rates, both traded on Liffe. They are virtually identical in operation and design as the Euribor or Eurodollar, with slightly differing contract specifications. Understand Euribor and Eurodollar futures and you will understand all STIR futures.

As can be seen in the contracts table in the Appendices, some like Eurodollar and Euribor are traded on two or even three exchanges. Most exchanges will try to capture business from other exchanges where they think they may have a competitive advantage, such as time zone or cross-margin incentives. However, even though the computerisation of futures trading has become a global phenomenon, the main pool of liquidity usually remains with the domestic exchange. The UK-based Liffe, hosting the European Euribor contract, is not really an exception given London's status as the capital of Europe's financial markets.

Trading is now computerised

STIR futures used to be traded by open outcry, mainly by loud young men in even louder coloured jackets on crowded trading floors. With the advent of computerisation, the vast majority of STIR futures are now traded electronically. The exceptions tend to be where some degree of negotiation is required during a transitional phase from floor to screen – examples being back-month trading or complex strategies.

Most exchanges' computer systems have an application program interface (API) architecture that allows third parties to build software to run on it. This has led to a market of independent software vendors (ISV) plying a variety of commercial packages, offering the trader connectivity to the majority of exchanges from most major locations. However, unless the trader is a full clearing member of an exchange, he will need to appoint a clearing agent to process and guarantee his trades. This agent is usually a larger financial entity and will assume the trader's risk based on a capital deposit in return for transaction-based commissions.

Directories of clearing members/agents and ISVs can be found on the accompanying website **www.stirfutures.co.uk**.

Contract structure and general specifications

The selling and buying of STIR futures represents a notional borrowing or lending from the money markets. They confer the borrowing or lending at a rate determined by the price at which the future was transacted, for a period of three months after the expiry and settlement of the contract, effectively a forward interest rate.

They are notional in the sense that they are cash settled and so a holding of STIR futures is not used to physically lend or borrow money from the markets. Instead, this notional value or unit of trading, usually a denomination of one million, is used as a proxy. The futures will mirror movements in the underlying market and provide a representative profit and loss.

Contract specifications for the four main STIR futures can found in the appendices. The US Eurodollar specifications are listed below for illustration.

Contract specifications for the Eurodollar contract

Table 1.1 – US Eurodollar contract specifications

Contract	Eurodollar
Exchange	CME
Notional value/unit of trading	$1,000,000
Delivery months	March, June, Sept, Dec, four serial, making a total of 40 delivery months
Price quotation	100.00 minus rate of interest
Minimum price movement	0.005 (0.0025 on front month)
Tick value	$12.50 per half basis point
Last trading day	Second business day preceding the third Wednesday of the contract month
Delivery day	Two business days after the last trading day
Margins (November 2011)	
Initial margin	$608–$1013
Maintenance margin	$450–$750

Explanation of the contract specifications

Exchange

The Eurodollar is traded on CME, part of CME group, a regulated futures exchange. CME Group is comprised of four designated contract markets (DCMs): CME, CBOT, NYMEX and COMEX. The Eurodollar contract is also listed on Liffe.

Notional value/unit of trading

The unit of trading is the *notional value* attached to each STIR future, normally in denominations of one million dollars, euros or Swiss francs or £500,000 in the case of Liffe Short Sterling. This unit of trading is the notional amount that would be nominally deposited or borrowed for three months at the contract's expiry. But since STIR futures are cash settled, these amounts never actually change hands. These units of trading are never at risk and are integral to the contract design only in that they permit a minimum movement increment to be derived.

A Eurodollar future has a notional value of $1,000,000 and this number is used to calculate its minimum movement, usually one or one half of a basis point. The figure of $1,000,000 is multiplied by the minimum permitted increment as designated by the exchange, in this case 0.005% (half a basis point), and then by the quarterly expiry cycle, to give:

$$\$1,000,000 \times 0.005/100 \times 0.25 = \$12.50$$

A *basis point* is one one-hundredth of one per cent (for example, the difference between 4.00% and 4.01%).

Delivery months/Expiry cycle

Each STIR future has a finite life and trades on a quarterly expiration cycle: **March, June, September** and **December** (usually denoted by the symbols H, M, U and Z respectively). The year is usually added to these symbols, so that the cycle in 2012 would be H2, M2, U2 and Z2 going into 2013 as H3, M3 and so on. Serial months in between do exist but are mainly aimed at specific users such as hedgers and often have much less liquidity than the quarterly expiries.

Price quotation and minimum price movements

Method of quotation

STIR futures trade as a quote of 100% minus the interest rate. For example, if interest rates were 4.50 %, the futures would be quoted as 95.500.

This methodology provides price synchronicity to other interest rate products such as bonds, which fall as interest rates rise and rise as interest rates fall. If interest rates were suddenly cut by 0.25% or 25 basis points to 4.25%, the STIR future would rise to approximately 95.75.

Alternatively, the price of the STIR future can be used to back out an implied forward rate by 100% minus the STIR future price%. In the above case, 100% - 95.75% = 4.25%. This STIR futures price implies a forward interest rate of 4.25%, which should be interpreted as a forward starting deposit or borrowing rate and not as to what the market expects three-month LIBOR or EURIBOR to be in the future.

Can STIR futures ever trade above 100?

Yes, although by necessity this would infer a negative implied forward rate. However, this is exactly what happened in 2011 in the Euroswiss STIR future. As a consequence of the 2010/11 European sovereign debt crisis, global investors tended to avoid the euro and invest in 'safe haven' currencies like the US dollar, British pound and Swiss franc. Switzerland is a relatively small global economy and the effect of investors buying the franc drove it to high levels against the euro. The effect of an overvalued currency is to make exports uncompetitive and this affected the profitability of Swiss companies exporting into the European market.

The Swiss National Bank (SNB) responded in August 2011 by pegging the Swiss franc to the euro at a rate of €/CHF 1.20, meaning that if the franc were to appreciate (<1.20) against the euro, the SNB would intervene to sell unlimited amounts of Swiss francs against buying euros. One of the ways that the SNB facilitated this peg was to intervene in the forward FX market, selling Swiss francs for future delivery at a rate which implied negative interest rates against the spot exchange rate (see the later section on FX Swaps).

The Euroswiss futures responded by trading well above 100 during late 2011 and then normalised to around 100 since the three-month Swiss LIBOR, to which the contract settles at expiry, never actually went negative, only the forward rates.

Fig. 1.2 – Chart showing front-month Liffe Euroswiss STIR future (thick black line, upper pane, RH scale), €/CHF exchange rate (thin black line, upper pane, LH scale) and three-month Swiss LIBOR (black line, lower pane, RH scale)

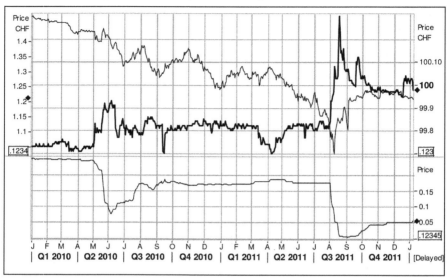

Tick size

The smallest permitted increment is known as the *minimum price movement* and is expressed in basis points. Derived from this figure and the notional value of the contract is the *tick value* which is the monetary value of the minimum price movement.

In the case of the Eurodollar contract, the minimum movement is half a basis point with a tick value of $12.50. This can be expressed as:

$1,000,000 (unit of trading) x 0.005/100 (minimum price movement) x 0.25 (quarterly expiry cycle) = $12.50

The nearest-dated Eurodollar front-month contract can trade in a quarter-of-a-basis-point tick value worth $6.25.

Tick values are known figures and do not need to be calculated by the trader. They are used to determine profit and loss and the risk sensitivity of the contract to changes in interest rates.

For example: If a trader were to buy one Eurodollar future at 95.50 and sell it at 95.51, they would have a profit of 2 ticks (1 basis point) or 2 x $12.50 = $25. If they had bought and sold two contracts at the same prices, the profit would be $50.

Price quotations

A quick look in the financial pages or exchange website might show the following quotes.

Table 1.2 – STIR futures example quote

Month	Symbol	Price	High	Low
Mar	H	95.50	95.48	95.53
Jun	M	95.45	95.43	95.48
Sep	U	95.41	95.39	95.44
Dec	Z	95.38	95.35	95.41

Each quarterly month has a price, which is the settlement price or closing price for that day's business. Note that all four quarterly expiries trade concurrently and in relation to each other. The high and low values show the day's range or the minimum and maximum prices traded during that session. However, this display is of historical prices from a previous trading session and if current price data were to be used, then the prices would appear something like this.

Table 1.3 – STIR futures example quote with current price data

Month	Symbol	Bid	Offer	Last	Volume	Change
Mar	H	95.50	95.51	95.51	40555	+0.01
Jun	M	95.46	95.47	95.47	30667	+0.02
Sep	U	95.41	95.42	95.42	28909	+0.02
Dec	Z	95.39	95.40	95.40	18909	+0.02

Some notes on the quote:

- **Bid/offer spread**
  The notable difference with the historic quote is the bid/offer spread. These are the selling/buying prices. The trader could sell March at 95.50 or buy it at 95.51, similar to the way shares are traded.

  The difference between the bid price and offer price usually reduces to the minimum price movement, in this example 0.01; but in Eurodollar or Euribor would be 0.005, such as 95.505 bid 95.510 offered.

- **Last price**

  The last price shows where business is currently being transacted. In this case it appears to be buying at the offer price and this is supported by the change column depicting the positive difference between the last traded price and the previous settlement price.

- **Volume**

  The volume shows the liquidity in the market. In this example, the combined four months have traded a total of 119,040 contracts, each contract being based on a notional value of $1 million, €1 million or £500,000, depending on the contract specifications.

The examples above have only used the first four months for the sake of expediency. In reality, the prices extend out for several years on the same quarterly cycle to the extent dictated by their individual contract specifications.

The quarterly cycle is also colour coded, the first four quarters being called the whites, the next four being the reds, the next four being the greens, the next four being the blues and the next four being the golds – contract specifications permitting. Sequences of STIR futures are generically called *strips* and so the first four quarterly expiries can be called the white strip, followed by the red and green strips. However, strips can comprise any number of futures and not just be determined by colour.

Table 1.4 – Example of coloured yearly sequences as seen at the beginning of 2012

Code	Expiry year	Colour
H2	First quarterly expiry	WHITE
M2		WHITE
U2		WHITE
Z2		WHITE
H3	Year 2 quarterly expiry	RED
M3		RED
U3		RED
Z3		RED
H4	Year 3 quarterly expiry	GREEN
M4		GREEN
U4		GREEN
Z4		GREEN

As time progresses, and the front contract expires, the contracts will move forward one place so that, for example, on the expiry of the H2, the M2, U2, Z2 and H3 will be the new white strip.

Last trading day and settlement

The last trading day is the expiry of the STIR future and is normally 11am (London time) to coincide with the LIBOR fixing for that day. That LIBOR fixing will determine the exchange delivery settlement price (EDSP) as:

100 - three-month LIBOR fixing on expiry day

The settlement day is normally two business days after the last trading day to reflect the T (trade) + 2 days settlement convention in the London Interbank money markets. However, the settlement for any STIR futures is cash-based and never results in an actual borrowing or lending.

Margins

Buyers and sellers of STIR futures deposit margin with the clearing house, which acts as a guarantor of trades and largely removes counterparty risk from the exchange-trading process. Margin can be regarded as collateral against possible losses and the amount of margin depends on the size of open positions; it can be posted in cash or securities.

There are two primary forms of margin.

- **Initial margin** (also known as scanning risk)
  This is the deposit required to initiate either a short or long futures position reflecting the risk of the underlying future.

- **Variation margin**
  This is a daily profit and loss calculated on a mark to market basis.

Any profit will be credited to the margin account and may be withdrawn but any losses will be debited to the margin account and these losses might have to be covered if there is a margin shortfall.

There is another form of margin called **maintenance margin**.

If the funds remaining available in the margin account are reduced by losses to below a certain level, known as the maintenance margin requirement, a trader will be required to deposit additional funds to bring the account back to the level of the initial margin.

Maintenance margin levels tend to be around 75% of initial margins and act as a buffer for exchange members.

The Eurodollar futures contract specifications list the initial margin in December 2011 as being $608 to $1,013 and the maintenance margin as being $450–$750. The exact amount of margin will vary with the expiry month but the general premise is that the more volatile the contract, the higher the margin, and vice versa.

The following table shows four days of price movements for the Eurodollar to illustrate the margin cash flows process.

The initial margin is assumed to be $1,000 and the maintenance margin is $750. The tick size for the Eurodollar is $12.50 per half basis point.

Day 1 – One Eurodollar is purchased to open at a price of 95.50 and the contract settles (closes) at the same price for that day. Consequently, there is no profit or loss and therefore no variation margin requirement but $1,000 must be lodged with the clearing house as initial margin.

Day 2 – The price has gone up to 95.55, giving a mark-to-market profit of $125 (10 ticks x $12.50) which is credited to the margin account and could be withdrawn if required.

Table 1.5 – four days of price movements for Eurodollar

	Closing price	Change on day (ticks)	P&L on day	Variation margin	Total margin
Day 1	95.500	0	0	0	$1,000
Day 2	95.550	+10	$125	$125	$1,125
Day 3	95.450	-20	-$250	-$125	$875
Day 4	95.350	-20	-$250	-€375	$625

Day 3 – The price has now fallen to 95.45, a loss of 20 ticks from the previous close. This is a loss of $250 (20 x $12.50), which is deducted from the margin account which is now reduced to $875. This is lower than the initial margin but higher than the maintenance margin so no action needs to be taken.

Day 4 – The price has fallen further to 95.35, adding a further loss of $250. This reduces the total margin to $625, which is lower than the maintenance margin of $750 and therefore more cash needs to be added to restore the balance to the initial margin level ($1,000). Failure to do so might result in foreclosure of the position by the clearing house.

Buying and selling STIR futures

The principles of buying and selling STIR futures and spreads are similar to those of stocks, bonds or commodities. Buying low and selling high will return a profit, and selling high and buying low will do the same.

Futures are transacted to *open* or *close*. This is market terminology for entering and exiting trades. A purchase or sale to open is entering a new trade or position. A purchase or sale to close is exiting an existing trade or position. Remember that in futures markets, it is as easy to sell to open, as it is to buy to open.

For example: If one STIR future is purchased at 95.50 to open and sold at 95.51 to close, a profit is made.

- If this were a Liffe Short Sterling future, where one tick is equivalent to one basis point then the profit on the trade would be £12.50.

- If it were a CME Eurodollar, where one tick is equal to half a basis point with a tick value of $12.50, then the profit would $25 (2 x $12.50).

It is sometimes easier to think of STIR futures profits and losses in terms of basis point values (BPV). This is often referred to as *duration*, expressed per basis point, also known as DV01 (dollar value of one basis point) and is a measure of the sensitivity of the underlying instrument to a change of one basis point in interest rates.

One basis point on the Eurodollar and Euribor would be €25 and $25 respectively. Remember that these contracts have a tick value of €12.50 and $12.50 due to the fact that their minimum price increment is half a basis point. Therefore two ticks make a basis point.

One basis point on the Euroswiss and Short Sterling is worth CHF25 and £12.50 respectively, since both these contracts have a tick value equal to one basis point (Short Sterling is £500,000 contract size).

Consequently, the profit or loss on any STIR future can be calculated by:

Number of contracts x difference between opening price and closing price in basis points x BPV

For example, if 100 Euribor are sold to open at 96.62 and bought back to close the position at 96.605, the profit would be:

100 x 1.5 x €25 = €3,750

If 50 Short Sterling are bought at 95.45 and sold at 95.44, the loss would be:

50 x 1 x £12.50 = £625

Note how the difference between opening price and closing price is expressed in basis points; otherwise the results need to be multiplied by 100 to compensate for the basis point convention. The difference between 95.45 and 95.44 is one basis point.

Buying and selling STIR futures as notional borrowings and lendings

It is hardwired into STIR futures contract specifications that:

- selling = notional borrowing

- buying = notional lending.

This can be shown by extending the previous examples of buying and selling STIR futures and determining the resulting profit or loss.

A previous example stated that:

If 100 Euribor are sold to open at 96.62 and bought back to close the position at 96.605, the profit would be:

100 x 1.5 x €25 = €3,750

An alternative way to look at this is that the opening sale is a proxy for a notional borrowing of €100 million (100 x €1million contract size) at a rate of 3.38% (100 - 95.62) for three months after the futures expiry.

The closing purchase is a proxy for a notional lending of €100 million (100 x €1 million contract size) at a rate of 3.395% (100 - 95.605) for three months (0.25 year) after the futures expiry.

Putting both sides of the trade together means that €100 million has been borrowed at 3.38% and lent out at 3.395% over the same forward period (three months being a standardised 0.25 of a year).

This would result in a profit of €100 million x (3.395% - 3.38%) x 0.25 = €3,750, the same as above.

Introduction to spreads and strategies

STIR futures are unique amongst financial markets in that they have many different expiry months trading simultaneously as part of the same contract. For example, a

STIR future such as the CME Eurodollar can have as many as 40 different quarterly expiries trading at the same time. All of these expiries are based on the same STIR future, and will have the same specifications, but will differ slightly in that they all have different expiries and so their prices will change at slightly differing rates according to underlying drivers such as changes in the term structure of interest rates.

These small differences in the price action between expiries give rise to the spread markets and related trading strategies.

Spreads

A *spread* is simply the differential between two expiries, created by buying one month and selling another. For example, a H2 future can be purchased and a M2 future sold in equal quantity, which will result in a H2M2 spread. If H2 was purchased at 95.51 and M2 sold at 95.46, the spread would be bought at a difference of 0.05 (95.51 - 95.46). This spread is called a three-month spread since there is three months' difference between expiries. Spreads can have many different permutations such as six-month, nine-month and 12-months but are subject to some common rules.

The nearest dated expiry is always quoted first in the calculation of the spread price so that its formula will appear as:

$$Future_{nearestdated} - Future_{furthestdated}$$

Spreads are quoted with a bid and offer price just like the outright futures contracts, but are quoted as a differential. They can be positive or negative and are quoted as separate instruments so that, for example, the H2 and M2 expiries will have individual quotations and so will the H2M2 spread. Trading the spread as an independently quoted contract involves the simultaneous transaction in both underlying months but with no execution risk.

The table shows some prices for the outright futures in the top box and some strategies in the lower box.

Table 1.6 – Quotes for standard STIR futures

Futures	Symbol	Bid	Offer
March	H2	95.50	95.51
June	M2	95.46	95.47
Sept	U2	95.41	95.42
Dec	Z2	95.39	95.40

Table 1.7 – Quotes for standard STIR spreads

Strategies	Symbol	Bid	Offer
3 month spread	H2M2	0.03	0.05
3 month spread	M2U2	0.04	0.06
6 month spread	H2U2	0.08	0.10
Butterfly	H2M2U2	-0.03	0.01

The three-month and six-month spreads are the differentials between the outright futures. Note how the bid/offer spreads in the two component outright futures of a spread will create a wider spread bid/offer, totalling the combined bid/offer spreads of the two futures. In reality, market participants would tighten these quotes.

Butterfly

The last entry in the lower table is a *butterfly*, which is a variation on a spread. Whereas a spread is the differential between two futures contracts, a butterfly is the differential between two spreads. It can be quoted in two ways, firstly as the difference between two spreads so that in the example above, it would be created by:

H2M2 - M2U2

Since the individual spreads are quoted as 0.03/0.05 and 0.04/0.06 respectively, the butterfly quote will be buying the first spread at 0.05 and selling the second spread at 0.04 to give an offer price of 0.01 (0.05 - 0.04) and a bid price of 0.03 - 0.06, equalling -0.03.

The second method of quoting the butterfly is by using the outright futures in the following formula:

$$(Future_{nearestdated} + Future_{furthestdated}) - (2 \times Futures_{middledated})$$

So that the butterfly offer price would be:

(buying H2 at 95.51 + buying U2 at 95.42) - (2 x selling M2 at 95.46) = 0.01

And the butterfly bid price would be:

(selling H2 95.50 + selling U2 at 95.41) - (2 x buying M2 at 95.47) = -0.03

Spreads and other trading strategies will be examined in much more detail later in the book, but hopefully this introduction will have highlighted the many trading permutations that spreads and strategies offer, as opposed to purely directional outright trading.

Spreads and butterflies carry lower risk than outright futures and can move in more predictable fashions, making them ideal instruments for the professional trader.

A typical trader's screen

Although there are many different software packages offering access to the STIR futures markets, they are usually of a typical layout, and will be considered in greater depth later.

Fig. 1.3 – A typical STIR trading screen featuring Easy Active Trade from Easyscreen (www.easyscreen.com). Used with permission

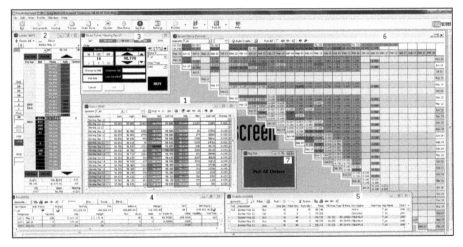

This screenshot shows a Windows-based display with the principal trading windows as follows:

1. watch window showing Liffe Short Sterling futures

2. ladder window showing a single Liffe Euribor future

3. order ticket, in this case to buy 16 Z3 Short Sterling futures at 98.77

4. risk window showing positions, margin requirements and profit/loss

5. order book showing working and completed orders

6. spread matrix displaying permutations of Euribor spreads

7. big pull window, enabling deletion of all working orders across all markets.

The advantages of trading STIR futures compared to other financial products

Be a price maker, not a taker

The modern trader is faced with the choice of many products to trade. There are stocks and shares, contracts for difference, foreign exchange and options to name a few. However, there always seems to be a middleman getting in between the trader and the market, be it someone obvious like a stockbroker or something less tangible like a wide bid/offer spread on a currency quote. Most markets will only offer the non-institutional trader agency access, meaning that the trader will usually be required to trade off someone else's price quotes, which creates an instant disadvantage. If a security is bought with a quoted selling/buying price of 50–52 at 52, there is an immediate loss since the selling price to exit the position is now 50. The trader might not want to sell immediately but there's no denying that paper loss on a mark-to-market basis. Furthermore, the market needs to rise two points before a break-even point is reached. Add in a commission, if applicable, and it's easy to understand why many traders fail. A trader would need to be right seven or eight trades out of ten to get ahead.

Futures offer a different approach to trading. Traders can still be price takers like in the example above, but they can also be a price maker. This means that the trader can be the party quoting 50–52, hoping that someone sells to him at 50 or buys from him at 52. It's immediately apparent that this can be a much more advantageous way to trade, particularly when, in reality, the huge liquidity of STIR futures markets creates a tight bid/offer spread which gives guidance as to where the market is and, most importantly, has other buyers and sellers bidding and offering the same prices in case the trader wishes to close out the position. Traders also have the benefit of being able to sell short just as easily as buying long. There are no additional costs involved.

Deep liquidity

STIR futures are amongst the most liquid financial markets in the world. It is virtually unheard of not to have a liquid market in all conditions, even in times of economic or political turmoil. Indeed, events that might cause problems in other financial markets, such as 9/11 (which closed the NYSE), led to huge trading volumes in global STIR futures. STIR futures also remained liquid during the worst moments of the financial crisis of 2007/8.

The liquidity of STIR futures is based on the cumulative order flow of thousands of traders and institutions, and not just quotes provided by a few market makers. This means that large orders, for example trades of between 1000 and 10,000 lots (1 to 10 billion of notional value) can trade at any one time, particularly in the larger Euribor or Eurodollar contracts and are usually easily absorbed by the markets.

A mathematical dependency

STIR future prices have a very clear reference to their underlying interest rates and market expectations for future interest rate levels, which provides traders with a good idea of their value, either absolutely or relative to each other, as in the case of spread trading.

Low costs

Trading costs are low for trading relatively large amounts of interest rate futures. To buy and sell one lot of Euribor (which is €1m notional of interest rate futures) would cost approximately €0.75 to €1.50, but would yield a potential profit (or loss) of €12.50 on a minimum movement. Trading rebate schemes can reduce these fees substantially.

Lower volatility

STIR futures have much lower volatilities than most other financial markets, meaning that they move around a lot less. The following chart shows the volatilities for the Eurostoxx 50, a European stock market index and Euribor futures. The Eurostoxx 50 volatilities range from a norm of around 20% to almost 100% in times of financial turmoil, whereas the Euribor futures are much less volatile (annualised price volatilities usually less than 1%) perhaps making it a more predictable product to trade.

Fig. 1.4 – Volatilities (close-to-close with 10-day observations) for Eurostoxx 50 (thick black upper line) and Euribor futures (lower) from 2006 to 2012 using logarithmic scale

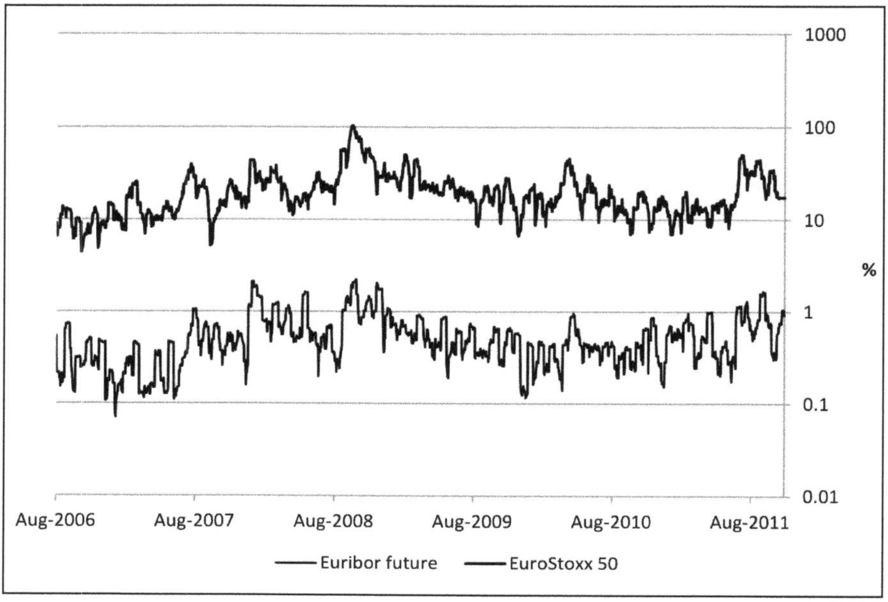

Many trading permutations

All these advantages can apply to most financial futures, but STIR futures offer further trading advantages. Because they have multiple expiries listed on the same contract, this offers the trader more choices. He could sell H2 or M2, or buy red September or buy green December. Indeed, many traders specialise in trading certain maturity cycles such as the reds or greens, rarely trading the front whites. Traders can also trade one maturity or expiry against another. For example, you might purchase H2 and sell M2 against it to trade the spread between the two contracts. You might buy H2, sell M2, sell M2 and buy U2 and trade the differential between the two spreads. It doesn't stop there. There are many trading permutations within STIR futures, which allow the traders to find a niche for themselves. However, make no mistake, there is little easy money in STIR futures. Subsequent chapters will look at the trading of STIR futures in much greater detail but first it is important to appreciate how STIR futures are priced relative to the underlying interest rates.

STIR Futures Pricing

Spot and forward rates

STIR futures settle to three-month LIBOR or EURIBOR and their prices should be derived from the rates underlying the LIBOR/EURIBOR fixing process, and those interest rates are short-term rates from the money markets. Money markets comprise both cash deposits rates (also known as depos or spot rates) and money market instruments. It is the former with which this section is primarily concerned.

Deposit rates

Most readers will be familiar with the concept of deposit rates. A bank will offer the depositor a choice of term and interest rate for the money. Usually, but not always, the longer the money is left, the higher the interest rate that is received. This depends on the outlook for interest rates but, generally, depositors will be rewarded with higher rates for the longer they leave their money. This shape of the deposit rate structure (or *yield curve*) where long-term rates are higher than short-term rates is termed *positively sloping*. The deposit rate will be fixed for the term of the deposit. The following table shows the some example deposit rates for euros.

Table 1.8 – Example of Euro Interbank rates

Term	Rate %
1 month	4.45
2 months	4.52
3 months	4.54
6 months	4.58
9 months	4.62
12 months	4.66

Let's say an author agreed a €200 advance for a book. Half is receivable today, and the other half in nine months' time when the manuscript is delivered. The first €100 could be deposited at a fixed rate and be assured that the rate quoted at inception would be the rate for the term of the deposit, whether it be one month or three.

Continuing this analogy, €100 is duly deposited today at the rate of 4.54% for three months. The author is happy, although a bit concerned about newspaper reports suggesting lower UK interest rates in the future. He is increasingly concerned that in nine months' time, deposit rates may not be as high as they are today. Since he will not receive the other £100 for nine months, the deposits market is not applicable and he really wants to lock in an interest rate for, say, three months that starts, not today as in the case of deposits, but in nine months' time – which introduces the forwards market.

Forwards market

The forwards market is concerned with forward-starting interest rates. These are contracts where a deposit or borrowing rate is determined today for a deposit or borrowing starting on some predefined date in the future for a specified period.

The author is then faced with the problem of determining the three-month interest rate starting in nine-months' time. The diagram below shows that the nine-month rate is 4.62% and the 12-month rate is 4.66%, so it's just a question of working out the value of the missing three-month period between nine and 12 months. This can be viewed diagrammatically as:

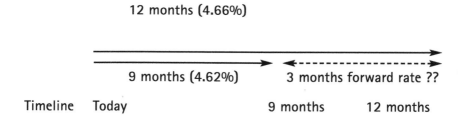

It is possible to mathematically solve for the 'missing' three-month period between 12 months and nine months by working through the cash flows if €100 were deposited in two different ways.

1. Since the 12-month rate is known to be 4.66%, funds could be deposited for that period at that rate. Depositing €100 for 12 months at 4.66% would provide €4.725 interest at maturity (€100 x 4.66% x 365/360) (using a European money market date convention of Act/360 and assuming 365 days in the year).

2. A similar sum could also be deposited for nine months starting from now until nine months hence at the rate of 4.62%. Depositing €100 for nine months at 4.62% will give €3.465 (€100 x 4.62% x 270/360) (assuming nine months is 270 days).

What needs to be done now is to solve for the rate at which the nine-month deposit could be reinvested for a further three months so that the total of interest received from both nine-month and three-month deposits is the same as that of the single 12-month deposit. This rate will be the nine-month forward rate.

Working this through gives the following cash flows:

- The nine-month deposit needs an additional €1.26 (€4.725 - €3.465) to be earned by reinvesting the nine-month deposit for a further three months so that this method equals the amount that could have been made by just investing in the 12-month deposit.

- However, the original €100 is now worth €103.465 after nine months and so this is reinvested for a further three months. This concept of earning interest on the interest is called compound interest. The rate at which it is reinvested for the €103.45 to generate €1.26 in interest is then calculated by:

- €1.26 / (€103.465 x 90/360) = 4.87 % (assuming 90 days in the three-month period) and this is the forward rate for three months, starting in nine months' time.

This concept can be expressed mathematically as a closed form formula using the relative of discount factors. These are effectively the present value of €1 at time t.

For example, if 9M EURIBOR is 5%, then the value today of €1 in nine months' time can be calculated as:

$$\frac{1}{1+(5\% \times \text{Act}/360)}$$

This would be the nine-month discount factor and if the 12-month discount factor were known, the three-month forward rate starting in nine months' time could be calculated by:

$$\text{Forward Rate}_{tn,\,tn+1} = \frac{\left(\dfrac{Df_{tn}}{Df_{tn+1}} - 1\right)}{\text{AccrualFactor}_{tn,tn+1}}$$

Where *Df* is the discount factor either at the start or end of the forward period and the accrual factor is the proportion of the year which the forward rate covers (tn to tn+1), incorporating the correct year base convention (360 days in the case of the euro and USD and 365 days for GBP)

Populating this equation with the numbers from the above example gives:

$$\frac{\left[\dfrac{\dfrac{1}{1+4.62\% \times \dfrac{270}{360}}}{\dfrac{1}{1+4.66\% \times \dfrac{365}{360}}} - 1 \right]}{\dfrac{90}{360}} = 4.87\%$$

This allows for the easy calculation of forward rates by use of a spreadsheet, omitting the need to work out individual cash flows each time, and gives the same answer as the manually calculated example using the cash flows. 4.87% is the forward rate that could be expected based upon the given deposit rates and this is the rate, fixed today, at which the author could expect to place €100, receivable in nine months' time, on deposit for three months.

In theory, there needs to be no advantage in depositing in either a single 12-month deposit or by investing in a nine-month deposit rate and a nine-month forward for three months. However, in reality the market forward rate is always a little less than its theoretical rate since the market attaches risk to progressively longer-term fully-funded unsecured deposits.

Forward rates are very dependent on the shape of the spot yield curve. If the yield curve is positively sloped, then forward rates will be higher than spot rates. Conversely, in a negatively sloped curve, forward rates will be lower than spot. This means that a derivative based upon forward rates like a Euribor or Eurodollar future might appear to be predicting higher or lower rates in the future but not necessarily so. The forward curve is a mathematical equilibrium that has to hold a particular relationship to the spot yield curve and doesn't necessarily contain any information about the market's future expectations of interest rates.

STIR Futures Valuation

Basic pricing concepts

STIR futures:

confer the borrowing or lending at a rate determined by the price at which the future was transacted, for a period of three months after the expiry and settlement of the contract.

This is the same concept as the forward rate except that the STIR future is a derivative and so its traded price will *imply* a forward rate.

Implied forward rates from STIR futures can be calculated as:

100% – STIR futures market price%

The value basis

Value basis is the difference between an equivalent term LIBOR or EURIBOR derived forward rate and the implied forward rate from a STIR future:

Equivalent term LIBOR/EURIBOR derived forward rate – STIR futures implied forward rate

The value basis is a measurement of the implied forward rate of the STIR futures contract relative to the equivalent term forward rate.

Using the previous forward pricing example, the three-month forward rate starting in nine months' time was found to be 4.87%. If the actual market price of an equivalent term STIR future was 95.15 (giving an implied forward rate of 4.85%), then the value basis would be 0.02% (4.87% - 4.85%). This could be interpreted as the STIR futures trading *expensively* in price terms (95.15 versus 95.13) or *cheaply* in rates terms (4.85% versus 4.87%).

Valuing Euribor futures

Valuing STIR futures is complex, incorporating several concepts that are cornerstones of financial modelling but complicated in theory and application. However, it is not essential to the understanding or application of STIR futures. Readers can skip it if they prefer.

The following sections depict how traditional STIR futures valuations models work. The process is contained within Bloomberg Professional, specifically the EUS <GO> page for the Euribor contract.

So far, two discount factors have been calculated (nine-month and 12-month discount factors) and used to calculate a three-month forward rate starting in nine months' time and then compared to the implied forward rate of an equivalent-term STIR future.

This process needs to be accurately replicated for all the required futures expiry dates. This will allow the comparison of the sequential forward rates with the implied forward rates from the STIR futures.

The process is as follows:

1. Determine a discount curve. This is a plot of discount factors of various maturities.

2. Interpolate the discount factors to match the futures dates.

3. Compare the forward rates with the implied forward rates from the STIR futures and identify any areas on the futures strip that might be considered under- or over-valued.

The discount curve

The discount curve needs to be calculated from spot rates on AA-rated securities in the currency of the relevant STIR future.

In the case of the Euribor STIR future, this would comprise EURIBOR fixings (or more specifically EURIBOR depo rates since EURIBOR is a survey-based fixing not an actual borrowing rate) and euro swaps. A swap is an interest rate derivative that replicates a fixed borrowing or lending at a weighted average of forward EURIBOR rates. It is a very liquid market, representative of the interbank AA credit curve (as determined by credit rating agencies like Standard & Poor's or Fitch).

Euribor rates are quoted in maturities from overnight to 12 months and euro swaps are quoted from one year to 50 years.

Discount factors from deposit rates can be calculated from:

$$Df_{deposits} = \frac{1}{1 + EURIBOR \times AccrualFactor}$$

Where EURIBOR is the relevant term Euribor rate and the accrual factor is the year fraction incorporating the correct day count convention – in the case of Euribor, this would be Act/360.

Extracting discount factors from swap rates is more complicated but the standard industry methodology is:

$$DF_n = \frac{1 - Swap_n \times \sum_{t=1}^{n-1} DF_t \times A_t}{1 + Swap_n \times A_n}$$

Where $Swap_n$ is the relevant term swap rate and

$$\sum_{t=1}^{n-1} DF_t \times A_t$$

this is the sum of the preceding discount factors (DF) times the accrual factor (A) at time $_t$.

It is beyond the scope of this book to derive this formula but a good book or course on swaps pricing should make this standard process clearer. What this formula does do is extend the discount curve beyond the 12-month limitation of EURIBOR rates by incorporating swap rates until a discount curve is produced covering a range of maturities.

Table 1.9 – Euro AA-rated discount curve on 28 October 2011 for value 1 November using EURIBOR rates for spot/next, one, three and six-month and swaps for one year onwards

Trade date	28-Oct-11 Fri	Spot Value	2	Spot date	1-Nov-11 Tue
Depos & Swap term	Dates	Rates (%)	A/360 Deposit Accrual	30/360 Swap Accrual	Discount Factors (DF)
SN	2-Nov-11 Wed	1.1360	0.0028	0.0028	0.999968
1M	1-Dec-11 Thu	1.3660	0.0833	0.0833	0.998863
3M	1-Feb-12 Wed	1.5920	0.2556	0.2500	0.995948
6M	1-May-12 Tue	1.7930	0.5056	0.5000	0.991017
1Y	1-Nov-12 Thu	1.6700		1.0000	0.983574
2Y	1-Nov-13 Fri	1.5650		1.0000	0.969435
3Y	3-Nov-14 Mon	1.7300		1.0056	0.949692
4Y	2-Nov-15 Mon	1.8800		0.9972	0.927933
5Y	1-Nov-16 Tue	2.0560		0.9972	0.902679
6Y	1-Nov-17 Wed	2.2800		1.0000	0.872190
7Y	1-Nov-18 Thu	2.3900		1.0000	0.845809
8Y	1-Nov-19 Fri	2.5000		1.0000	0.818256
9Y	2-Nov-20 Mon	2.6200		1.0028	0.788808
10Y	1-Nov-21 Mon	2.6800		0.9972	0.763565

Interpolating discount factors to match the futures dates

Once the discount curve has been produced, the discount factors need to be interpolated to match the futures expiry dates.

Interpolation is the method of constructing new data points within the range of a discrete set of known data points. The known data points are the discount factors derived from EURIBOR and swap rates and the new data points are the futures expiry dates and the superseding three-month period.

There are various interpolation methods available including:

- linear interpolation of discount factors

- linear interpolation of the logs of the discount factors

- cubic spline interpolation on the zero yield curve or discount functions

Generally the second and third methods give more consistent results but are more complex to implement.

Table 1.10 – Implied forwards from futures and theoretical forwards derived from linear interpolation of the logs of the discount factors from EURIBOR rates and swaps

Dates	Futures	Futures	100−F (convexity adjusted)	Interpolated discount factors	Implied forwards from futures	Theoretical forwards
	3W Euribor		1.297%	1.00000	1.297%	1.297%
21-Nov-11 Mon	X1	98.465	1.535%	0.99928	1.535%	1.362%
19-Dec-11 Mon	Z1	98.600	1.400%	0.99809	1.400%	1.582%
19-Mar-12 Mon	H2	98.785	1.213%	0.99461	1.213%	1.850%
18-Jun-12 Mon	M2	98.835	1.161%	0.99160	1.161%	1.726%
17-Sep-12 Mon	U2	98.825	1.169%	0.98873	1.169%	1.490%
17-Dec-12 Mon	Z2	98.770	1.221%	0.98585	1.221%	1.457%
18-Mar-13 Mon	H3	98.695	1.292%	0.98285	1.292%	1.424%
17-Jun-13 Mon	M3	98.595	1.388%	0.97968	1.388%	1.424%
16-Sep-13 Mon	U3	98.495	1.483%	0.97630	1.483%	1.424%
16-Dec-13 Mon	Z3	98.355	1.618%	0.97269	1.618%	1.721%
17-Mar-14 Mon	H4	98.225	1.742%	0.96877	1.742%	2.024%
16-Jun-14 Mon	M4	98.070	1.891%	0.96457	1.891%	2.024%
15-Sep-14 Mon	U4	97.905	2.049%	0.96003	2.049%	2.024%

Table 1.10 shows the futures expiry dates for the November 2011 (X1) contract out until the September 2014 contract (U4). The implied forward rate from the futures is derived from 100 - Price (convexity adjusted – see subsequent pages) and the theoretical forward rates derived from interpolated discount factors from EURIBOR rates and swap rates using:

$$\text{Forward Rate}_{tn, \, tn+1} = \frac{\left(\dfrac{Df_{tn}}{Df_{tn+1}} - 1 \right)}{AccrualFactor_{tn, tn+1}}$$

Where Df is the discount factor either at the start or end of the forward period and the accrual factor is the proportion of the year which the forward rate covers (tn to tn+1), incorporating the correct year base (360 days in the case of the euro).

Implied forward rates from futures versus theoretical forward rates

The last two columns of the table show the implied forward rates from the STIR futures and the **theoretical** forwards derived from the discount curve based on

EURIBOR and swap rates. These forwards from discount factors are theoretical since they are not market quotes.

Graphing these shows the disparity between them. The difference between them is the value basis.

Fig. 1.5 – Euribor futures implied forward rates versus theoretical forward rates – 1 November 2011

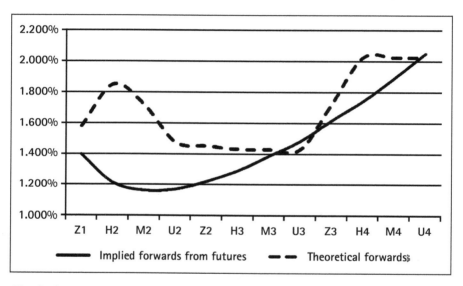

Clearly there is not much of a link between them. And yet there should be. Both are supposedly the same thing; namely a three-month forward rate starting at specified time in the future. The value basis is the difference between these two curves and is wide with no discernible pattern.

Drivers of the value basis

What is being observed here is a dislocation between the forwards derived from EURIBOR rates and the implied forwards from the STIR futures based upon them.

Prior to the financial crisis of 2007/8 the forward curve and implied forward curve from the futures were almost identical, with arbitrage being cited as the prime reason why these two curves should not diverge.

However, all this changed in the financial crisis. The effects remain today. From 2007, interbank lending linked to EURIBOR and LIBOR rates largely dried up and counterparty risk was transformed from a relatively minor and unlikely risk into a major risk. Banks that had traditionally partially funded themselves by borrowing via interbank transactions found that counterparty banks no longer wanted to lend, since interbank transactions are fully funded but unsecured. A default by the borrower could have serious ramifications.

Central banks responded to this drying up of interbank liquidity by offering unlimited overnight money and term repo transactions (secured lending) to banks, meaning they no longer had to rely on the interbank markets for funding. This led to a collapse of volume and business in interbank markets, meaning that EURIBOR and LIBOR quotes (and therefore EURIBOR and LIBOR-derived forward quotes) were largely arbitrary.

However, STIR futures, being derivatives, continued to actively trade – and paradoxically became a market proxy for the three-month forward curve, even though it was a derivative on a market that had largely ceased to function.

The two forward curves in the chart now show a value basis reflecting the risk between a EURIBOR forward curve effectively constructed from cash borrowings and lendings that carry multiple hazards of counterparty risk, funding risk and term risk (see following sections) compared to the forward curve from futures containing none of these hazards.

Advanced pricing concepts

Convexity and the convexity bias

Changes in the prices of STIR futures like Eurodollars and Euribor futures are driven by changes in the underlying interest rates. STIR futures trade at a fixed basis point value ($25 or €25) irrespective of the level of interest rates and therefore their price sensitivity to a change in rates is linear and has no convexity.

> **For example:** A change in interest rates from 5% to 5.01% would imply a change in STIR future value from 95.00 to 94.99, which on one contract such as the Euribor would be worth €25. This would be the same if interest rates changed from 2% to 2.01%, therefore showing that the basis point value does not change relative to the level of interest rates.

STIR futures are often used to hedge instruments like bonds and interest rates swaps (see later chapters). Bonds and swaps do not have fixed basis point values as underlying rates change and therefore exhibit convexity in their price/rate relationship. Generally, the value of a basis point on a bond or swap diminishes as rates increase and increases as rates fall.

This means there can be an inherent advantage in receiving the fixed rate on an interest rate swap, which is a convex instrument, and hedging the interest rate risk by being short STIR futures with no convexity.

Receiving the fixed rate on a swap is like lending via a sequential series of LIBOR or EURIBOR-linked forward rates, and this could be hedged by being short STIR futures (a notional borrowing).

- As interest rates increase, the basis point value of the swap will decrease whereas the STIR future basis point value will remain constant, leading to a small potential profit on the hedge. Being short STIR futures in a rising interest rate environment will make a trader money and receiving fixed on an interest rate swap in a falling interest rate environment will lose a trader money but at a diminishing rate.

- As interest rates fall, the basis point value of the swap will increase, whereas the STIR future basis point value will remain constant, leading to a small potential profit on the hedge. Being short STIR futures in a falling interest rate environment will lose money and receiving fixed on an interest rate swap in a falling interest rate environment will make money at an increasing rate.

However, the situation is made more complex due to the different settlement procedures between STIR futures and swaps.

Futures are settled daily and their profit or loss added or subtracted to or from the margin account, whereas the floating side of a swap settles only on the swap's setting dates.

- If interest rates increase, the futures price will fall, leading to a profit on the short STIR futures position and a margin credit that can be reinvested at higher rates.

- If interest rates fall, the futures price will increase, leading to a loss on the short STIR futures position and a margin deficit; but this can be financed at the lower rates.

The advantages in being short STIR futures against receiving fixed swaps result in the markets quoting implied forward rates from STIR futures at higher rates (making the STIR futures price lower) than they would otherwise be. This effect is termed the *convexity bias*.

There are several methods of calculating the convexity bias, most of which are complex, and readers with further interest are directed to the recommended reading below.[1] Convexity bias generally increases with term and is driven by volatility and mean reversion of interest rates.

---

[1] 'Convexity Conundrums', Risk (March 1997), **www.powerfinance.com/convexity**

The pricing example in Table 1.10 has a convexity bias for the Euribor U4 futures of 4.6 basis points.

The markets are well aware of the convexity bias and therefore the implied forward rate of the U4 future has to be adjusted. 4.6 basis points is deducted from the forward rate implied by the future to obtain an unbiased implied forward rate. The Euribor U4 was trading at 97.905, implying a forward rate of 2.095%, which is reduced to a convexity-adjusted 2.045%.

Another method: stringing/chaining

Comparing forward rates derived from a discount curve to the equivalent implied forward rates from STIR futures can be problematic due to the sensitivity of the forward curve in relation to changes in the discount curve and interpolation methodologies.

An alternative valuation methodology is stringing or chaining. Here, a zero coupon yield is determined for a particular maturity derived from a discount curve based on deposit rates and swaps and compared to an equivalent term strip of futures linked (hence 'stringed' or 'chained') together to match the maturity.

The diagram shows two timelines:

Fig. 1.6 – Stringing/chaining

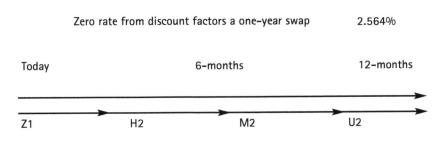

The top timeline is a one-year swap expressed as a zero rate (for example, 2.564%) and the bottom timeline is a strip of four STIR futures linked together to give a zero rate (for example, 2.167%). Comparison of the two zero rates can identify cheap or expensive parts of the strip (in this case, the futures strip appears cheap in rate terms compared to the swaps).

A zero rate is essentially the yield to maturity on a zero coupon bond which is devoid of reinvestment risk. Reinvestment risk is a feature of any asset like a swap that throws off intermediate cash flows that have to be reinvested at the original return. Otherwise the total return if held to maturity can be distorted. Zero rates are considered pure and homogenous interest rates ideal for financial modelling.

Zero rates can be backed out of discount factors derived from deposits and swaps by:

$$Z_n = \left[\frac{1}{DF_t} \right]^{\left[1/\sum_{t=1}^{n-1} t,t_t \right]} - 1$$

Where Z_n is the n term zero rate, DF is the discount factor at time t and

$$\sum_{t=1}^{n-1} t,t_t$$

is the sum of the accrual factors to time t.

For example, the zero rate from a one-year swap with a discount factor of 0.975 where $t = 1$ would be:

$(1/0.975)^{(1/1)} - 1 = 2.564\%$

The STIR futures can be linked together to form a zero rate by:

$$[(1 + IFR_1 \times accrual) \times (1 + IFR_2 \times accrual) \times (1 + IFR_3 \times accrual)...\times(1 + IFR_n \times accrual)] - 1$$

Where IFR is the implied forward rate from the futures (100% - Price%) and the accrual is the year fraction covered by the future (0.25).

For example, using the following prices:

Table 1.11 – Example prices

	Market price (P)	IFR (100% – P%)
Z1	98.00	2.0%
H2	97.90	2.1%
M2	97.80	2.2%
U2	97.70	2.3%

And stringing the futures together …

$$[(1+2.0\% \times 0.25) \times (1+2.1\% \times 0.25) \times (1+2.2\% \times 0.25) \times (1+2.3\% \times 0.25)] - 1 = 2.167\%$$

In this simplified case, the zero rate from the futures strip at the one-year term appears cheap and undervalued compared to the zero rate from the one-year swap. It is effectively saying that if €1 were invested in the swap, there would be a return after one year of 2.564%, but if the same €1 were invested in a quarterly compounded strip of four STIR futures, the return would only be 2.167%.

This process, refined for market accrual conventions, start dates and futures expiries can be extended along the entire futures strip and the results viewed graphically as a term structure of zero rates between swaps and futures. Using the data for the previous study on Euribor futures on 1 November 2011, the cash and futures strings appear as in the graph.

Fig. 1.7 – Cash string (chains) from swaps compared to futures strings – Euribor futures 1 November 2011

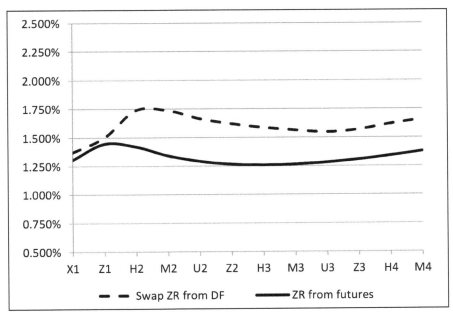

The graph shows a similar pattern to the prior graph of Euribor futures implied forward rates versus theoretical forward rates on 1 November 2011. This methodology gives smoother results but a basis is still evident with a difference of approximately 0.25% at the two-year point, which is due to term risk.

Term risk (tenor basis)

At first sight this appears to be an arbitrage opportunity – for example, the opportunity to enter into a two-year swap to receive a higher rate than what would be paid out by stringing together a strip of equivalent- term STIR futures. However, the word arbitrage denotes a risk-free profit – but in this case a trader attempting to monetarise this difference is taking on a hidden risk which accounts for the 0.25% difference.

The trade would be constructed by first receiving the fixed rate on the two-year euro swap. A swap denominated in euros is a bilateral derivative made up of two sides: one side is the exchange of an annual fixed rate of interest in return for the other side, which is a semi-annual floating rate of interest based on six-month EURIBOR. The trader would elect to enter into the swap transaction as the fixed rate receiver, meaning that they have an obligation to lend out the semi-annual floating payments based on six-month EURIBOR. The fixed rate received on the swap at inception would actually be the weighted average of these six-month EURIBOR forward rates being paid out. Secondly, the trader would borrow every three months for two years at three-month EURIBOR, with forward rates locked in by constructing a two-year strip of Euribor futures from individual contracts strung together.

The hidden risk here that accounts for the 0.25% difference between receiving the higher rate on the swap and borrowing at the lower rate in the Euribor strip is due to term risk. Remember that EURIBOR is an unsecured rate and consequently a credit premium exists for term lending versus rolling funding in shorter intervals. A trader that rolls three-month borrowings for three months has the option to cancel every three months, whereas a trader who lends for a six-month term does not. The difference of 0.25% is the credit premium demanded by the markets to reflect the credit and liquidity perceptions between three- and six-month EURIBOR in November 2011.

This risk can be hedged out by use of another derivative – a basis swap. A EURIBOR/EURIBOR basis swap is a floating-for-floating exchange of (netted) cash flows, where each floating side references a distinct EURIBOR fixing – in this case three- and six-month EURIBOR rates. Basis swaps are quoted as a spread against the shorter underlying tenor and the payment is determined by the longer tenor. For example, the 6s3s (sixes into threes) EURIBOR/EURIBOR basis swap is quoted as the three-month EURIBOR + spread with the payment frequency being six-monthly (with the three-month side being compounded). In November 2011, the 6s3s EURIBOR basis swaps were unsurprisingly trading around 0.25%, thus negating any scope for profit if a true risk-free arbitrage was required.

It should be noted that this example has been simplified to highlight the concept of term risk and has not touched upon other issues like the fact that a swap transaction would start almost immediately, whereas the STIR strip is forward starting. This issue and others will be explored later.

In conclusion, STIR futures pricing has evolved through the financial crisis from what was formerly a fairly simple comparison between forward rates derived from LIBOR and EURIBOR rates and the implied forward rates from STIR futures, to a complex methodology which draws in relative value comparisons and adjustments using other complex derivatives. Traders should try to be aware of these new influences on STIR pricing.

Hedging with STIR futures

Hedging is where an existing financial risk is offset by taking an opposite position in another instrument or market.

For example, a company might have an existing borrowing requirement and they hedge by selling interest-rate futures contracts.

If interest rates rise, the higher borrowing cost will be offset by profits on the futures position. However, a futures hedge will offset both losses and gains and in the example above, if interest rates fall, the lower borrowing cost will also be offset, this time by losses on the futures position.

A simple hedging example

It is March and a European Hotel Group has agreed to acquire a German hotel for €25m in June. The company plans to issue permanent capital to finance the purchase three months later in September. The treasurer has established a EURIBOR flat line of credit to finance the gap from June until September but fears that interest rates may rise between now and June.

The treasurer could sell 25 Euribor June futures at 97.00, implying a borrowing rate of 3% starting from the expiry of the June future (which is assumed to be the same as the start of the three-month borrowing period) for 0.25 years.

Fig. 1.8 – Diagram of hedging example

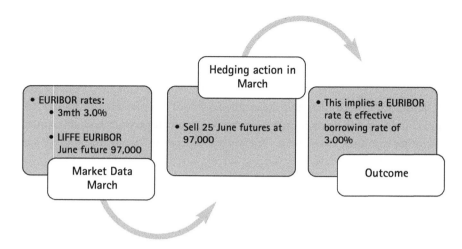

Fast-forward to June and the treasurer's fears have been confirmed. The three-month EURIBOR rate has risen to 3.25%, leading to higher three-month borrowing costs. The expiring futures on the same day as the borrowing starting would have an EDSP of 96.75 (100 - 3.25) which would result in a profit of €15,625.

25 contracts x €25 (BPV) x 25 basis points = €15,625

The cost of borrowing €25 million for three months (say 90 days) would be €203,125:

25,000,000 x 3.25% x 90/360 = €203,125

Meaning that the net borrowing cost was only €187,500 (203,125 - 15,625).

This amount expressed relative to the amount borrowed results in a net annualised borrowing rate of 3%, exactly the same as implied by the futures price of 97.00 when sold in March.

187,500/25,000,000 x 360/90 = 3%

Hedging considerations

This hedging transaction worked perfectly for a variety of reasons, all to do with the hedge requirements being met perfectly by the standard features of the STIR future, notably:

Principal at risk

- 25 futures exactly matched the borrowing exposure of €25 million.

Exposure period

- The borrowing period of 90 days in a 360-day year was exactly the same year fraction as that of the futures contract.

- The start and end of the borrowing period coincided with the futures expiry dates.

- Zero basis risk as convergence between cash and futures was complete.

Exposure basis

- The company was borrowing at a EURIBOR-linked rate and there was no basis risk on the relationship between the borrowing rate and EURIBOR.

Margin flows

- The futures profit or loss is always received or paid before the loss or profit on the underlying borrowing.

- If any of these conditions do not apply the hedge will not be as perfect.

A more complex hedge...

Consider a more complex but realistic hedging variation on the above example ...

> It is March and a hotel group has agreed to acquire a German hotel for €25m in **mid-May**. The Company plans to issue permanent capital to finance the purchase **two months later in July**. The Treasurer has established a **credit line linked to two-month commercial paper rates to finance the gap from May until July** but fears that interest rates may rise between now and May.

In this situation, using a June Euribor future would introduce basis risk if the June futures price was not exactly the same as three-month EURIBOR on the borrowing date in May. The June futures would have to be sold in mid-May, which is about one month before the futures expiry date, and there is no reason for the futures price to have converged to the three-month EURIBOR rate by then. Any difference between the implied rate from the future and the actual borrowing rate will affect the overall effective borrowing rate on the hedge.

Furthermore, 25 contracts would not be applicable since the treasurer only wants to borrow €25 million for two months, not three, and the company is borrowing at a rate linked to commercial paper rates not EURIBOR rates.

Solution

This is an example of where STIR serial futures are applicable. A *May* future could be used instead, and even though the expiry day of the future might not be exactly the same as the borrowing day in mid-May, the implied rate from the future would be very close to the three-month EURIBOR rate.

However, the treasurer is not borrowing at three-month EURIBOR but a two-month commercial paper rate, so a regression analysis would be necessary to quantify how one rate changes in relation the other, resulting in a Beta statistic, assumed here to be 1.05, meaning that if EURIBOR rates increase by one basis point, then two-month commercial paper rates would increase by 1.05 basis points.

Also, only a two-month borrowing period is required, so the sensitivity of the borrowing to a basis point change in rates (BPV or basis point value) is required. Assuming that the two-month borrowing period is 62 days, then the BPV of the borrowing would be:

€25,000,000 x 0.01% x 62/360 = €430.56

Dividing this BPV by the BPV of the May future (€25) returns 17.22 (430.56/25) and this is the approximate number of May futures that should be sold. Approximate because two-month commercial paper rates might be assumed to be more volatile than EURIBOR rates as shown by the Beta of 1.05 and therefore the hedge should be increased accordingly.

17.22 x 1.05 = 18.08

There is also the comparatively minor issue of tailing the hedge.

Variation margin flows occur on the futures during the operation of the hedge and interest can be earned or paid on these flows, depending on whether these flows are positive or negative. In contrast, interest on the actual borrowing is only settled at the end of the borrowing/lending period. The effect of margin flow interest will increase the magnitude of the flows and so the hedge must be scaled down by applying a variation margin leverage factor such as:

$$\cfrac{1}{1+i\left[\cfrac{\dfrac{D_h}{2}+D_b}{B}\right]}$$

Where i is the short term interest rate, B is the number of days per year, D_h is the length of the hedging period and D_b is the length of the borrowing period.

In this case, using a short rate of 3% with the hedging period being from March to mid-May, (say 60 days) and the borrowing period being 62 days, the variation margin leverage factor is 0.9924.

$$\cfrac{1}{1+3\%\ x\left[\cfrac{\dfrac{60}{2}+62}{360}\right]} = 0.9924$$

and the hedge ratio should be reduced accordingly to compensate for the margin flows benefits.

18.08 x 0.9924 = 17.94

Of course, it is not possible to sell 17.94 May futures but the tailing hedge and Beta factors can be useful in deciding to round up or down. In this case 18 May futures should be sold.

Populating the example

March: In March, three-month EURIBOR was observed to be 3% and two-month commercial paper rates were 3.13%. 18 May futures were sold to hedge the borrowing exposure of €25 million for 62 days starting in mid-May.

Mid-May: By mid-May interest rates had increased as feared. Three-month EURIBOR is now 3.25% and two-month commercial paper has increased to 3.39% (hence a beta of 1.05). The futures are repurchased at 96.74. This is not quite the same as 100 - 3.25 since an assumption is made that the borrowing date and futures expiry date is not quite the same and so there is a small basis. This would result in a profit of:

18 contracts x €25 x 26 basis point = €11,700

This would be sat in the margin account accruing interest whilst the cash borrowing of €25 million at 3.39% for 62 days would result in interest due of €145.958.

€25,000,000 x 3.39% x 62/360 = €145,958

The net borrowing cost was €134,258 (145,958 - 11,700).

This amount expressed relative to the amount borrowed results in a net annualised borrowing rate of 3.12%:

134,258/25,000,000 x 360/62 = 3.12%

Fig. 1.9 – Diagram of the populated example

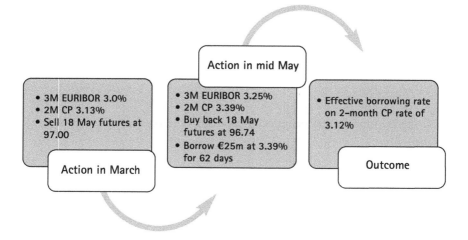

This is very close to the two-month commercial paper rate in March of 3.13%, which the treasurer via the hedge was trying to lock in. It is not perfect due to the basis between the price that the futures were bought back at (96.74) and the three-month EURIBOR rate on that day (3.25%). In this case the futures were implying a EURIBOR rate of 3.26%, which gave an improvement of one basis point on the effective borrowing rate on two-month commercial paper.

Basis can affect the effective borrowing rate when the futures have to be repurchased to close before their expiry. If the basis is wide it can either improve the effective borrowing rate by making it lower or increase it by making it higher.

In reality, the basis within the final month to expiry is usually +/-10 basis points, decreasing toward zero in the final week. Provided a STIR future with an expiry date within two weeks of the borrowing date is used, then basis risk can be contained within an acceptable tolerance. However, other factors like whether the beta between three-month EURIBOR and two-month commercial paper calculated from a backwards-looking data sample was actually representative of the borrowing period can be an additional influence on the accuracy of the hedge.

When hedging non-standard exposures with standardised instruments like STIR futures, hedging can be more of an art form than a science!

Fig. 1.10 – Basis between September 2011 futures and three-month EURIBOR June 2011 to September 19 2011 (basis RH axis)

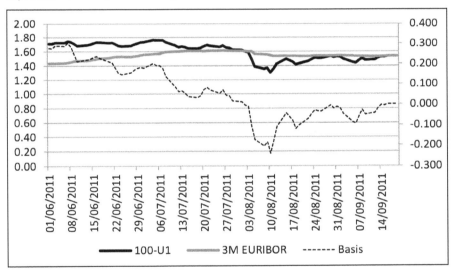

The Drivers of STIR Futures Prices

There are two broad categories of drivers behind the prices (and change in the prices) of STIR futures: changes in the futures curve and price-sensitive effects.

The changing shape of the futures curve

STIR futures are implied forward rates and sequential strips of STIR futures are representative of a three-month forward curve based on derivatives. These sequential STIR futures prices can contain market expectations of future interests

The curve is constantly changing

Although it has been said earlier that curves tend to be positively sloping, that is, longer-dated rates tend to be higher than nearer dated rates, the curve can take many shapes. In times of falling interest rates, all or part of the curve might be negatively sloping, where the longer-dated rates are lower than the near-dated ones. Curves can move sharply from one shape to another as illustrated by the chart that shows data from 2006–2008.

Fig. 1.11 – Euribor implied forward curve (100% – Price%) 2006–2008

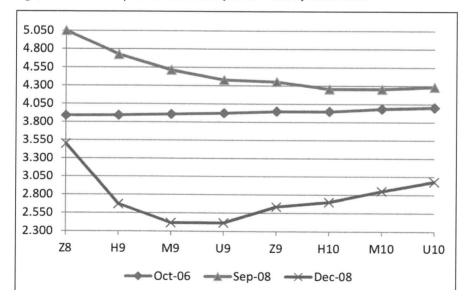

The October 2006 curve shows the implied forward curve from Euribor futures starting Z8 until U10 and the curve is slightly positive with no great expectations built in.

Fast-forward two years to September 2008 and the Lehman crisis. Expectations of future interest rate cuts produce a negatively shaped curve. This effect is magnified by December 2008 when a rapidly slowing global economy increases expectations of even lower rates, resulting in a curve which is partly steeply negative and partly positive. Here the futures curve is suggesting that rate cuts will bottom in the euro zone around 2.30% during early 2009 before moving back up later in the year or early 2010. History proved that rates were to move lower (1%) and stay there for a considerable period.

However, futures curves are normally not static for long. New data and forecasts, right or wrong, constantly influence the outlook for rates and hence the STIR futures price curve. The yield curve will always be a melting pot of opinion and expectations, ensuring that STIR futures will be active products to trade!

Liquidity considerations of the micro-curve

The micro-curve can be considered to be the local effects on a small segment of the curve. STIR futures are generally liquid to around three to five years but differing levels of liquidity along with market expectations can give rise to small distortions. These distortions can create opportunities in certain trades such as spreads and strategies.

These distortions are based upon the concept of liquidity preference. Users of STIR futures often tend to trade the front, white months, which reflect about a year's interest rate expectations. Consequently these months or contracts tend to have the highest traded volume and be the most liquid markets, in turn attracting new trade for precisely that reason.

The following table shows the Eurodollar data from the close of business on 8 December 2011. The data includes the contract, settlement (closing) price, net change from the previous day's settlement price, total traded volume and open interest (number of open contracts).

Table 1.12 – Selected Eurodollar data – 8 December 2011

Month	Settle	Change	Volume	Open interest
Dec–11	99.4475	0.005	164,537	973,289
Jan–12	99.435	0.010	4,096	28,177
Feb–12	99.420	0.015	62	6,557
Mar–12	99.390	0.010	241,149	906,333
Apr–12	99.390	0.015	–	426
May–12	99.375	0.015	–	255
Jun–12	99.360	0.015	256,590	1,092,429
Sep–12	99.350	0.020	185,540	779,396
Dec–12	99.350	0.020	171,105	758,081
Mar–13	99.360	0.020	171,582	770,612
Jun–13	99.345	0.025	146,899	569,078
Sep–13	99.315	0.035	109,552	445,338
Dec–13	99.240	0.045	111,480	521,817
Mar–14	99.130	0.050	87,211	365,495
Jun–14	98.975	0.055	74,571	304,308
Sep–14	98.805	0.060	71,170	214,183

Source: CME

The Eurodollar shows how H2 and M2 have the highest volume and open interest and are the main points of liquidity on the STIR price curve – not the front month Z1 that is close to expiry (note how the December contract trades in quarter basis points in line with its contract specifications and how only the first serial month has any volume or open interest). Volumes steadily decline from these points onwards until around the 2018 contracts, where volumes are very low but there is tangible open interest. Arguably, a trader wishing to execute a large order would be more inclined towards trading H2 to Z3 contracts simply because the market is more able to accommodate the business.

The net change shows a general curve flattening where longer-dated rates have declined more than shorter-dated rates (longer-dated futures have gone up more in price than shorter-dated futures).Often, the back months might be higher or lower than the front, reflecting changing curve shapes but usually in progressive amounts. However, the incidence of a large trade in a particular month can sometimes differentiate prices, particularly intra-day. Traders can take advantage of these small kinks in the price curve with a variety of trades.

Seasonal influences

Sometimes, the contracts covering the year-end, namely the December contracts, can trade at a slightly higher yield than those surrounding them. This is put down to tighter credit conditions in the inter-bank money markets and hence a slight rate premium in the banking system over the Christmas and New Year period. It first became apparent due to a botched liquidity operation from the Federal Reserve Bank in the US during the 1980s and consequently became a pricing characteristic of the market structure, although its effects did diminish during the 1990s. The notion of tighter year-end rates was reinvigorated over the millennium when the December 2000 contracts of all major STIR futures contracts fell sharply on Y2K and bank financing fears, which ultimately proved unfounded. However, the markets do have a memory and, on balance, the December contracts do tend to trade relatively cheaper to their adjacent expiries.

Turning to the other driver of STIR futures …

Price-sensitive effects

Price-sensitive effects are causes that influence the STIR futures price. They include economic data, interest rate sensitive comments by central bankers, influences of other markets and event and systemic risks.

Economic data

STIR futures prices are influenced by the interest rate outlook which, in turn, is dependent on the state of the underlying economy. Economic statistics, reflecting the state of the economy, are released on a monthly basis and some are eagerly anticipated by the markets looking for new direction. Banks, brokers and information vendors provide calendars of impending economic releases and their corresponding forecasts. Some are available free over the internet. (See the Appendices for details.)

Economic releases are usually released at the following times:

- UK: 0930 GMT

- US: 1330 GMT and 1500 GMT (0830 ET and 1000 ET)

- Eurozone: 0700, 0900, 1000 GMT (0800, 1000, 1100 CET)

Economists provide forecasts of upcoming economic releases and financial markets can move significantly in reaction to figures that deviate from their consensus. Some figures are consistently more important than others and some are of more cyclical importance. Sentiment surveys tend to be cyclical indicators of economic turning points. Most international markets closely watch US economic releases since America is the world's largest economy and if America catches a cold – as they say – everybody sneezes.

Below is a list of the main economic releases. This is not meant to be a comprehensive list, but includes the main and most consistent market movers. The figures relate to all three economic areas of the United States, Europe and UK unless a release is indicated as being country specific.

Employment

The US figure, Non-Farm Payrolls is probably the most closely watched indicator in world financial markets. It is usually released on the first Friday of each month and is a barometer of whether the economy is creating jobs or not, and so is a reflection of the health of the economy itself. The figure includes both the private and public job data and so needs to be analysed beyond the headline number to see whether one sector has unduly influenced the figure. The private business sector payrolls will be most important and revisions of the previous month's data can also have price-moving effects. A lower than anticipated Non-Farm Payroll number will tend to cause the STIR futures prices to increase, reflecting the possibility of a slowing economy and lower interest rates. The reverse holds true for a higher-than-anticipated figure.

A weekly jobless figure is released every Thursday but has less influence.

Domestic employment data for other countries will normally have a lesser, local effect.

Gross Domestic Product (GDP)

Gross domestic product is a national report measuring how quickly an economy is growing. It is issued quarterly and is a reflection of economic output. A weaker than expected figure will tend to cause the STIR futures prices to increase. However, bear in mind that the quarterly GDP lags other monthly indicators. This means that the market may well have already anticipated its effect. The figure is released in a series of estimates and then later revised. Watch out for the GDP deflator and price index constituents which are broad indicators of inflationary pressures.

Retail Sales

Retail sales are a monthly report of consumer spending. Retail sales account for approximately 30% of all consumer spending and that itself can account for up to

75% of economic activity. The figures are subject to large revisions in subsequent months. A lower than consensus number will tend to cause the STIR futures prices to increase, indicating economic weakness.

Consumer Price Index (CPI)

A very important number for financial markets, being the most popular measure of inflation in retail goods and services. It is released monthly and a lower figure will boost markets whilst a higher number will infer higher interest rates since the majority of central banks target inflation via the setting of interest rate levels. No monthly revisions.

Producer Price Index (PPI)

PPI, like CPI, is another price level indicator but measures the change in prices paid by businesses. It is a composite of several PPIs, but the most important component tends to be the finished goods PPI that can reflect price pressures in the manufacturing process. It will have the same effects on markets as CPI – some consider PPI changes to be a precursor for CPI changes. Watch out for the core PPI number.

Purchasing Managers Index (PMI)

The main US PMI is the Institute for Supply Management (ISM) Manufacturing Survey, important because it is a private survey issued on the first business day of the month and represents demand for manufactured products. This in itself is an indicator of economic activity.

PMIs are also issued by the euro zone and the UK and have similar characteristics.

A number strongly above the median of 50 can cause STIR futures to sell off and a weak number well below 50 can have the opposite effect.

University of Michigan Sentiment

This US survey is a private indicator of consumer attitudes on the business climate, personal finance and retail, reflecting a sample of 500 individuals. It is regarded as being a superior consumer confidence figure and it is released at 0945 (ET) on the second Friday of each month. It tends to be a more closely watched number at turning points in the growth of the economy.

Consumer Confidence

Another indicator of consumer outlook. It differs from the University of Michigan figure in that it concentrates more on attitudes to employment and is drawn from a new sample each month.

Durable Goods

A monthly US figure based on future manufacturing activity. Important since it is a forward-looking indicator, gauging production in the months ahead. Durables are goods lasting three years or more. It can be one of the first numbers to indicate a forthcoming change in the state of the manufacturing economy.

Industrial Production

A monthly figure of industrial output, issued in the US, UK, and Europe in the main form of the German industrial production number.

German IFO Business Survey

An important figure issued by the largest economy in the euro zone, and therefore closely watched by Euribor STIR futures traders. It is a predictive indicator of economic performance based upon survey answers from 7,000 German business leaders in the main sectors of manufacturing, retail, construction and wholesale. The figure is presented in three forms: Climate, Situation and the most widely watched Expectations index. The Expectations component is a forward-looking indicator of industrial production and has a good history of forecasting changes.

It is issued in the fourth week of every month. A higher than consensus number will cause Euribor futures to sell off.

German ZEW Economic Sentiment Indicator

The ZEW Economic Sentiment Indicator is released monthly, usually on the second or third Tuesday of the month. Up to 350 financial experts take part in the survey and the indicator reflects the difference between the share of analysts that are optimistic and the share of analysts that are pessimistic for the expected economic development in Germany over the course of six months.

Housing

Housing statistics are regarded as being a good indicator of the state of the economy. The US issues New Home Sales (sales of new single family homes), Existing Home Sales (sales of previously owned single family homes) and Housing Starts (numbers of new homes being built and future construction permits). The main UK figures are the Royal Institute of Chartered Surveyors (RICS) Survey (300 surveyors and estate agents in England & Wales are asked if they feel prices are falling or rising) and a monthly House Price Index issued by the Office of the Deputy Prime Minister. Other surveys are supplied by Nationwide, Halifax, Hometrack and Rightmove.

Table 1.13 – Summary of the effects on STIR futures prices caused by economic releases

Economic release	Country	Higher than consensus forecasts	Lower than consensus forecasts	Market effect ranking
Non Farm Payrolls	US	↓	↑	High
US Weekly Jobless claims	US	↑	↓	Low
GDP	All	↓	↑	Med/Low
Retail Sales	All	↓	↑	High
CPI	All	↓	↑	High
PPI	All	↓	↑	Med High
PMI	All	↓	↑	Med
Consumer confidence	US	↓	↑	Med/High
University of Michigan	US	↓	↑	Med/High
Durable goods	US	↓	↑	Med
Industrial production	All	↓	↑	Med
Housing	All	↓	↑	Med

Interest rate announcements

Interest rate announcements by the main central banks are of great importance to the STIR futures markets. They are made at regular intervals and are eagerly awaited by the markets. Central bankers do not decide in advance of a meeting as to whether interest rates should be increased or decreased. Instead they analyse the latest statistics and reports, discuss, and then decide. Market expectations are usually guided by central bankers' rhetoric to align the consensus with the outcome.

U.S. Federal Reserve ('Fed')

The Federal Open Market Committee (FOMC) consists of the seven-member Board of Governors and five of the 12 regional Fed presidents. They vote on monetary policy by simple majority. The FOMC holds eight regularly scheduled meetings during the year, and other meetings as needed. They release the result of the vote, along with names of how each person voted, at the same time as they announce the interest-rate decision. The Federal Reserve releases its meeting minutes three weeks later and these are eagerly awaited for indications of future interest rate expectations.

European Central Bank (ECB)

The Governing Council of the ECB meets twice-monthly, but interest rate decisions are usually taken at the first meeting, typically the first Thursday of the month. The ECB decides by consensus, rather than formal vote, of its 18 Governing Council members and a majority carries decisions. However, if there is a tie, the president has the casting vote.

No detailed information is available about how decisions are taken, since no minutes are released and no breakdown of a vote provided.

Bank of England (BOE)

UK interest rate decisions are made by the nine-member Monetary Policy Committee comprising the Governor, the two Deputy Governors, the Bank's Chief Economist, the Executive Director for Markets and four external members appointed directly by the Chancellor. The interest rate decisions are announced at noon on the Thursday of the first or second week of the month. Decisions of the Monetary Policy Committee are made on a one-person one-vote basis, with the Governor having the casting vote if there is no majority.

BOE policy meeting minutes are usually released on the third or final Wednesday on the month of the policy meeting and are eagerly received by the markets. Policy meeting minutes can be one of the most influential releases for shaping market interest rate expectations.

Central banker rhetoric

The main function of a central bank and its central bankers is the monitoring and regulating of interest rates in the economy.

An old joke goes:

> **Q.** How many central bankers does it take to screw in a light bulb?
>
> **A.** Just one. He holds the light bulb and the whole earth revolves around him.

In financial markets, it is not so much light bulbs as comments on interest rate policy around which the financial world revolves. Announcements from central bankers are followed closely; every nuance is examined for an indication of the future direction of interest rates. Central bankers have cultivated the art of sometimes saying a lot but revealing little. Speeches can be deliberately obtuse – rarely will bankers be explicit in their commentary.

However, central bankers do inform market participants when their behaviour is not consistent with that of the central bank, or when market expectations need guidance. Sometimes markets will price in a rate rise or cut too aggressively and the bankers need to communicate this via speeches or interviews. This managing of expectations is done in the hope that markets can be smoothly guided to a homogenous viewpoint. The aim is to achieve this with the minimum of price volatility, but it can often create price action in the STIR futures markets.

Case Study: An example of managing expectations – European Central Bank (ECB) 2011

In March of 2011, European central bankers discussed an increase of eurozone interest rates to 1.25% in April 2011 in response to perceived inflationary pressures having kept them frozen at a record low of 1.0% for almost two years.

The press conference of the ECB meeting held on March 3rd provided the platform, resulting in a one-day fall in the Euribor M11 futures of almost 20 basis points (40 ticks) as markets reappraised future rate expectations.

The following are selected ECB board members' and central bankers' comments after this meeting.

"Keeping interest rate policy unchanged while headline inflation rises – even if core inflation remains unchanged – implies a de facto allowing for the monetary stance to become more accommodative. Over time this is likely to impact on core inflation."

LORENZO BINI SMAGHI (EXECUTIVE BOARD), MARCH 4

"A rate hike next month is possible but not certain at this point."

"Clearly the risks to inflation are on the upside and it is the mission of the ECB to prevent those from materialising, so we are ready."

JOSE MANUEL GONZALEZ-PARAMO (EXECUTIVE BOARD), MARCH 4

"So far, inflation expectations have remained fairly well anchored, but we know that there are risks with having a number of months with an excessive inflation rate due to the cost of commodities and energy."

"Some question marks start to arise that some pressure for second-round effects develops, some pass-through is being seen."

CHRISTIAN NOYER (FRANCE), MARCH 4

"I think President Trichet said the right thing: it's possible but not on auto-pilot" [on being asked whether a rate hike should be expected]. *"I wouldn't do anything to try to correct market expectations at this point"* [on being asked if he is comfortable with market anticipations of an ECB rate rise to 1.75% by year-end].

AXEL WEBER (GERMANY), MARCH 8

"An increase in interest rates at the next meeting of the Governing Council in April is possible, but it is not certain."

"This is certainly not a decision on the start of a series of interest rate increases."

JOZEF MAKUCH (SLOVAKIA), MARCH 10

"Strong vigilance is the message that has been given and that is still relevant."

EWALD NOWOTNY (AUSTRIA), MARCH 14

"The ECB needs to be ready to react immediately to prevent any increase in inflation expectations."

"We indicated to markets that they should prepare for a re-normalisation of interest rates ... It's better to do it gradually."

LORENZO BINI SMAGHI (EXECUTIVE BOARD), MARCH 14

The ECB duly raised euro zone interest rates from 1% to 1.25% on 7 April 2011 and went on to increase them further to 1.5% in July. However, the worsening of the European sovereign debt crisis in late summer 2011 and increased likelihood of a global recession resulted in the ECB under the new presidency of Mario Draghi responding by cutting interest rates to 1.25% on 3 November, surprising markets with only a little guidance in advance.

"The role of a central bank under any circumstances, and in crisis times in particular, is to inflexibly pursue its main objective, which in the ECB's case is price stability, and to perform as a key anchor of stability."

JOSE MANUEL GONZALEZ-PARAMO (EXECUTIVE BOARD), OCT 12

"As the euro area's banking problems have grown worse, changing the central bank's interest rates might not have a significant influence on the financing conditions of companies and individuals."

ANDRES LIPSTOK (ESTONIA), OCT 18

After November, the rate cut was justified ...

On the ECB's decision to cut rates:

"We anticipated the deterioration of the economic situation over the next couple of weeks, so this was a pre-emptive decision. We never pre-commit, but I would like to stress this was a pre-emptive decision."

JUERGEN STARK (EXECUTIVE BOARD), NOV 4

And rhetoric started guiding markets to expect further rate cuts to 1% in December 2011.

"If there is a situation that we see a serious downturn, or the danger of a serious downturn in Europe, taken together with the perspective of price stability, then I think it's time to rethink and to act maybe in a more decisive way."

EWALD NOWOTNY (AUSTRIA), NOV 11

Federal Reserve to Publish Rate Forecasts from 2012

Ben Bernanke, the US Federal Reserve Chairman, has signalled a move away from using rhetoric to communicate to markets by announcing a decision to publish internal interest rate forecasts to the markets, thereby creating more specific and unambiguous guidance.

The Federal Reserve Open Markets Committee (FOMC) stated in the minutes of its December 2011 meeting that it was changing the way it communicates with markets.

From January 2012, the US Federal Reserve will replace its current rhetoric of "exceptionally low interest rates … through mid-2013" with interest rate forecasts from each member. All 17 members of the FOMC will also forecast when they expect rates to rise for the first time.

Correlated markets

It has been shown how STIR markets are influenced by yield curve effects, economic news, central banker rhetoric and interest rate announcements. However, the movements of other STIR futures can also affect them and this effect can be observed by the use of the statistical measure *correlation*.

Correlation is the causal relationship between two comparable entities. It is expressed as either being positive with a value between zero and one, or negative between zero and minus one. An example of a positive correlation is the relationship between smoking and lung cancer, whilst a negative correlation could be that between age and normal vision. The relationship, either positive or negative, is strongest closest to the respective boundaries of 1 and -1.

International STIR futures markets are highly correlated because of their interest rate parity relationship. Simply put, this means that an equilibrium must hold between the interest rates of two currencies if there are to be no arbitrage opportunities.

The table shows the correlation coefficients between the four main STIR futures representing the currencies of the US Dollar, British pound, the euro and the Swiss franc.

Table 1.14 – Correlation matrix daily data (January 2008 to September 2011)

	Euribor	Eurodollar	Short Sterling	EuroSwiss
Euribor	1	0.956	0.9844	0.9682
Eurodollar	0.956	1	0.9781	0.9598
Short Sterling	0.9844	0.9781	1	0.987
EuroSwiss	0.9682	0.9598	0.987	1

It can be seen that most markets have a strong positive relationship to each other over longer periods of time. As one moves the others tend to move in line, with the Eurodollar and Euribor being the main drivers. The EuroSwiss tends to follow the Euribor very closely, since its currency and economy are inextricably linked to the euro.

However, viewing a correlation matrix over a shorter period can reveal a different story ...

Table 1.15 – Correlation matrix daily data (January 2011 to Sept 2011)

	Euribor	Eurodollar	Short Sterling	EuroSwiss
Euribor	1	-0.3188	-0.1459	0.3376
Eurodollar	-0.3188	1	0.2157	-0.8212
Short Sterling	-0.1459	0.2157	1	0.0508
EuroSwiss	0.3376	-0.8212	0.0508	1

... showing that correlations are highly variable and are affected by differing economic cycles. For example, during early 2011, the ECB was raising interest rates when most other rates were stationary or decreasing.

Since the advent of electronic trading, trading correlations between contracts has been made easier as most trading software packages allow multi-exchange connectivity from one platform, making it comparatively simple to click and trade, for example, Eurodollar and Euribor.

Uncorrelated markets

The influences of correlated markets are quite clear; they tend to be intrinsically linked by their currencies and interest rates. Other markets, such as equities and oil, would appear at first to have little to do with STIR futures and have meaningless correlation coefficients to each other. However, in uncertain times, with (for example) stock market volatility or oil price shocks, STIR futures can focus very closely on a particular agent such as stock index futures or oil prices.

Equities

Generally, stock indices are negatively correlated to STIR futures, meaning for example as the FTSE 100 increases, the Short Sterling future might be expected to fall as rates are increased to slow the economy; but the relationship is broad only. Mostly, the causal relationship is not close. However, the effects of 2008/9 on the FTSE 100 reinforced the negative correlation as rates were cut sharply in response.

Fig. 1.12 – FTSE 100 v Short Sterling 1997 to 2011 (thin line – Short Sterling RH Scale, thick line FTSE-100 LH scale, lower pane 50-day rolling correlation)

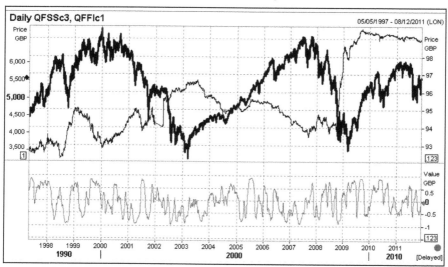

Source: Reuters

This is the effect that rapidly falling stock markets or event risks tend to be countered by interest rate cuts from central banks to bolster the financial system.

Oil

The next chart shows a similar negative correlation effect between the Euribor Z8 contract and the price of oil, which reached an all-time high in July 2008. The largely negative correlation is due to the economic argument that high oil prices can be inflationary and so interest rates should rise and Euribor futures fall.

Fig. 1.13 – Brent Crude Oil v Euribor Z8 2007-2008 (thin line – Euribor Z8 LH scale, thick line – Brent oil RH scale, lower pane 50 day rolling correlation)

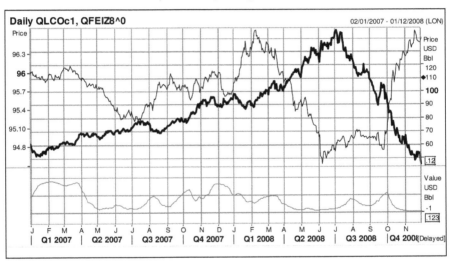

Source: Reuters

Event risk

Event risk is the term applied to the effect of unforeseen events on the STIR futures price, usually natural disasters or acts of terrorism.

Ever since, the World Trade Centre attacks of 11 Sep 2001, event risk premium due to the flight to quality has become more prevalent. Events or rumours of events will rally STIR futures prices as investors seek out safe havens and less volatile environments for their funds. Speculators also magnify this effect, trading instruments like STIR futures and bonds that will benefit from central bank intervention. Both the European Central Bank and Federal Reserve cut interest rates in the aftermath of 9/11 to restore confidence to financial markets and ease credit.

Event-risk premium tends to be short-lived and its influence is usually restricted to the period of perceived threat. In past years, 9/11, the Madrid train bombing and the London Underground bombings have all affected the STIR futures markets.

The next chart shows the effects of the London bombings on 7 July 2005 on Short Sterling M6 STIR futures. A 25-tick spike on the day, driven on a flight to quality sentiment, was soon corrected as traders realised there were unlikely to be any significant knock-on economic effects. Sentiment-driven markets tend to become pragmatic rather quickly.

Fig. 1.14 – Short Sterling M6 June 2005 to July 2005 intra–day tick

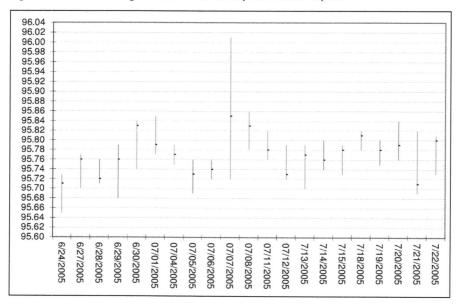

Systemic risk contagion

STIR futures can also influence each other via systemic risk. This is the risk that a localised problem in a financial market could cause a chain of events that has a knock-on effect on other markets. For example, a default by a major market participant, such as the bankruptcy of hedge fund Long-Term Capital Management in 1998, can cause liquidity problems for a number of counterparties to those funds. This can cause those counterparties to fail on their own obligations, prompting a liquidity crisis in the financial markets. This is usually countered by interest rate cuts and so STIR futures rise on a global basis.

Conclusion

In conclusion, the reader should now hopefully be aware of what STIR futures are, how they are priced and what influences cause them to move. They might also have awareness that they are unlike most other kinds of financial instrument and can offer a myriad of different trading approaches and risk profiles. The next section deals with the mechanics of STIR futures markets, which includes clearing and settlement, and how the markets are accessed.

Mechanics of STIR Futures

2

Accessing the Markets

Most financial markets require the individual trader to transact through an intermediary, such as a broker or bank, who is a member of a particular market. Exchange-traded financial futures markets are almost unique in that they permit individuals or smaller entities to trade and compete at a professional level, on the same terms and at similar costs as those of a bank or institution. An individual can post bids and offers and transact with all other participants in exactly the same way as a trader employed by a major bank or broker. There are no layers of intermediation, and no tiered access levels or cost structures favouring one class of participant over another. It is as level a playing field as can be found in the financial markets.

The exchanges have long recognised the importance of smaller market participants as liquidity providers. Capitalised individuals or small groups assume the risk of other traders by taking on the other side of their trades in return for the prospect of financial gain. Their activities promote liquidity, particularly in areas such as further dated contracts or spreads, and this is attractive to other market users. Clearly, there is an issue of counterparty risk. A small trader trading with a bank might not be worried about the bank's ability to settle the trade, but the bank most certainly will be worried about the small trader's ability to do so. This is where the clearing structure removes the counterparty risk and guarantees the settlement procedure.

Clearing and settlement

The clearing and settlement procedure is the trade-matching and processing part of a trader's business and this is usually outsourced by the trader. There are several types of institution involved in this process, including *clearing members* and the *clearing house*.

Clearing member

Clearing members are normally full members of the futures exchanges and fully regulated by the local financial regulatory body, who ensures that they are fit and proper to conduct business. Clearing members tend to be banks or well-capitalised clearing companies which specialise in processing and settling trades, and they have all the necessary trade-processing systems to match and settle a trader's business. Each trader or market participant who is not a clearing member must appoint one and their trades will be processed, matched and settled by them in return for a commission. The clearing member will usually provide a fully integrated service, offering the trader office space, trading systems and trade settlement. The clearing member is effectively attaching their name and capital to the activities of the trader and so they must ensure that they cover their own risks by demanding a capital deposit from each trader that is consistent with their activity level and risk profile. The clearing member will also utilise risk management software to monitor trader activity.

Clearing house

The clearing house is the institution to which the clearing members submit all their trades, and here they are guaranteed against default. Clearing houses are also known as *central counterparty clearing houses* (CCP) since they remove the counterparty risk from the trading process. Once a trade has been matched and cleared by a clearing member and submitted to the clearing house, there is no risk attached to the position of a default by any party to the trade.

Clearing houses such as NYSE Clearing, which acts as CCP to the Liffe (London) markets, are substantial institutions. Clearing members are required to deposit cash or near-cash securities with the clearing house as collateral or margin against their trades. The clearing houses are responsible for setting these margin levels for futures, which is collateral reflecting the risk of a trader's position.

Clearing process

Fig. 2.1 – Simplified clearing process

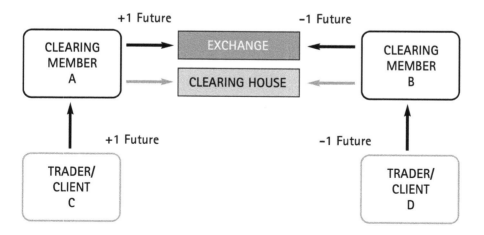

The diagram illustrates the trading and clearing process. Traders C and D can trade with each other via the exchange mechanism without fear of default by each other. Since neither of them are clearing members, they have appointed clearing members A and B to clear and settle their business. The terms and conditions of their relationship with their clearing member will be set out in a *clearing agreement* document that will define the amount of capital they need to deposit with the clearing member. Usually, this is a minimum of £25,000 and is considered a minimum liquidity balance that must be maintained at all times. The clearing member will also process and settle trade transaction in return for a commission usually expressed as an amount per lot (buy or sell one contract). This amount varies according to trade volume and further amounts for exchange fees and a clearing house fee are added. (See the Appendices for a list of clearing members.)

In this diagram, trader C has bought one future, either by routing the order via the clearing member or by direct market access (DMA) supported by the clearing member. Trader D has sold one future at the same price and the two orders are matched together and instantaneously transferred to the clearing house, which now stands as counterparty to each side of the trade. This means that trader C is not concerned about the creditworthiness of trader D and vice–versa, since the counterparty to each side of the trade is now the clearing house. The clearing house will cover its counterparty risk by demanding margins from the clearing members (A and B) who in turn will demand margins from the traders (C and D).

However, the whole process is not risk free. Traders C and D have no fear of each other defaulting since the clearing house is now the counterparty to each side of the trade. But from the perspective of the clearing house, its counterparties are clearing members A and B and not traders C and D.

This means that traders C and D have credit-risk exposure to the clearing members with whom they have pledged margin as collateral against their trades. Should the clearing members default, it is by no means certain that the traders' monies will always be ring-fenced from the clearing members' operational cash balances. They may not receive back monies pledged as collateral.

The following examples show how fraud along with related financial troubles at a clearing member can result in customer losses …

Refco Inc.

Refco was the largest broker and clearing member on the CME Group and had over $4 billion in approximately 200,000 customer accounts. Refco entered crisis on 10 October 2005, when it announced that its chief executive officer and chairman, Phillip R. Bennett, had hidden $430 million in bad debts from the company's auditors and investors.

He was sentenced to 16 years in federal prison.

The business was eventually sold to Man Financial, with Refco Overseas Ltd being relaunched as Marex Financial Limited.

MF Global

MF Global (formerly known as Man Financial) was a major global futures broker and exchange clearing member.

On 30 October 2011, a unit of the New York-based brokerage reported a "material shortfall" in customer funds. Customer accounts with $5.45 billion were frozen on 31 October, the same day the parent company, MF Global Inc., filed the eighth-largest bankruptcy in US history. The shortfall in customer accounts may have been as large as $1.2 billion, or 22%, according to the trustee overseeing liquidation.

MF Global allegedly improperly mixed customer funds and used them for its own account for at least several days before the bankruptcy.

Non-clearing members

A non-clearing member is an exchange member but not a full clearing member. The non-clearing member still has to appoint a clearing member to process their business but might benefit from economies of scale if they have several traders attached to their company. This structure is common where smaller trading companies might be clearing members of one exchange but only qualify for non-clearing status on another exchange. They will accept this arrangement in order to facilitate business for their customers who might want access to multiple exchanges.

Trading arcades

Trading arcades or bureaus are facilitation-based organisations that provide the technological access and trading support, sometimes in the form of training, to traders. They have a similar clearing structure to the non-clearing member in that they also need to appoint an exchange clearing member, but might not have the exchange membership or regulatory approval of the non-clearing member. Trading arcades are useful organisations for traders seeking training or support or financing, or for those traders looking to trade remotely from the clearing member's facilities, perhaps closer to home or in a lifestyle-enhancing or taxation-beneficial foreign domicile. Several trading arcades run recruitment schemes. There are some important considerations in the decision to use a trading arcade. Some are structured so that the trader can open an account directly with a clearing member and just use the services of the arcade to access and execute their business. The arcade will usually have a wholesale commission deal with a clearing member and might be able to offer a more advantageous deal, plus they might be more adapted at servicing the needs of the trader, from technological support to creating the right atmosphere. However, a lot of trading arcades will require the trader to become their client or trainee, especially if taken on as part of a recruitment drive. This is fine if no capital is required, but if a trading deposit is necessary, it might be considered as part of the assets of the arcade, which will usually be a much less substantial organisation than the clearing member. This type of trading arcade might be considered a single account by its clearing member and its deposit with the clearing member will cover the activities of several traders at the trading arcade. If one trader has a bad day and loses everything, it could possibly take the rest of the account and hence the trading arcade with it. It has happened in the past and might happen again. Even though the counterparty risk has been removed between traders, credit risk can still exist in the clearing structure. Sometimes it might be more prudent to accept a less favourable commission deal from a large international bank acting as clearing member rather than a great deal offered by a newly established arcade.

Margin requirements

Each futures contract held from one day to another will require a deposit, reflecting its inherent value and risk. This deposit is called *margin* and is posted by the clearing member to the clearing house for futures positions carried overnight (sometimes, in times of market volatility, intra-day margins can also be requested by the clearing house). The futures contract margin requirements are also used by clearing members to impose a trader's trading limits based upon the amount of capital a trader has in his account.

SPAN

The most popular method of calculating margin requirements for STIR futures is called SPAN. This stands for **S**tandard **P**ortfolio **AN**alysis of Risk and was developed by the CME Group in 1988 and adopted by Liffe in 1990. It is a margining system that calculates the effects of a range of possible changes in price and volatility on portfolios of futures and futures-based options. The worst possible loss calculated by the system is then used as the margin requirement.

SPAN replaced an older system of charging a pre-determined initial margin for each contract and then a variation margin, which was essentially the profit or loss of the position when marked to market. SPAN calculates an initial margin by quantifying the risk and the potential for loss for all futures positions in a portfolio but also takes into account the offsetting effects of intra-contract and inter-market products. This means that portfolios that incorporate a futures position that partially offsets the risks of another futures position are fully recognised by the system and the trader is not burdened with margin overlap or duplication.

SPAN calculates its margin requirements by constructing a series of 16 scenarios of changing underlying prices and volatilities to produce a risk array. This risk array will contain a number of probable outcomes based on price and volatility factors over time. The clearing house will determine on a daily basis which range of outcomes is most appropriate and it will use the worst outcome as its margin figure or scanning loss for a particular product. Furthermore, a charge, termed an *intra-contact* or *inter-month spread charge* will be added to the margin where, for example, a long Euribor for March expiry is partially offset by a short position in the Euribor June contract. Where an inter-contract position reduces the overall risk, a credit to the overall margin call is added. For example, a future with similar risk characteristic such as a Swapnote future included in a portfolio of Euribor STIR futures will reduce the overall risk profile.

For example:

- A single Euribor future might attract an initial margin of €850.

- Inter-month charges are tiered according to the expiry month. A Tier 1 spread comprising, say, a long Euribor front-month contract and a short further-dated front-month Euribor contract would attract a charge of €250, reflecting the reduced risk of the spread versus the outright future.

- A portfolio of different products would be margined as above but benefit from an inter-contract charge. A portfolio including a long Euribor future and a short two-year Swapnote future would attract margin of €850 and €600 accordingly. However, both would benefit from a 65% credit per leg in recognition of their offsetting risk characteristics.

SPAN is used by the clearing house to set margin levels. The clearing members will be required to post margin to that amount on a daily basis for the cumulative position of its traders. Clearing members will also use a PC software version of SPAN to manage their overall risk position for a range of traders. They might use the clearing house margin requirements as a basis for their own, either increasing them if appropriate or allowing a leverage effect. A clearing member will sometimes allow traders to trade a multiple of their maximum overnight margin facility on an intra-day basis. This recognises the fact that traders can buy and sell many contracts per day and the inherent liquidity of short-term trading can support larger transaction sizes.

Comparison of futures settlement with equities and CFDs

An investor buying a share through a traditional stockbroker experiences a different clearing and margining procedure to that of the futures trader. An equity trade is usually settled in full a few days after the trade and the total monetary consideration of the deal has to be delivered. For example, an investor buying 1,000 shares of Vodafone at £1.80 will have to pay a total consideration of £1,800 plus expenses when settlement is due.

Contracts for difference (CFDs) on equities introduce a futures-type settlement procedure which is much more capital-efficient than buying shares outright. An investor could buy 1,000 shares in Vodafone at £1.80 and only have to post a small margin amount, reflecting the risk of the position. This margin requirement will increase if Vodafone shares decline in value from the purchase price of £1.80 but, ultimately, the investor is only financially responsible for the difference between the purchase price and the selling price of the shares.

STIR futures (and futures in general) are very similar in their settlement procedure to CFDs. Once a position is established, an initial margin is payable and then the difference between the traded price and the current price is added or subtracted from the margin account, depending on whether the trade is in loss or profit.

Although there are similarities between the way futures and CFDs are settled, there are also some notable differences:

- Futures and shares are traded on recognised and regulated exchanges, whereas CFDs are traded within the activities of a regulated financial broker or bank.

- Futures are matched by a central clearing house which acts as a guarantor of the position, thereby removing counterparty risk. In contrast, a CFD is a contract between the investor and a financial broker or bank and is subject to the credit risk associated with that organisation.

- The clearing house is totally impartial in its decisions regarding margin levels as to the positions held by market participants, whereas the CFD broker might have an opposite position to that of its traders.

Fixed and variable costs

Traders face two types of cost structures:

- **fixed costs** are made up of regularly repeating costs such as software, communications and office space rental

- **variable costs** are the transaction fees, including exchange fees and commissions.

Fixed costs

Software costs vary according to the level of sophistication of the software package and its connectivity. A base cost for a software package that connects to one or two exchanges will vary from £250 to £500 per month, with connectivity to four or more exchanges and more advanced trading features raising this to £900 to £1,250 per month. Communication charges will normally be included in an overall desk or administration charge if using the office facilities of a clearing member or trading arcade. They only really become a stand-alone factor for a trader, usually working from home, and costs can vary from £25 per month for a simple broadband connection to approximately £750 per month for a leased telephone line depending on location and distance. The desk or administration charge for a clearing member or arcade-based trader will amount to approximately £350 per month, but can be incorporated into a single overall charge including everything, and will usually be a similar amount.

Variable costs

The variable costs are made up of commissions and exchange fees, usually quoted as a single rate by the clearing member or arcade. They are negotiated either as a flat rate based on estimated volumes or on a sliding scale, starting quite high and rapidly dropping as volume thresholds are reached. Note that all business for the month is usually put through at the lowest rate for the volume achieved. The total amount payable per transaction will incorporate an exchange fee, which is the portion charged by the futures exchange, a clearing house fee, which is the amount charged by a clearing house responsible for guaranteeing trades and arranging margins, and a clearing member commission.

STIR futures traded on Liffe attract exchange fees of £0.25 per lot and a clearing house fee of £0.03 per lot. Commissions for an active trader will vary from £0.03 to £0.25 per lot. Commissions for international exchanges might be higher than for those trading in the country of domicile, reflecting the higher cost of communications and international clearing procedures.

Like any business, everything is negotiable. Clearing futures is a competitive business and clearing members are eager for business, especially from volume players. For those traders or collective groups of traders offering a significant transaction-based revenue stream, a clearing member might waive a substantial portion of fixed costs in expectation of larger fee income. Smaller, new traders might be offered lower fixed costs in return for higher commission levels. Whichever way a clearing deal is structured, most traders will have to base their cost structure on an estimated monthly spend of approximately £1,000, with commissions adding several thousand pounds to this amount.

Liquidity and rebate schemes

The previous section has highlighted the potential expense of futures trading. Fixed costs are high but it is exchange fees and commissions that make up the bulk of a traders' costs.

The largest portion of a trader's variable costs go to the futures exchanges in the form of exchange fees. The exchanges have a large cost base, having to provide and support the market infrastructure, but they are mindful of the liquidity benefits that short-term trading by speculative traders brings to their markets. Some exchanges address this issue by offering rebate schemes for volume trading or attempting to attract liquidity to less popular areas of the markets or products by offering incentives. Rebate and incentive schemes vary from time to time, but at present Liffe and CME Group offer the following schemes of interest to the STIR futures trader.

STIR Liquidity Provider (LP)

This is a volume discount programme, whereby approved applicants can benefit from reduced exchange trading fees on proprietary business above defined volume threshold levels, in addition to lower exchange trading fees in the back delivery months of these contracts.

An Individual LP is an individual who, through his trading activity, supports and enhances the liquidity of Liffe's STIR futures contracts. Specifically Liffe defines an Individual LP as an individual:

"(a) whose principal activities include trading futures on a discretionary basis for his own account, or for the proprietary account of an employer in which he has an interest;

"(b) whose trading activity contributes to price discovery and satisfies the futures order flow of other market participants; and

"(c) who can demonstrate that they have met the appropriate minimum volume threshold requirement in any calendar month during the six-month period prior to the calendar month in which the LP benefits are due to commence."

This scheme is designed to promote STIR liquidity in the back or deferred expiry months, with declining exchange fees for deferred month trading. This starts in the red months with a saving of up to £0.10 per lot, increasing to £0.15 and £0.20 per lot for green and blue months respectively.

STIR Discount Schedule

The STIR discount schedule runs alongside the STIR LP programs to offer eligible firms further potential exchange fee rebates via a discount schedule.

Full details are available on Liffe's website (see Appendices) and these schemes are significant because although the clearing house fee and the clearing member commission will be unaffected, the overall cost of buying and selling back-month STIR futures can be reduced by approximately one third to a half. This means that trades which the trader might have previously considered prohibitive due to high fees or marginal due to uncertain profitability can now be considered part of a trader's repertoire.

The total savings available to a trader willing to concentrate on back months are shown in the following chart, which illustrates the total percentage savings provided by both schemes for the Euribor contract.

Fig. 2.2 – Percentage saving in total exchange fees for Liffe Euribor, based on variable monthly volumes

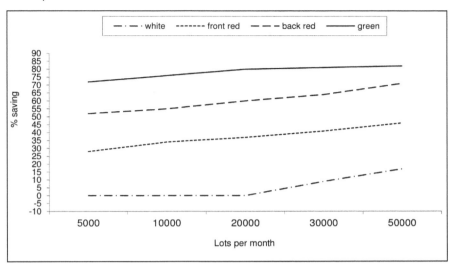

It is clear that even a relatively small monthly volume in anything but the front white contracts quickly attracts large percentage savings over the standard fee schedule. As volumes increase, the savings rise proportionally.

New Market Participants Scheme (NMP)

The Liffe NMP scheme is aimed at new trainee proprietary traders with no prior trading experience. Participants benefit from fully rebated exchange clearing fees, subject to a monthly cap for a maximum period of six months.

International Incentive Program (IIP)

CME Group operates an International Incentive Program scheme for non-US based traders trading on their electronic Globex market. Presently, individual non-member accounts are assessed at different rates from institutional and member accounts. This can result in unregistered Eurodollar traders paying exchange fees as high as $1.19 per lot. This reduces to $0.44 per lot on the IIP scheme.

New Trader Incentive Program (NTIP)

The CME Group New Trader Incentive Program provides fee incentives for new traders at proprietary firms operating in regions not traditionally actively involved in CME Group futures markets.

The choice of Clearing Member or Trading Arcade

The well-capitalised aspiring trader has the choice of several clearing members and trading arcades. The main selection criteria are:

Customer classification

Futures traders are usually regarded by the financial regulatory authorities as being professional traders who do not need to be directly regulated but must have a certain level of relevant experience before being allowed to open an account with an exchange clearing member. A trader with prior experience, perhaps working for someone else, would be deemed 'expert status' by the Financial Services Authority, the UK financial regulator, but this might vary according to international regulations. Those aspiring traders with no prior futures experience might be directed to training or mentoring schemes, or perhaps have to accept a retail client contract rather than a professional trading contract. The compliance department of the clearing member has the responsibility of ensuring that traders have this level of experience and status and will make enquiries accordingly at the account-opening stage. Aspiring traders should check with the clearing member or trading arcade to determine their potential classification.

The criterion for an experienced trader is governed by the compliance department of a clearing member and is based on guidance from the regulatory authority. As a guide, here are some typical requirements for acceptability, as might be specified by a UK based clearing member.

- The trader should have a general knowledge of the products that they intend to trade, and they should show that they have read the relevant information regarding contract specification and mechanisms.

- The trader should have a general overview of the exchanges they intend to trade on. They should know where the exchanges are based, how they are run and the exchange trading rules.

- The trader should have knowledge of the FSA code of conduct and relevant sections for trading.

- The trader should have sufficient training on the trading system that he intends to use so that he understands how to place outright trades, spreads and how to pull orders.

- The trader should be able to trade in single lots under the supervision of an experienced trader. This can be achieved by the experienced trader having a sub-account in which the trainee can trade in single lots, thus providing an audit trail for the trader's ability to place and pull orders and their profitability/loss over the training period.

- The trader should have a fundamental knowledge of economic figures and how they will influence the products he is trading.

- The trader should be able to explain why he has taken a position and why that position should make money and the same when the position is closed. If this results in a loss the experienced trader should determine if the logic applied to the taking of that position was correct.

Financial probity

The trader needs to assure himself or herself of the financial standing of a clearing member or, more importantly, a trading arcade. The clearing member will have to have met certain criteria to qualify for regulation by the local financial regulator in order to qualify for exchange membership. A trading arcade only has to meet the financial requirements of the clearing member. That's not to say that trading arcades should be avoided. Many provide a very high level of service and are run by traders for traders.

The largest institutions are not always the most secure, Refco and MF Global being recent examples that prove this (see earlier).

Usually it is a question of meeting the people, talking to their traders and others in the market, and using judgement. The internet can be useful for opinion. There are several traders' forums like Trade2Win or Elitetrader where participants are not reluctant to share their views.

Financial protection

Futures traders are normally considered professional traders by the regulatory authorities and so do not benefit from segregated funds protection offered to the retail investor. This means that futures clients' money can be pooled and at risk in the case of clearing member default. It can be useful to be aware of how funds are regarded and to enquire whether any protection or guarantees can be put in place.

Capital requirements and commissions

Cheapest is not always best and this should not be the sole factor in determining choice. Commissions on futures will always be on a per-lot or per-round-trip basis (buy and sell one lot) and never on capital value. Look out for hidden charges such as tiered commission schedules not defaulting to the lowest tier for all business at the end of the trading month, no (or low) interest being paid on capital deposits, or punitive financing for traders requiring financial backing.

Check to see if interest is paid on margin deposits. This can be significant for spread traders carrying large inventories. Clearing members effectively receive interest from the clearing house by posting bonds as security and so they are in a position to pay interest to clients, but this tends to be by negotiation.

It is also worth checking to ensure that any eligible rebate and liquidity schemes are passed on in full to the trader.

Technological ability

Speed can be everything in futures trading. A poorly constructed or overcrowded network can cause slowdowns and outages.

Trading arcades

Trading arcades usually offer training schemes for new traders and financing for suitably qualified traders.

Training schemes operate by a crop of trainees recruited from web sites, newspaper adverts and referrals. They may or may not be paid a salary, but they normally should not be required to provide capital. They are placed on a training scheme and paper trade for a time, which involves trading a simulated market whilst their performance is monitored. Those showing promise are retained and the rest let go – a process of selection that continues through to their graduation to trading real markets.

Those who graduate are placed on a contract defining the terms of their deal and these are regularly renegotiated as the trader's star rises or falls. Many trainees choose to stay with their original trainers and several have gone on to become major players in the futures markets.

Financing deals are variable and normally involve a profit-share deal defined by how much capital is provided. They are usually offered to experienced traders looking for more capital to trade in bigger-sized or other more capital-intensive markets, but some arcades will offer financing deals for those with less capital. Such deals are not always attractive to either party. The arcade will be asking why an experienced trader is in need of financing – are they any good at their job? The trader seeking financing will need to ensure it is an equitable deal.

Software and hardware

The two main STIR futures exchanges operate two similar trading systems. Liffe calls their electronic trading system *Connect*, and the CME Group platform is called *Globex*. Both are based on open host system architecture with an application program interface (API) that allows users to build trading applications directly on the exchange trading platform. Some larger users such as banks have built their own propriety front-end trading applications. But the most popular way of accessing the markets for the smaller trader is by commercially built software developed by independent software vendors (ISV). This integrates trading, settlement and risk management in one off-the-shelf package.

The system architecture has multiple traders using the same ISV software connecting directly to the ISV server, either by internal network, if situated in the same offices, or remotely via an external network such as a leased line or via the internet. The server connects directly into the exchange gateway, which is usually a server-based exchange network hub. This can be located in a clearing member's office or as a designated hub on an international network, allowing quick access for traders based in foreign countries. The gateway connects directly to the exchange host, where orders are matched or placed in the market according to price level and priority as determined by the trading algorithms.

Trading algorithms

These are controlled by the exchanges and usually operate on a time priority or pro-rata basis. A

- *time priority* based algorithm (also known as first in first out, FIFO), will give precedence to the earliest placed orders at a given price, and a

- *pro-rata* algorithm will give an equal preference to all orders, irrespective of when they were placed.

Both Liffe and CME operate a similar pro-rata algorithm for STIR futures, but they can both be altered, with notice, to accommodate different preferences. Such preferences can include a top order priority, where an order, of any or a maximum designated quantity, is placed at a price before all others and so is given preference over all other orders. Another is a preference recently introduced by the CME to their algorithm that gives an element of FIFO to their pro-rata algorithm for trades allocated after the top order.

Algorithms can be modified frequently by the exchanges to enhance host performance, give preference to a certain class of trader such as those fulfilling a market-making obligation, or to attempt to gain a competitive advantage over another exchange's products in the case of a dual listing. Consequently, it is advisable to check the current algorithm in use from the exchanges' websites and notices.

Implied pricing functionality

The exchange host trading platforms on both Connect and Globex support functionality called *implied pricing*. This is where the prices from outright futures contracts can be used to imply prices for a spread or similar trading strategy, and vice versa.

Strategies such as calendar spreads and butterflies are quoted as instruments in their own right, rather than just being a by-product of the futures strip. The concept of implying prices in these strategies directly from futures prices was pioneered by Liffe during the development of Connect. Implied prices help promote liquidity in the order books. The exchanges guarantee the fill of all sides of a transaction involving implied prices.

There are two types of exchange-supported implied pricing:

1. *implied-in pricing* – where prices are implied into the spreads from the outright futures

2. *implied-out pricing* – where spread prices are used to imply prices into the outright futures.

There is a third kind which is *implied upon implied pricing*, where prices are created based upon implied prices elsewhere. The exchanges do not support implied upon implied prices and do not guarantee execution of all component positions of this kind of trade. Implied upon implied functionality is usually a feature of ISV trading software and can be useful to the trader in that it can indicate additional liquidity, provided they are aware of the inherent execution risk. Liffe only supports implied out pricing to calendar spreads whereas CME extends this to cover butterfly spreads.

Examples

The following table illustrates the implied-in functionality. Three outright contracts, H2, M2 and U2 are quoted in quantities of 100 lots on both bid and offer. The quoted bid/offer spread is one tick for the first two contracts but two ticks for the U2 expiry. All of these prices are used by the exchange host computer to calculate implied-in prices to populate the strategies, in this case the H2M2 and M2U2 spreads.

Table 2.1 – Implied-in functionality for STIR futures (implied-in prices are shown in italics)

Contract	Bid qty	Bid	Offer	Offer qty
H2	100	98.78	98.79	100
M2	100	98.55	98.56	100
U2	100	98.37	98.39	100
H2M2	100	*0.22*	0.23	50
M2U2	50	0.17	*0.19*	100

Table 2.2 – Implied-in and out functionality for STIR futures (implied-in prices are shown in italics and implied-out prices are in bold)

Contract	Bid qty	Bid	Offer	Offer qty
H2	100	98.78	**98.79**	150
M2	150	**98.55**	98.56	100
U2	100	98.37	**98.39**	150
H2M2	100	*0.22*	0.23	50
M2U2	50	0.17	*0.19*	100

Since spreads are a function of the bid/offer prices of the component outright futures, the implied-in price for the H2M2 will be 0.22 bid and 0.24 offered as shown by:

Fig. 2.3 – Components of H2M2 spread

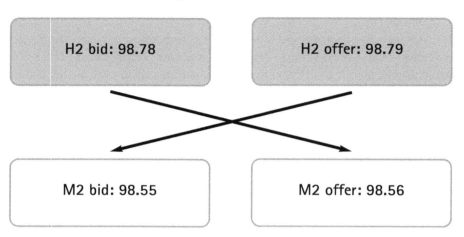

The spread H2M2:

- the **bid price** is given by the bid of H2 subtracting the offer of M2 (98.78 - 98.56 = 0.22), and

- the **offer price** is given by the offer of H2 subtracting the bid of M2 (98.79 - 98.55 = 0.24).

This makes an implied-in quote of 0.22 bid and 0.24 offered in 100 lots per side (since those are the quantities available in the outright futures).

However, the spread-implied bid and offer price has been improved upon by a market participant who has placed an offer to sell 50 lots at 0.23. This then creates a true spread price of 0.22 bid in 100 lots, which is all implied-in, and a trader's offer of 50 lots at 0.23.

A similar situation occurs in the M2U2 spread, which has implied-in prices of 0.16 bid and 0.19 offered, again derived from the bids and offers of the component outright futures. The three-tick-wide implied-in price reflects the totals of the bid/offer spreads in the M2 and U2 contracts, the U2 having a two-tick-wide spread, perhaps reflecting less liquidity. A market participant has improved this three-tick-wide implied-in spread quote by bidding 0.17 for 50 lots, making a true M2U2 spread price of 0.17 bid and 0.19 offered, which is all implied-in.

If the market participants had not improved upon those spread prices, then the market prices available would be the outright futures, as quoted in price and size in the table. The spreads would all be implied-in and quoted as the function of their component outright futures bids and offers. All the outright futures and spreads would have a quoted size of 100 lots. However, the presence of those two trader orders, to sell 50 H2M2 at 0.23 and buy 50 M2U2 at 0.17, have the effect of implying out additional quantities into the outright futures. The offer to sell 50 H2M2 at 0.23 will imply out an offer to sell 50 H2 at 98.79 against buying the M2 offer at 98.56 (98.79 - 98.56 = 0.23). This adds an additional 50 lots to the existing offer of 100 lots, making a total of 150 lots available at 98.79, of which 100 lots is a trader order and 50 lots is implied out. This is shown in the table and is represented by bold font.

The offer to sell 50 H2M2 at 0.23 can also work the other side of the spread as well. A bid to buy 50 lots of M2 at 98.55 is implied out against the trader bid in H2 to buy 100 lots at 98.78 (98.78 - 98.55 = 0.23). This will add an additional 50 lots to the existing trader's bid of 100 lots.

The order to buy 50 M2U2 at 0.17 will imply out another 50 lots of U2 at 98.39, making a total of 150 lots at 98.39, against buying the M2 offer at 98.56 (98.56 - 98.39 = 0.17). However, it will not be able to imply a bid into the M2 since it would need to purchase at a price of 98.54 against the U2 bid of 98.37 (98.54 - 98.37 = 0.17) but the M2 is 98.55 bid already.

Implied prices – traders' friend or foe?

The good

The development of implied pricing was an inspirational enhancement for the trading of STIR futures. It immediately brought liquidity from outright futures contracts into the strategies markets. It also defined arbitrage boundaries for all types of spreads, preventing the possibility of trading a spread or similar strategy at prices outside of those implied by the component outright futures. The implied-out prices returned a lot of the liquidity from more stable and liquid spreads (such as three-month calendar spreads) into the outright futures strip, creating a more liquid market all round. Traders also had the assurance that if they traded a spread based upon implied prices, they were guaranteed a fill of all sides of the trade at the required prices. This effectively removed execution risk from transacting a spread trade in the outright futures.

The bad

However, these benefits of implied prices are also something of an Achilles heel: the improved pricing efficiency of the market means reduced opportunities for traders. Nevertheless, implied pricing can help traders in that trades can be triggered by price action elsewhere. A spread seller might inadvertently trigger two outright futures trades if that spread price were made up of only implied-in prices.

It is important to be aware of where the implied prices are and how much of the outright or spread bid or offer quantities they make up. Implied prices can disappear instantaneously if the providing bid or offer is removed. Consequently, care must be taken if legging spreads, particularly in the back months of STIR futures where incidence of implied pricing is higher.

Selecting an ISV

There are many commercially available ISV software packages, of which about seven are the most popular (see appendix or **www.stirfutures.co.uk**). Some specialise in different products, such as options, but to a large extent they are similar in design and functionality. The choice of ISV might be limited to those offered by the trader's clearing member or trading arcade, but usually the trader will have a choice of around two to five different ISVs.

The majority of ISV software will offer similar features, with most resources having gone into the design of the trading functionality. Some ISV software includes more advanced features such as algorithm creators, complex order management, and links into Excel for automation, but all will share common trading features such as trade history, position management and working order books, as well as additional information sources such as exchange tickers and messaging.

- The **trade history** is an audit of all completed trades with relevant order numbers and execution time.

- **Position management** indicates the open futures positions currently held, displayed as a total and detailed by individual contract or expiry. The position management function often incorporates a real-time profit and loss on open and closed positions.

- The **order book** shows all futures orders currently being worked in the market and indicates whether part of the order has been filled or not.

- **Exchange tickers** are price and time histories for futures contracts.

- **Messaging** is an information flow indicating market and software status.

But it is the price display functionality that is of most importance to the trader. This is where the futures price action is observed and trades entered and deleted. Every trader probably has their own idea of how they would ideally like to view the markets, but some commonality is unavoidable. The essential requirements are an economical use of screen space, easy and quick order entry and deletion, and clearly viewable information.

Price displays

STIR futures traders tend to look at several delivery months at once, as well as strategies such as spreads, so a market grid layout is a popular choice for the price display functionality.

Table 2.3 – Market grid display of STIR futures and strategies

Product	Bid qty	Bid	Offer	Offer qty	Last trade	Last qty	Volume
H2	1171	98.79	98.80	3758	98.80	1	1692
M2	23	98.59	98.60	6208	98.59	10	7124
U2	1695	98.40	98.41	100	98.41	100	3507
Z2	43	98.23	98.24	717	98.24	53	1416
H2M2	3260	0.20	0.21	349	0.20	18	937
M2U2	2054	0.18	0.19	63	0.19	28	1206
U2Z2	121	0.17	0.18	3269	0.18	1	428

The table shows a typical market grid layout.

Product column

In the left column, the products are titled and usually presented in a user-defined order, the most popular approach being to have the outright futures in descending sequential order followed by a similar display of the strategies. The strategies shown here are the three-month calendar spreads, but any combination or other strategies can be included, as can other futures contracts.

Bid and offer quantity columns

The bid and offer quantity columns show the amount of futures contracts bid and offered for purchase and sale by market participants. These quantities will normally include implied pricing as well as the trader bid and offers. Usually it is possible to see exactly how much implied pricing is present by a variety of methods, including a mouse tool tip display, a check box that turns the implied prices on or off, an indicative colour display or the implied prices additionally displaying in separate columns, as shown in the table.

Table 2.4 – Example of Implied price functionality from Liffe Short Sterling (L) 10 Feb 2006, 10.01am

Product	Bid qty	BID	OFFER	Offer qty	Implied bid qty	Imp. bid price	Imp. offer price	Imp. offer qty
L H6	21996	95.42	95.43	23232	887	95.42		
L M6	11869	95.48	95.49	8241	125	95.48		
L U6	8068	95.48	95.49	856	2660	95.48		
L Z6	1607	95.44	95.45	5656			95.45	1117
L H6M6	887	-0.06	-0.05	13969			-0.05	11869
L M6U6	17769	-0.01	0.00	761	856	-0.01		
L U6Z6	3724	0.04	0.05	30627			0.05	856

Here it can be seen from a real-time snapshot of Liffe Short Sterling STIR futures that the bulk of the front months are made up of outright trader orders. In the H6 contract, out of the total of 21,996 contracts on the bid, only 887 are implied-out prices. However, the H6M6 spread has a very high proportion of its offer quantity (13,969) as implied-in (11,869), generated by the bid for 11,869 lots in M6. This means that the spread, although seemingly very well offered, could lose the majority of its offer quantity if sellers sold out the M6 bid. If this happened, the H6M6 would be left with a trader offer quantity of only 2,100 lots. Not as liquid as it first appeared!

The trader offer of 856 U6 at 95.49 is implying-in a M6U6 spread bid of -0.01 for 856 lots, adding to the 16,913 lots already bid by traders. It is also implying-in an offer in the U6Z6 spread at 0.05, adding to the 29,771 already there.

To take things further, the combination of these two implied-in spread bid and offers could imply-out a bid of -0.06 for 856 lots (-0.01 - 0.05) for the M6U6Z6 butterfly spread. In this case, the butterfly would be -0.06 bid for thousands anyway, because of the existing trader bid of -0.01 in the M6U6 spread and the existing 0.05 offer in the U6Z6 spread, but it highlights the extension possibilities of implied pricing.

Although these implied-in spread prices could imply-out a butterfly price of -0.06, this functionality is not supported by all exchanges. Liffe does not support implied-out pricing on any strategy other than calendar spreads, whereas CME does support implied-out pricing on butterflies. However, it is all slightly academic since the butterfly spread would be-0.06 bid in size anyway since that would permit traders to effectively buy the M6U6 spread on the bid and sell the U6Z6 spread on the offer. In fact, bidding -0.06 for the M6U6Z6 butterfly would be so attractive that there was actually a better -0.05 trader bid in the market at the time of writing!

Finally, there is a big implied-out bid for 95.48 in U6 for 2,660 lots created partly by the 0.00 offer in 761 lots in the M6U6 spread (bidding 95.48 in the U6 against selling 95.48 in the M6) and the 0.04 bid for 3,724 in the U6Z6 spread (bidding 95.48 in the U6 against selling Z6 at 95.44).

It must be apparent by now that the concept and identification of implied pricing can be tricky but it is worth taking the time and using an ISV package where inter-dependencies on implied prices can be spotted with a bit of practice. Implied prices will often lean against trader prices and are easily triggered by price action elsewhere. Again it is important in back months, where the liquidity is less than the front-month examples shown above, to be aware of what is generating the implied price and gauging how reliable it might be.

Two or one-click dealing

Going back to the earlier market price grid display, the bid and offer show the current market prices. Most ISV packages allow the trader to click the price and execute the order. This might feature two-click dealing, where (for example) clicking the offer price will bring up a buy ticket, usually colour coded blue, with the trade price and a pre-defined quantity, and a second click will send the order to market. Most ISVs, however, also have one-click trading functionality for speed advantage.

From this display, traders can normally view the depth of a market by a dropdown function within the software. This will show the prices and quantities above and below the current market prices, as shown in the table.

Market depth

Table 2.5 – Market depth display of STIR futures

Product	Bid qty	BID	OFFER	Offer qty	Last trade	Last qty	Volume
H2	1171	98.79	98.80	3758	98.80	1	1692
	567	98.78	98.81	1256			
	245	98.77	98.82	768			
	43	98.76	98.83	435			
	85	98.75	98.84	324			

The top price is the same bid/offer price and quantity as shown for the H2 contract, but underneath a dropdown shows the market depth depicted in italics. These are the prices either side of the bid and offer and are tradable in the same way as the top-level prices. This is a useful function in faster moving markets, where it might be necessary to click above or below a current price in order to stand a better chance of being filled on the trade.

Most exchanges employ a price-match function where an order will always be filled at the best price (within limits). For example, if the market was rising quickly and a trader clicked to buy 200 lots at 98.82 in the market depth, the order would be filled at a better price of 98.80 or 98.81 if those offers were still available. The exchange host algorithms will not normally allow a trade to be filled at an off-market price.

Note: implied prices will not be a constituent of the market depth liquidity; they will only be generated for top-level best market prices only.

Market depth can also be useful as a technical indicator to determine order flow. Should there be larger offers than bids in the market depth then it might indicate some reluctance by the market to go up, since it is likely that resistance will be met from sellers. Often key technical levels attract market depth volumes and this can be useful to the trader.

The popularity of trading in the market depth for faster moving products such as bond futures has led to the development by ISV of trading applications specifically tailored to fast execution within the market depth. These can be of interest to the STIR trader for outright trading in times of volatility.

Table 2.6 – ISV market (ladder) depth display

B. QTY	BID	OFFER	O QTY
		98.84	324
		98.83	435
		98.82	768
		98.81	1256
1171	98.79	98.80	3758
567	98.78		
245	98.77		
43	98.76		
85	98.75		

This table shows a typical layout of these trading tools. They tend to be single contract displays, showing the market depth in a permanent vertical profile that automatically re-centres as the price moves. Orders are executed by fast one-click trading in a pre-determined quantity, usually on the blank space to the side of the price. Orders to sell an offer or join a bid are normally done by single clicking the price. Additional functionally such as drag-and-drop order movement, cumulative traded volumes and quick delete of all orders, bids or offers varies between products.

Last trade and volume

Finally, the remaining columns on the market grid display shown in Table 2.4 are the market information displays of last trade and quantity (total volume traded) and can be expanded to include additional columns such as contract highs and lows, previous settlement price, net change of the day and open positions. All columns and rows in the market grid display are usually user-customisable and moveable to the trader's specifications.

Spread matrix

Most ISVs include a spread matrix as part of their software. This is a display where all the permutations of calendar spreads for a STIR future are shown in a tradable matrix as shown in the table.

Spread matrices are presented in a slightly different format depending on the ISV. Some are a fixed display mechanism and some are highly customisable so that the user can configure the display to their own liking, with prices and quantities presented horizontally or vertically.

Generally, all matrices will be the same to the extent of featuring a two-axes display, with the sequential futures' quarterly expiries displayed along each side. The prices of the outright futures are normally displayed and will be clickable and tradable in the usual manner. Here, they are shown on the top row in a vertical format, where the bid price and quantity is on the lower cell and the offer price and quantity is on the higher cell. Implied prices can be shown either by colour coding, mouse tool tip or by a check box that turns the implied prices on or off.

Table 2.7 – Example STIR spread matrix

PRICE	QTY	PRICE	QTY	PRICE	QTY	PRICE	QTY
98.79	3060	98.58	1569	98.40	2453	98.23	275
98.78	601	98.57	692	98.39	409	98.22	319
H2		M2		U2		Z2	
H2		0.22	1779	0.40	409	0.57	319
		0.21	478	0.38	601	0.55	275
		M2		0.19	1507	0.36	598
				0.18	684	0.34	379
				U2		0.17	302
						0.16	1465
						Z2	

The spread prices are generated against the relevant futures, so that the first spread, the H2M2 spread, is quoted as 0.21 bid for 478 lots and 0.22 offered in 1,779 lots. Following down and across the matrix returns the other three-month spreads, the M2U2 and U2Z2. Going up one level gives the six-month calendar spreads, the first one being H2U2 and then M2Z2. Another level higher returns the nine-month spread, which is the H2Z2 spread.

The implied pricing in this example is shown as italics on the price, where the implied pricing is only a part of the total order quantity and shown as italics on both the price and quantity when it is all an implied price. It can be observed that implied pricing is present as part of a larger quantity in the three-month spreads but can be the sole price and quantity in the less liquid and less traded six- and nine-month spreads. The nine-month H2Z2 is a purely implied-in price of 0.55 bid, 0.57 offered and its quantities are limited to the quantities available in the outright Z2 contract.

Auto-spreaders and price injection models

Some ISVs offers *auto spreaders* and *price injection* models. These are usually optional extras and can be expensive additions.

Auto-spreader model

The auto-spreader is a simple concept to understand, but a complex piece of software. It works by creating its own spread or similar strategy based upon the contracts entered by the user. It can work spreads based on existing strategies, such as calendar spreads, or hybrid spreads, such as a bond future against one or more STIR futures. Most auto-spreaders are customisable so that several spread legs can be entered and worked at once. For example, the three legs of a butterfly can be worked simultaneously or more complex multi-leg trades such as trading packs and bundles against interest rate swaps or bond futures. Some auto-spreaders even permit strategies such as calendar spreads to be entered so that a butterfly spread can be worked as the two component spreads as well as the individual outright legs.

The auto-spreader will effectively create an implied-in price for a spread or strategy based upon the inputted component legs. But this is not an implied-in price like those generated by the exchange host, and there is no guarantee of execution of both sides. The auto-spreader can be configured to work one or all sides of the spread or strategy by showing a bid or offer to the market in those selected contracts. It can also look for a certain amount of volume on the other side to the trade or to avoid leaning against just implied prices to reduce the risk of being legged out. This is where one side of the spread or strategy is completed but the other side is missed, usually by another trader beating you to it or, more commonly, by an exchange-implied price being used preferentially to guarantee the fill on an exchange spread or strategy that is trading at the same time.

Auto-spreader

Using the prices from spread matrix, a trader decides that he wishes to buy 50 lots of M2U2 spread at 0.18. He could join the bid of 684 lots with everyone else and be guaranteed a fill on both sides in a pro-rata allocation when that price traded. Alternatively, he could use an auto-spreader to inject prices into the outright futures. This would effectively bid 98.57 in the M2, against selling 98.39 in the U2 if partially or fully filled on the M6. It could also simultaneously offer 98.40 in the U2 against buying 98.58 in the M2 if partially or fully filled on the U6. If the outright prices were to change, the auto-spreader would automatically re-submit the orders at revised prices. The auto-spreader could be configured to look for a multiple of more than one times the order size before entering the leg order. If it were set to two times, it would ensure that the U2 bid of 98.39 was at least bid for 100 lots before submitting its order to bid 98.57 for 50 lots in the M2 and do the same on the other working side of the order. It might also be programmed to ignore any implied prices that were part of the total quantity. However, if the figure is set too high, the auto-spreader might be unable to enter the order since insufficient size would be available on the other side.

The astute reader who has fully understood the concept of implied-out pricing might be wondering what the point of the auto-spreader is. It is effectively doing exactly the same as the implied-out functionality of joining the M2U2 spread bid at 0.18. The exchange host will imply out a bid into the M2 and an offer into the U2 at the same prices but with no execution risk. Contracts such as Euribor and Eurodollar can commonly have three-month spreads bid or offered in 10,000 or more lots per side, whereas the outright futures might only be bid and offered in quantities of perhaps a thousand. In this scenario, joining a large spread bid would yield proportionally less fill than working the orders in the outrights, and particularly so if the exchange host algorithm gives a preference to the outright prices rather than the implied-out prices.

Price-injection model

Price-injection models are very similar to auto-spreaders and work on similar logic but might be tailored towards option hedging or market-making. Market-making might just require the constant injection of prices to fulfil a market-making mandate but will not necessarily require a fill to spread off against another contract or expiry.

Both auto-spreaders and price injection models can create a lot of network traffic and demands upon the exchange-trading host. It is common to have to be registered to use such an application and the traffic levels of the trader will be monitored. If too many auto-spreader orders are being placed in the market, perhaps at price levels which are not close to being filled, then the exchanges can take punitive measures. Most ISV auto-spreaders have some functionality to minimise order change traffic.

The use of auto-spreaders requires the acceptance of the additional risk of being legged out. It does happen frequently, the usual causes being the entire bid or offer being traded in one clip causing a fill on one side but the other being missed due to implied order preference or technical issues such as system slowdowns. They are useful tools but should be used cautiously and not in times of volatility.

Auto-traders

Auto-trading interfaces are available on a few ISV trading platforms. They can take the form of a real-time data (RTD) protocol in Microsoft Excel, an algorithmic trading interface or direct coding to an application programming interface (API). These allow the programming, usually in Visual Basic or C++, of a fully user-customisable automated trading model.

Risk management considerations

All ISV software will have a risk management solution that provides both pre-trade and post-trade risk management for the trader.

Pre-trade risk management

Pre-trade risk management is determined by the risk manager and partially by the trader. Futures position limits are based on the trader's experience, their capital, the futures margin requirement and an intra-day multiple, if offered, based on the current market volatility. These limits will be entered into the ISV risk management software and then will relate to a specific trader, only allowing them to trade a maximum clip size or build an inventory of a maximum amount. The system will check each order before it is allowed to market to ensure it conforms, otherwise it will be rejected. The trader can adjust these amounts downward, so that their clip size might be less than their maximum permitted.

Post-trade risk management

Post-trade risk management is the analysis of a trader's open futures positions that have already been traded and permitted by the pre-trade risk management. Most systems mark positions to market based upon either the last traded price, the current bid or offer price, or settlement prices if the market has closed, and operate a warning system if absolute levels of loss or cash balances are breached. Some post-trade risk management systems can be more sophisticated and use a correlation, SPAN or value-at-risk (VaR)-type discipline and some are capable of analysing firm-wide risk for larger clearing members, who might have several ISV packages.

Many ISV risk management packages operate on the principle that all working orders can be executed simultaneously. That is to say, for example, if ten orders were being worked then in theory all might be instantaneously filled in times of severe market volatility. That would be true if all ten orders were all bids or all offers since volatility tends to manifest itself directionally, but unfortunately many ISV risk management systems include both bid and offer orders as part of their calculation. This means that the trader with a pre-trade position limit of 100 lots could enter ten orders of ten lots, either bid or offered and run the possibility that all could be hit, but only enter five bids and five offers before reaching their maximum threshold. It is very difficult to envisage a situation where both bids and offers are executed almost simultaneously. Wouldn't the trader be pleased with that outcome? However, for lack of a better model, many ISV risk management software programs run on the above principle and traders should be aware of the constraints that it can impose.

Limitations of some ISV risk management systems

Some ISV companies have put most of their resources into their trading applications and given little further consideration to their risk management solutions once they've been 'proven' robust. Consequently, some contain risk management principles of dubious merit. An example that affects STIR futures traders is the inclusion of strategies as outright futures risk. For example, a trader with a pre-trade position limit of 100 lots might not be able to enter an order into a calendar spread for 100 lots since the risk management software will consider it to be two 100-lot positions (long/short 100 lots of one expiry, short/long 100 lots of another expiry). This is despite there being no execution risk, being guaranteed by the exchange algorithm and the clearing house SPAN margin system regarding a spread strategy as having approximately only 25% of the risk of an outright future. This can result in the dichotomy of the trader having to request higher than usually allowable position limits from their risk manager to facilitate their business at normal levels.

Accordingly, spread traders should check to see how their ISV risk management system manages strategy-based trading.

Rogue traders – when risk management fails

Virtually all risk management software packages and procedures are proven and robust nowadays, after about five years of continual use and refinement. It hasn't always been like that, though; particularly in the early days of electronic trading. The case studies below serve as a reminder that software, people and arcades aren't infallible, especially when there is a specific aim to defraud.

Griffin Trading Company

Griffin Trading Company was a Chicago-incorporated company specialising in providing clearing services to futures traders. It was a non-clearing member of Eurex and had in place an arrangement with a clearing member of Eurex to clear the trades of GLH Derivatives Ltd, which comprised a number of traders trading on Eurex and Liffe, including a John Ho Park.

John Ho Park had been in breach of his pre-trade position limits several times from July 1998 to December 1998 by trading positions up to 20 times his permitted daily trading limits. Griffin and GLH had inadequate risk management software and procedures, and John Ho Park was aware of this and exploited it. Although being warned about his position limit breaches, Park continued to over trade and on 21 December 1998 had an intra-day position of 10,176 Eurex futures when his allowable position limit was restricted to 978 lots. His overnight position limit was 50 lots but he actually carried 10,128 lots over the night of 21 December, resulting in a loss of £6.3m on 22 December as prices moved against him.

The failure by Griffin and GLH to meet margin calls from their clearing member resulted in default and ultimately the liquidation of Griffin.

Sussex Futures Ltd

Sussex Futures Ltd acted as an arcade for traders trading Eurex and Liffe. On 6 August 1999, a trader called Stephen Humphries, trading as SPH Futures Ltd, exceeded his ten-lot intra-day position limit in the Liffe Gilt future by building a position of 1,129 lots, which resulted in a loss of £743,000. Sussex Futures Ltd had an automated risk management system but on that day it had been disconnected due to malfunctions and there was insufficient staff numbers for manually monitoring his activities.

Sussex Futures Ltd ceased trading but no other customer was disadvantaged since the owner made arrangements to cover all the losses by making a substantial personal financial contribution. Stephen Humphries of SPH Futures Ltd served a prison sentence for fraudulent trading.

TRX Futures Ltd

Shaun Oates worked for TRX Futures, a UK-based futures broker and clearing member of several exchanges, and lost £4.8 million (30% of TRX's capital) with fraudulent and unauthorised trades.

Oates broke company rules by setting up a trading account for his own front company and then faking records to show it had deposited $5m. Oates also deleted successful trades from real clients' records, before diverting the profits to himself and buying two houses with £775,000 of ill-gotten gains. The losses became apparent in the market turbulence of 2008 and Oates was tried and jailed for five years in 2011.

Influences Regarding the Trader's Choice of Markets and Contracts

STIR futures traders have the choice of several exchanges and contracts to trade, but there can be advantages or incentives that influence the decision.

There are two principal STIR futures exchanges, Liffe in London, offering Euribor, Short Sterling and Euroswiss, and CME in Chicago offering Eurodollars. There are also Euroyen STIR futures traded on Tokyo Financial Exchange (TFX) in Japan, but difficult and expensive access, plus anti-social trading hours (for western traders), rule this out as a viable choice.

The majority of traders tend to stay close to home in their choice of markets and contracts, usually for reasons of domicile, time zone and connectivity, but the more mobile trader can choose to trade from different locations for reasons such as lifestyle and taxation considerations.

Domicile and time zones

The exchanges operate their electronic trading platforms on a global network with access points in most countries and major cities. Liffe, for example, operates Connect in over 831 sites covering 31 countries and all time zones.

This makes connectivity and market access relatively easy and the trading hours of the major STIR futures contracts tend to overlap with time zones of other major financial centres to facilitate business. Eurodollar and Euribor are available almost 24 hours a day. Smaller, indigenous STIR futures contracts tend to have trading hours matching the usual local working day. However, despite round-the-clock or extended trading hours being available in the larger global contracts, the vast majority of business is conducted during a domestic time zone. Eurodollar is relatively inactive during the Far Eastern trading day (US night) and moderately active during European trading hours (US very early morning), as traders might trade or spread Eurodollars against moves in Euribor. However, the bulk of business is transacted during the US working day (the European afternoon and evening). Euribor is also usually quiet after European working hours, despite being available to US traders during their afternoon.

Consequently, it is not unusual to find mobile US traders relocating to London or Europe to access those markets, and vice versa, despite the markets being available globally.

Remote Trading

Remote trading includes any trading outside of the clearing member's internal network. It can include most trading arcades, either located locally or abroad, and individual traders working from home or a small office. All remote trading organisations or individuals will need to have some form of connectivity to connect to the internal network of the clearing member, unless they host their own exchange gateways or hubs.

Internet

The simplest form of connectivity is via a simple broadband internet link – popular with home-based traders because of the low cost, short contract period but relatively fast performance. Larger futures brokers tend to offer ISV trading software with internet connectivity for the remote trader.

It should be remembered that all broadband internet connections are *asymmetrical digital subscriber line* (ADSL) which means that although a service might be advertised as having a 10MB (megabyte) or 20MB bandwidth, that only applies to its downstream capability. Its upstream bandwidth will normally be limited to just 750k, which might be fine for a single user connecting to one or two exchanges, but will not have surplus upstream capacity for more users. *Symmetrical digital subscriber lines* (SDSL) are being rolled out in urban areas and offer the same upstream and downstream bandwidth but are many times more expensive.

Virtual private network (VPN)

A variation on the internet connection is the *virtual private network* (VPN), a secure internet connection by the use of encryption. VPN will be a more secure method of trading via the internet but might be fractionally slower due to the encryption process. Both internet and VPN users should be aware of their contention ratio, which is the ratio of total bandwidth available shared amongst subscribers. A residential internet connection might have a contention ratio of 40:1, meaning that there can be up to 39 other users sharing the service. This can be fine if there are only a few other daytime users competing for your bandwidth over Non-Farm Payrolls, but if music downloaders and file sharers surround you, then slowdowns are likely. Business broadband services are better options, being a little more expensive but offering lower contention ratios, better service back-up and usually a little more upstream bandwidth.

Digital private circuit

Top-level connectivity is via a *digital private circuit* such as British Telecom's Kilostream and Megastream services or by an *application service provider* (ASP) such as Radianz. These are the most expensive methods of connecting a remote office or arcade, but are also the quickest and most reliable. ASP connections tend to be fully managed with redundancy (back-up), meaning that the entire connection is supplied and managed, including the network, routers (device forwarding data between networks) and back-up in case of a partial failure. Some ASP connections use a network protocol such as *network address translation* (NAT) that is not supported by all ISVs, so it is necessary to check in advance to entering into a contract, which are usually of one year's duration, although discounts might be offered for longer commitments. Digital private circuits such as the Kilostream and Megastream services can be supplied on a network-only basis, where the client is responsible for supplying and configuring the routers. They usually involve a connection fee and annual rental charge dependent upon location and distance to point.

Connectivity speed

Connection speed is always of vital interest to remote traders. There can be several influences upon speed to market, the main ones being distance and quality of connection and network infrastructure integrity.

Connection speeds can be tested by Ping tests and Traceroute (tracert) commands, if the destination internet protocol (IP) address is known.

Ping

On Windows machines, ping tests are run in the RUN window of the operating system and will have the following syntax.

C:\> ping xxx.xxx.xx.xxx

Where xxx is the IP address of the remote server.

The ping test sends a data packet to its destination and measures how long it takes to come back, rather like an echo or sonar. Its round-trip is measured in milliseconds (thousandths of a second) and ping speeds are governed by network traffic, distance and bandwidth constraints. Very generally speaking, a remote trader based in the same city as their destination host should consistently ping at between 8ms and 20ms. Further distances such as London to Chicago might ping up to 100ms and trans-world can be approximately 300ms.

Not all networks can be pinged, since firewalls often block them as being intrusive security threats.

Traceroute

The traceroute command has similar syntax except 'ping' is replaced by 'tracert'.

This command provides details of the path between the two hosts and the number of nodes involved. The fewer nodes or hops between nodes, the more direct, and possibly *quicker*, the connection.

There is also a 'pathping' command that combines the ping and traceroute utilities. The difference is that each node of the connection is pinged as the result of a single command, and that the behaviour of nodes is studied over an extended time period, rather than the ping's default sample of four messages or Traceroute's default single route trace. The disadvantage is that it often takes more than five minutes to produce a result.

Trading STIR Futures | 3

Trading Opportunities: The Two Trades

There are two ways to trade STIR futures:

1. **outright trading**, which is the purchase or sale of a single contract only

2. **spread trading**, which is the trading of multiple contracts against each other. Spread trading (also known as *strategy trading*) can be either intra-contract, where trades are within the same futures contract or inter-contract, where one contract is traded against another correlated contract.

Outright trading

Outright trading is the simplest form of trading but also one of the most difficult. Someone once described futures trading as "being the hardest way to make easy money" and no doubt they were probably referring to outright trading.

On the face of it, trading outrights is fairly straightforward. You try to buy low and sell high, but it's a volatile form of trading and earnings can be erratic. It's possibly the area of highest failure amongst new traders, but it's also the arena of the trading legends.

Macro trading

Fundamentals-based macro view

Outright trading can be considered in two forms. The first is macro trading where a considered view is used to justify a purchase or sale. This view might be based on an economic incongruity, such as the trader thinking that the STIR futures prices were too low, driven down by the market's inflationary expectations of high oil prices but against a background of a rapidly weakening economy and the possibility of future interest rate cuts. George Soros, one of the most successful traders of all time, employed this kind of trading with great success and he attempted to quantify this discrepancy between market participants' expectations and the actual course of events by a theory of reflexivity in his book *The Alchemy of Finance*. It's an interesting read, mainly to learn more about how these discrepancies can build up in markets, but it is difficult to quantify this phenomenon.

Technically driven macro view

Alternatively, the macro view might be technically driven, where the decision to buy or sell is based upon chart patterns or trading indicators. Charts are graphical representations of price-time series and indicators are mainly mathematically derived measures of relative price movements. Many books have been written about each but the subject is beyond the scope of this one. Most traders look at charts and familiarise themselves with price levels, either to generate trading ideas or to be aware of what other more technically driven traders are watching. It really depends on whether the trader believes that historical price trends can influence future trends or whether mathematics can interpret price action.

CASE STUDY: A trading example

In November 2005 market expectations of an interest rate rise by the ECB were being supported by increasingly hawkish central banker rhetoric and at their 1 December meeting the ECB duly raised interest rates by 25bps.

The chart shows that, afterwards, the Euribor future was finding resistance at the 97.11 level, providing a good selling point in expectation that further interest rate rises would put downward pressure on the market. This view gathered momentum during December and the market fell to 96.90 on expectations that the euro zone was at the start of a cycle of monetary tightening.

Fig. 3.1 – Hourly chart of Euribor Z6 – November 2005 to January 2006

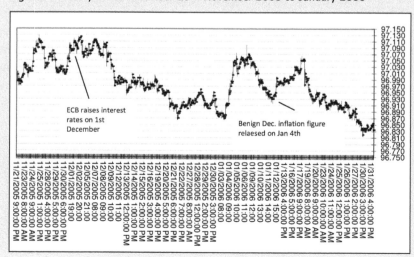

However, these expectations were temporarily reversed early in the New Year when the December inflation figure released on 4 January was lower than expected. This prompted a sharp inter-day rally as shorts covered their positions. This provided further selling opportunities for the brave, believing that this rally was mainly technically induced and the upward pressures on interest rates remained. This view was subsequently correct as the markets sold lower in January.

Trading example – the money flows

On 7 December, a week after the ECB rate rise, the Euribor Z6 future had bounced back to the 97.11 level. A decision was made to sell ten lots around this level with a view to further rate rise expectations driving the market lower. The trade is closed out five days later, on 12 December. The money flows are described below.

- **Commissions** are €2 per round trip (to buy and sell one lot), therefore totalling €10 to sell the opening position of ten lots.

- The **initial margin** requirement is €475 per contract, totalling €4,750 for the ten-lot position.

The market account will be marked to market with the closing prices of the position each day. If the position is showing a profit, this will be credited to the account. If it is showing a loss, it will be debited from the account. The prices for the trade period are shown in the table below.

Table 3.1 – Prices for the example trade period

Date	Open	High	Low	Close
7 Dec	97.11	97.12	97.06	97.07
8 Dec	97.07	97.11	97.03	97.055
9 Dec	97.06	97.075	96.97	96.97
12 Dec	96.98	97.00	96.97	96.99

- 7 Dec

Sell 10 Euribor Z6 at 97.06. Commission bill is €10. Initial margin requirement is €4,750, but since the market settles higher at 97.07, rather than the traded price of 97.06, there is an unrealised loss on the trade of ten ticks equalling -

€250 (10 x 97.06 - 97.07 x tick value of €25). This amount is added to the margin requirement, making a total of €5,000.

- 8 Dec

The market tracks a little lower, settling at 97.055. The margin account is now credited with the inherent profit on the trade, reducing the total requirement to €4,750 - €125, equalling €4,625 (10 x 97.06 - 97.055 x €25).

- 9 Dec

The market breaks lower and settles at 96.97. Margin requirement is now €4,750 - €2,250, totalling €2,500 (10 x 97.06 - 96.97 x €25). Now would have been a great time to close the trade but a decision is taken to run it over the weekend, in the hope of some rate rise commentary in the weekend press.

- 12 Dec

The market opens a little higher. The hoped-for negative press didn't materialise and a decision is taken to close the position. Ten lots are bought at 96.99, making a profit of seven ticks. The second part of the commission of €10 is now payable.

The total profit equals:

97.06 - 96.99 = 7 ticks x 10 lots = 70 ticks = 70 x €25 = €1,750

Commissions equalled €20, making an adjusted return of €1730.

Trading size is purely dependent on account size and the position limits imposed by the risk manager. The above trade could just as well have been done in one lot, ten lots, 500 lots or 1,000 lots. The liquidity is there in STIR futures at virtually all times. Commissions would naturally be larger, being charged on a per-lot or per-round-trip basis, but so would the accompanying profit and loss. For example, the commissions on a 1,000-lot trade would total €2,000, but the profit on the above trade would have been €175,000.

There is a funding cost of margin which is dealt with in different ways by different clearing members. Interest is usually payable on traders' accounts, but capital utilised as margin might not attract interest. However, for most STIR traders, these amounts are relatively insignificant given the trade's profit or loss potential.

Scalping

The second form of outright trading is scalping. This is short-term intensive price-action trading. Unlike macro trading, where a position is established based on a view and in looking for a significant movement, scalping is all about trading the bid/offer spread and trying to gain a quick tick here and there. Scalpers add liquidity to markets they operate in, acting in a market-making capacity, providing price quotes almost continually. Scalping is usually involved in the more volatile bond and equity futures markets but can be used with success in the liquid front months of STIR futures.

Scalping examples would be exactly the same as above (under *Macro Trading*), except on a much shorter time scale. And since most scalping is intra-day, it would not involve overnight margin.

Losing money

The problem with outright trading is the risk of losing money, either absolutely or in a drawdown. Losing money absolutely is easily understood and very easy to achieve, especially when the odds are stacked against the trader. A trader needs to be right about seven times out of ten in order to make money after fees. No mean feat, but those traders who have a firm grasp of limiting their losses and getting their view right most of the time and at the right time, can get ahead.

Drawdowns are the unrealised losses on a position. For example, a trader might buy futures at 95.50 and sell later for 95.55, making five ticks. If, however, whilst holding the position the price had dropped to 95.45 before going up to 95.55, the trader would have had a drawdown of five ticks.

Some traders can handle drawdowns, others can't. The legendary hedge fund trader Michael Steinhardt was renowned for *being able to see the mountain in the distance whilst ignoring the valleys in-between*. Others prefer to take the loss and start again.

In outright trading, most macro-traders tend to be hedge funds seeking higher returns whilst the scalpers tend to be independent traders using their own capital for smaller but more frequent profits. Perhaps it's easier taking drawdowns when it's someone else's money!

Trading considerations for outrights

1. Markets move between periods of volatility and inactivity. It is usually during the periods of volatility that the scalping and trading opportunities exist – but periods of extreme volatility are best avoided.

2. Economic releases often have big effects on STIR futures markets. Trading just before the figure, or carrying positions over numbers, carries additional risk.

3. STIR futures can move quickly but not as quickly as the more volatile bond futures at the longer end of the yield curve. Scalpers use them as leading indicators for STIR futures.

4. Markets frequently move on false rumours, usually based on what is fashionable at the time. At present it is terrorism and they are identified by sharp, sporadic price movements. Normally, the trader will only hear about the rumour after the market price action, making them difficult to trade. Real events are usually identified by consistent large-scale buying or selling.

5. Each STIR future has its own culture and influences. These can change from month to month. Price action is often a reflection of traders' cumulative positions. Sometimes, such as on Friday afternoons or before a bank holiday, prices can fall or squeeze higher as traders seek to square their positions.

Spread trading

Spread trading is the purchase or sale of one futures contract against an opposite position in another related contract. There are two classes of spread:

- **intra-contract** – where one series is traded against another within the same STIR futures contract

- **inter-contract** – which involves a spread between two or more different futures contracts.

Spread trading usually has a lower risk profile than outright trading, particularly intra-contract spreading which can be quantified via a statistical measurement such as standard deviation. An outright Euribor future might have a standard deviation of 0.23 whilst its three-month calendar spread might have a standard deviation of just 0.03.

Consequently, the outright is much more volatile than the spread, making the spread a lower-risk method of trading. Spread trading offers a more controlled exposure to the differential between two futures contracts, instead of trading a single contract and being fully exposed to its price action.

Spread trading offers a different kind of trading experience than outrights. There is less outright risk, numerous trade permutations, either within a contract or against others and they can be traded electronically as single strategies where both parts of the spread are transacted simultaneously, thus eliminating execution or leg risk.

Spread Trading: Intra-Contract Spreads

There are basically three types of intra-contract spreads (which are those that trade within the same STIR futures contract):

1. calendar spread

2. butterfly spread

3. condor spread.

They are characterised by the fact that their total position will always net out to zero since the component legs will counter-position each other. An example could be the long calendar spread that comprises a purchase of a near-dated future (+1) and a sale of a further-dated future (-1), netting out to zero. All these spreads can be traded either as the component legs or as strategies or single instruments on the leading futures exchanges.

Calendar spread

The calendar spread is the simultaneous purchase and sale to open of the same underlying contract but in different delivery months.

It is simply the difference between two delivery months in the same futures contact. They are also known as *legs* and can be expressed as:

$P_1 - P_2$

where P_1 is the price of the nearest delivery month in the spread and P_2 is the longer-dated delivery month in the spread.

Example

If H2 was trading 97.490 and M2 was trading 97.320, then the H2M2 spread is the difference between the H2 and the M2 or 97.490 - 97.320 = 0.170.

0.170 is the differential between these two contracts and is effectively 17 ticks or 17 basis points. This differential, or spread, can change as the two futures change in price since they are not perfectly correlated to each other because they represent different points on the yield curve.

Calendar spreads don't have to be limited to just P_1 - P_2, where there is only the difference of one delivery cycle or three months in-between. Another example might be:

P_1 - P_3

where P_3 would be U2, making the H2U2 spread with a six-month interval between expiries.

Calendar spreads are always priced by the convention of dealing the nearest month first so that buying the spread would involve buying the nearest-dated series, selling the far-dated series. Selling the spread would be selling the nearest-dated series and buying the far-dated series. Calendar spreads have a market bid/offer spread just like any single future. These can be determined by a simple process of using the bids and offers of the component futures:

• Spread **bid price** = bid price nearest future - offer price further future

• Spread **offer price** = offer price nearest future - bid price further future

So by using the following price quotes ...

Table 3.2 – Example STIR futures prices

	Bid price	Offer price
H2	97.490	97.495
M2	97.315	97.320
U2	97.210	97.215
Z2	97.160	97.165
H3	97.105	97.110

The buying price (or offer) and the selling price (or bid) of the H2M2 spread would be:

• H2M2 **bid price** = 97.490 - 97.320 = 0.170

• H2M2 **offer price** = 97.495 - 97.315 = 0.180

Continuing this process would give the following spread prices from the price table.

Table 3.3 – Spread prices implied by the STIR futures prices

	Bid price	Offer price
H2M2	0.170	0.180
M2U2	0.100	0.110
U2Z2	0.045	0.055
Z2H3	0.050	0.060

The calendar spread bid/offer spread will always be a maximum of the combined bid/offer spreads of the component futures. In this case, where Euribor has a half-tick spread, the spread bid/offer will be one tick. It could possibly be wider if a more illiquid future was used with a bid/offer of more than half a tick but will always be the sum of the individual bids and offers.

This spread is also the implied price since it is generated by the outright futures. In practice, the spread bid/offer in the market is narrower than the implied prices. The following table shows the market prices of the STIR spreads and, comparing these to those of the price table, it can be seen that the spread bid/offer is the minimum permitted increment of half a tick. The implied prices make up one side of the price, but the other price is improved upon by market participants. Spread markets are usually tight and highly liquid since they have less volatility than outright futures. Traders are more willing to trade for the minimum increment on an instrument that has less movement and usually in larger sizes hence promoting liquidity.

Table 3.4 – Actual market prices for STIR spreads (italics show implied prices)

	Bid price	Offer price
H2M2	0.175	*0.180*
M2U2	0.105	*0.110*
U2Z2	0.050	*0.055*
Z2H3	*0.050*	0.055

The market examples in the table are the actual exchange-traded strategies for the sequential three-month spreads. These spreads, in this form, can be traded as instruments just like individual futures. It is also possible to construct and trade spreads consisting of component futures that start and end with any delivery month within the cycle. However, a number of characteristics need to be observed.

1. A calendar spread with a larger interval between component delivery months will be more volatile than one with a shorter interval.

2. Shorter interval spreads tend to be more liquid than longer interval spreads (although one-year spreads are popular; for example, Z2Z3).

3. White pack spreads will be more volatile than red pack spreads, which in turn will be more volatile than spreads in the green pack.

4. Margin requirements will be higher on longer interval spreads and on white pack spreads, less so respectively on red and green pack spreads.

Volatility increases with wider spread intervals

The chart shows how a longer interval within the spread increases volatility by showing the declining correlation of the three-month (3M) sequential futures to the front month. It is clear how a spread between the front month and the next delivery month has a much lower net correlation (the difference between the two correlations) than one between the same front month and, say, a delivery month one year later. This widening net correlation, as the interval between the delivery months widens, is reflected by the increasing standard deviations. This means that as the interval between front month and the next series widens, the volatility and risk also increases.

Fig. 3.2 – Chart showing the correlations of sequential series against the front month plotted against the standard deviations of the spreads against front month

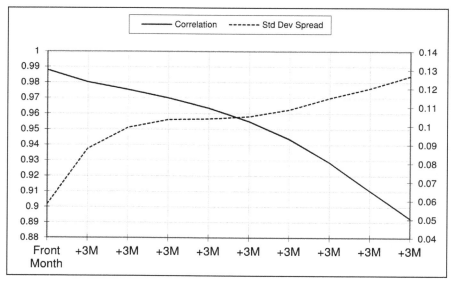

Spreads of any interval will be more volatile in the front white pack than spreads in the red pack, which in turn will be more volatile than spreads in the green pack. For example, a white pack spread might be twice as volatile as a red pack spread depending on the data sample.

Fig. 3.3 – Price movement for Euribor three-month spreads: white pack spread (thick black line), red pack spread (thick grey line) and green pack spread (thin black line)

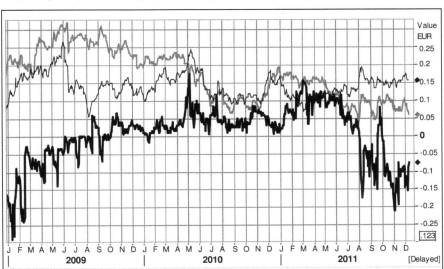

It is apparent how the front white spread moves more than the red and green spreads. This can be due to a number of factors driving the STIR futures prices, including liquidity, the economic outlook and incidence of interest rate expectations. Most of these factors tend to be concentrated into the first year of the STIR futures price curve, simply because forecasting is an imperfect science and making longer-dated forecasts is unreliable. This is often why the majority of curvature in the STIR futures price curve is present in the first four, and then the following four delivery months, representing the white and red packs or two years of the yield curve.

Calendar spreads are effectively yield curve capture trades, and the amount of curve being captured is dependent on the spread interval. Put another way, they are a price representation of a yield curve shape at a given time and the changing shape of the yield curve will drive their prices.

Yield curve effect on calendar spreads

Previous sections have shown how yield curves are usually positive. But they can be flat or even negative in times of impending recession. The table shows how calendar spreads will respond to a changing yield curve shape.

A **steepening curve** refers to a **widening** of the difference between a longer-term rate and a shorter-term rate and will cause calendar spreads to widen.

A **flattening curve** refers to a **narrowing** of the difference between a longer-term rate and a shorter-term rate and this will cause calendar spreads to narrow.

Table 3.5 – Yield curve effects on calendar spreads

	Calendar spreads price
Yield curve steepening	↑
Yield curve flattening	↓

It should be remembered from previous sections (*Liquidity considerations of the micro curve*) that segments of the yield curve, and hence the STIR futures price curve, can have both steepening and flattening effects within a section as small as two years. This can lead to the interesting situation of some spreads moving up and others moving down, making the butterfly spreads of particular relevance.

Following on from the earlier 2005 trading case study, another way of trading the euro zone interest rate rise expectations of December 2005 (instead of taking a macro view and trading the outrights, as shown in an earlier example), would be to trade the steepening shape of the yield curve by using calendar spreads.

The chart shows the Euribor H6M6 spread over the same time period. An anticipation of higher interest rates could prompt a purchase of the calendar spread, in expectation that the yield curve would steepen as the markets looked for further rate rises. This would cause the calendar spread to rise in value as the further-dated contract (M6) declined more quickly than the nearer H6.

Fig. 3.4 – Euribor H6M6 calendar spread – July 2005 to January 2006

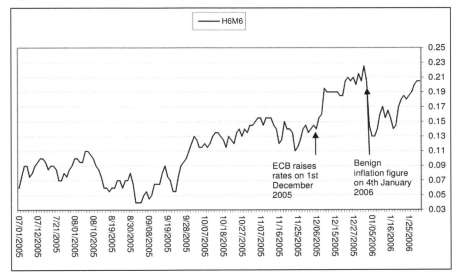

The spread could have been purchased at around 0.13 when rates were increased on 1 December 2005. The spread then mirrored the steepening yield curve and increased to 0.21, until being sharply corrected by the benign inflation figure on 4 January 2006.

Although the calendar spread is directional and will be influenced by the movements in the outright futures, it has a much lower risk profile than the outright future. The Z6 contract (in the earlier example) moved approximately 20 ticks, whereas the H6M6 spread moved just six ticks.

Calendar spread matrix

A useful way of presenting calendar spreads is via a matrix. Most ISVs incorporate them into their trading software and they have the advantage that all spreads, of all permutations and intervals, can be observed in a single space.

The next table shows a typical matrix layout. Different matrices will differ slightly, but generally all will display a sequential series of futures along the X and Y axes, with the spread prices embedded accordingly. The table shows the futures strip, with symbols and prices along the top row and the futures symbols diagonally across the matrix. The spread prices are stacked so that the offer is above the bid, although some matrices will exhibit these prices side by side or allow the user to customise.

Fig. 3.5 – STIR futures spread matrix

	H2	M2	U2	Z2	H3	M3	U3	Z3
OFFER	99.325	99.220	99.170	99.115	99.080	99.030	98.985	98.930
BID	99.320	99.215	99.165	99.110	99.075	99.025	98.980	98.925
	H2	M2	U2	Z2	H3	M3	U3	Z3
	H2	0.110	0.160	0.215	0.250	0.300	0.345	0.400
		0.105	0.155	0.210	0.245	0.290	0.335	0.390
		M2	0.055	0.110	0.145	0.195	0.240	0.295
			0.050	0.105	0.140	0.190	0.230	0.285
			U2	0.055	0.090	0.140	0.190	0.245
				0.050	0.085	0.135	0.180	0.235
				Z2	0.040	0.090	0.135	0.190
					0.035	0.085	0.130	0.185
					H3	0.050	0.095	0.155
						0.045	0.090	0.145
						M3	0.045	0.105
							0.040	0.100
							U3	0.060
								0.055
								Z3

Spread from spreads example:

Bidding the M2H3 at 0.140 against selling M2Z2 at 0.105 will result in being long Z2H3 0.035.

By following one symbol from the diagonal row to underneath another symbol on the top row, the market spread price for that combination can be found. For example, following the H2 on the diagonal row to where it is underneath M2 on the top row will give the three-month H2M2 spread as 0.105 bid, 0.110 offered. The diagonal row is always quoted first. It can be seen that the 0.110 offer is in italics and this is because it is an implied price. However, these can contain a quantity of market participants' orders, making a combination of implied and outright orders. Different ISVs have different ways of showing this order information. Generally, in the depths of the matrix, towards the top right-hand corner, prices are often implied with the bid/offer spread defaulting to the spread implied by the bid/offer prices of the outright futures. This is because spreads of such a large interval are not popular and so traded volumes are low and hence liquidity can be poor.

Conversely, prices towards the diagonal symbols tend to be tighter and more liquid since these are the three-month spreads. The diagonal row above these is the six-month spreads and the one above those are the nine-month spreads and so on. Generally, as mentioned earlier, spread liquidity will decline as the spread interval grows larger or, as displayed by the matrix, as one moves upwards from the diagonal symbols towards the apex of the matrix.

A spread matrix is not just a useful visual aid, allowing the trader to view all spreads in one space. It can also be used as an alternative trading mechanism.

The trader is faced with two simple choices when trading a spread. They can enter their order in the spread order book, and, if trying to join the bid or offer, join the queue of other orders all trying to do the same thing. Spreads tend to be highly liquid, particularly the low interval ones, with thousands or even tens of thousands of contracts on the bid and offer. Exchange-trading computerised algorithms will usually ensure a pro-rata trade allocation but can be geared towards preferential treatment for certain kinds of order. The reality is that the order is usually completed only when the entire spread price has traded out. That's fine if the trader really wants to buy or sell that price, if perhaps they have an absolute view on the curve, but if their motive is being able to buy the bid before everyone else or sell the offer whilst it is still offered, it is not much use. The second choice is to leg the trade via the individual component futures. This is a very effective method when done successfully, but is subject to outright or leg risk.

Creating spreads from spreads

There is a third way, however. It is possible to create spreads from spreads. A 12-month spread like the H2H3 must be the same as the four three-months spreads within its interval period, in this case H2M2 + M2U2 + U2Z2 + Z2H3. It must also be the same as:

- two six-month spreads (H2U2 + U2H3), or

- nine-month + three-month spread (H2U3 + U3Z3), or

- three-month + nine-month (H2M2+M2H3).

The wider the spread interval, the more trade permutations and ways of establishing other spreads there will be. Most traders will use this approach to either convert an existing spread into another that is perhaps more liquid, or has a shorter interval, or even to convert a long position in a spread into a short position if their views on the shape of the curve have changed.

An easier way to look at this and the trading possibilities is to reduce the matrix to show only the spread intervals.

Fig. 3.6 – Data from spread matrix, but only showing the spread intervals

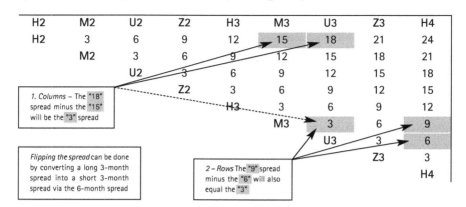

As with the spread matrix, the sequence of three-month spreads lies above the diagonal symbols, followed by the six-month spreads above, then the nine-month spreads, and so on, in a geometric pattern.

Converting longer interval spreads to three-month spreads

A trader can convert almost any spread into another. Taking an 18-month spread and subtracting a 15-month spread will leave a position in a three-month spread. Two "three" spreads will equal a "six" spread. Usually, though, most traders will want to convert other spreads into a three-month spread. The three-month spreads have liquidity barriers that make it unappealing to merely place a bid or offer in the order book in the first place – but those liquidity barriers also make it attractive for the trader to be long on the bid or short on the offer.

There are two easy patterns to look for in the matrix to find longer-dated spreads for conversion into three-month spreads.

1. Columns

First, select the target three-month spread, for example the M3U3 spread, and find the corresponding box with a "3" in it. Follow the *column* up to the top row with "18" in it underneath the U3 symbol. Going one cell left will be "15" for the H2M3 spread. Subtracting this from the "18" spread will result in the "3" spread of M3U3 (see textbox). Netting out the symbols can substantiate this: a H2U3 "18" spread minus a H2M3 "15" spread will net out to M3U3.

This process can be continued down the matrix column so that going a step down will give the "15"spread (M2U3) and going one cell left will be the "12" (M2M3). Again this will net out to the M3U3 spread. This procedure can be followed down the matrix column to do the same for "12" against "9", "9" against "6" and "6" against "3". That's five ways to establish a position in the three-month M3U3 spread. The same process can be used on any other three-month spread, the only constraint being the depth of the matrix limiting the number of permutations.

2. Rows

Again, a three-month spread is chosen and the M3U3 spread is used as an example. This time, instead of following the column upwards from the "3", the *row* is followed right to the end of the matrix where the cell is "9" for the M3H4 spread. Going one cell down to the "6" gives the U3H4 spread. Netting these two spreads will result in the M3U3 spread. This is the same process as *columns*, but using the rows instead of the columns (see textbox).

Both these methods complement each other in that they can offer increased trading permutations for three-month spreads. If one method is limited by the depth or width of the matrix limiting the number of permutations, then the other can be used. Note that in both cases, the second spread is of a lower interval than the first, and geometrically there will always be a downward progression towards the diagonal symbols. If a higher interval were chosen for the second spread than the first, it would just relate to an adjacent spread. Furthermore, these examples have used only one step left or down within the matrix. It is perfectly possible to use more steps, but the resulting spread will be longer dated than the three-month spreads used. The resulting spread will always be the difference between the two initiating spreads.

Reversing spread positions

Spreads can also be flipped or reversed in position. If a trader is long of a spread, for example M2U2, and the yield curve starts flattening, the value of the spread is likely to decrease, and the position can be shunted along to the next sequential spread and made short by use of the six-month spread. By being long of M2U2 and selling the six-month M2Z2, a short position is made in U2Z2. Netting out the positions illustrates the process …

Table 3.6 – Flipping a long M2U2 spread into a short U2Z2 spread via the M2Z2 spread

	M2U2	M6Z6	NET
H2			
M2	+	–	
U2	–		–
Z2		+	+

The process of using the intervals to convert longer-dated spreads into shorter-dated spreads can be easily transferred to the real matrix in Figure 3.5. By using the columns method it is possible to find an alternative way to buy M2U2. It is an attractive spread to buy on the bid and sell on the offer since the actual market quote on the day for the three-month spread is 0.050 bid on 26,450 lots and offered at 0.055 on 11,423 lots (the bid and offer sizes have not been included on the matrix for space considerations). The large-sized bid and offer on both sides of the spread means that a pro-rata trade allocation by placing an order into the order book is going to be poor. But it would be a very attractive and well-protected trade if it could be purchased on the bid before the majority of others have traded the three-month. One way would be to bid the H2U2 at the 0.155 that was only bid for 426 lots and, if filled, sell the H2M2 against it at 0.105 (bid for 203 lots) resulting in a long position in the target M2U2 at 0.050 (see textbox). The same spread might then be sold at 0.055 by using the rows approach, also shown as a textbox in figure 3.6. By selling M2M3 at 0.195 (831 lots on offer) against buying U2M3 at 0.140 (104 lots on offer), the three-month M2U2 can be effectively sold at 0.055 giving a profit of half a tick. Nice work if you can get it!

Traders' notes

1. Be aware of the impact of exchange fees and commissions on the potential profit of a matrix trade. The above example of buying and selling the M2U2 spread would have involved eight lots being traded compared to just four lots if the spread were bought and sold as a strategy. However, fee rebates are often available for high volumes of trade, particularly in further-dated contracts. Many 'matrix traders' live off the exchange rebates.

2. Beware of trading one spread against the price of another that is purely implied. The examples above all had 'paper' bids and offers in the quotes used, as well as a component of implied pricing. Implied prices have a nasty habit of disappearing just when you need them!

3. The trade allocation algorithm of each exchange is different and can be changed by the exchanges. The trader needs to be aware of how favourable the allocation would be for a longer-dated spread compared to a shorter-dated one, particularly when generated by a trade implied from a trade in the outright futures.

4. The implied pricing algorithms frequently generate trades in longer-dated spreads from price activity in the futures strip. It is therefore more favourable, and means a better chance of an order being filled, to bid when the offer is implied and vice versa, therefore 'leaning' against the implieds.

5. Remember that longer-dated spreads are more volatile than shorter-dated ones and can have poor liquidity. Often the prices can be purely implied and missing a leg deep within the matrix can be expensive! Look for opportunities closer to the target spread first before going deeper into the matrix.

6. Always 'net out' a matrix trade on paper first before entering the order to ensure that the result is what was envisaged.

7. Use the matrix as an escape route when prices are moving against the spread. Look for alternative ways to close an open spread by columns or rows or flip it into another spread.

International spread correlations

Comparing international calendar spreads

The relatively high correlations between international STIR futures contracts were presented earlier (*The drivers of STIR futures prices*). By association, it should be expected that the spreads will be highly correlated to each other as well. However, spreads are effectively a snapshot of a segment of a country's yield curve, which in turn is influenced by what stage it is at in its economic and interest rate cycle. Consequently, correlations of spreads can be very positive in times of similar economic outlook, but they can break down when divergence occurs.

Butterfly spread

Calendar spreads have been defined as the difference between two delivery months in the same futures contact and expressed as P_1 - P_2. Butterflies are an extension of the same logic, but instead are the difference between two sequential spreads in the same futures contact. They are expressed as:

$$(P_1 - P_2) - (P_2 - P3)$$

Or:

$$P_1 + P_3 - (2*P_2)$$

where P1 is the price of the nearest delivery month in the strategy and P2 is the next delivery month, and P3 the next delivery month.

The chart shows the Eurodollar M2U2 and U2Z2 spreads. The difference between them is the M2U2Z2 butterfly.

Fig. 3.7 – Eurodollar M2U2 spread (thick black) and U2Z2 spread (thin grey) and M2U2Z2 butterfly spread (lower pane) 2009–2011

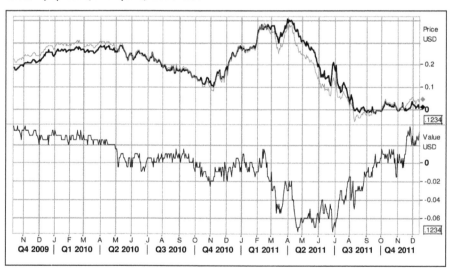

Source: Reuters

Again, as with calendar spreads, the pricing convention is of dealing the nearest month first. Buying the butterfly would involve buying the nearest-dated series, and selling it would be selling the nearest-dated series. Butterflies (also known as *flies* or *the fly*) don't just have to be two three-month spreads back to back. They can be six-month sequential spreads or even wider, provided the centre leg (P_2, also known as *the body*) is the same for both spreads and the first P_1 and third legs P_3 (also known as *the wings*) are equidistant from the body.

Butterfly spreads also have a market bid/offer spread just like any single future or calendar spread and these can be determined by the same process as shown before for calendar spreads. The bid/offer prices can be calculated for the M2U2Z2 butterfly using the prices displayed in the spread matrix in Figure 3.5:

M2U2Z2 bid $\quad$ = (M2(bid) – U2(offer)) – (U2(offer) – Z2(bid))

$\qquad$ = (97.215 - 97.170) - (97.170 - 97.110) = -0.015

M2U2Z2 offer = (M2(offer) - U2(bid)) - (U2(bid) - Z2(offer))

$\qquad$ = (97.220 - 97.165) - (97.165 - 97.115) = 0.005

The bid/offer spread is two-ticks wide because it is the sum of the bid/offer spreads in the four legs of the butterfly (4 x 0.005). This is similar to calendar spreads, whose bid/offer spreads were determined by the bid/offer spreads of the component futures (which were also the implied prices). However, their bid/offer spreads were often improved upon by market participants, reducing them to the minimum permitted increment. This much reduced bid/offer spread in calendar spreads can be used to improve the pricing of butterflies. Since butterflies are the difference between two sequential spreads they can also be priced as:

$S_1 - S_2$

where S1 is the price of the nearest spread (M2U2) and S2 is the next spread (U2Z2).

So, again using prices from the matrix in Figure 3.5:

M2U2Z2 bid = S_1(bid) – S_2(offer) = 0.050 - 0.055 = -0.005

M2U2Z2 offer = S_1(offer) – S_2(bid) = 0.055 - 0.050 = 0.005

The same butterfly now has a reduced bid/offer of just one tick, but is frequently improved upon by market participants to the minimum permitted increment. In the example using Euribor, this is half a tick or 0.005 basis points. If the butterfly is determined to be -0.005 bid and 0.005 offered by the component spreads, it would not be unusual to find the market price was actually 0.000 bid and 0.005 offered, or perhaps -0.005 bid and 0.000 offered. The price level of 0.000 is likely to be the aggregate of the last traded prices of the component futures. This is where the butterfly should trade, since any deviance from this trade level will present opportunities to the trader to trade the fly against either the outright futures or component spreads.

The most popular butterfly spreads are the sequential three-month and the sequential one-year strategies. Butterflies are usually lower risk and less volatile than their individual component spreads and therefore attract less margin.

Butterflies will still be a directional trade, driven by the curve becoming more or less curved around the body of the butterfly, as caused by steepening and flattening effects.

Butterflies are a useful tool for the spread trader:

1. They provide a trading mechanism for the relationship between the sequential calendar spreads: good for trading small distortions on the micro-curve.

2. Similar to using the spread matrix, they offer more avenues to enter or exit a trade. For example, the holder of a long position of a calendar spread that is beginning to suffer from the effects of a flattening yield curve has several choices. The position could be liquidated or flipped into another spread by the matrix, or be converted into a short butterfly by taking an additional short position in the preceding sequential spread.

3. Butterflies are a corner of the triangular price relationship between futures, calendar spreads and butterflies. The outright prices dictate the arbitrage boundaries via the implied-in prices and the calendar spreads improve this further. The level at which trade is going through the individual futures and the calendar spreads should harmonise with the price quotes in the butterfly. If these get slightly out of line, say by a large calendar spread trade or butterfly spread stressing this relationship, then the potential to price-improve can exist.

Traders' notes

1. As with matrix trading, be aware of the impact of trading expenses on the potential profit of trading a butterfly. There are four component legs in a butterfly and expenses can represent a very sizeable proportion of an expected profit.

2. Remember that butterflies can be priced as both a ratio of sequential futures and a combination of sequential calendar spreads. Deriving the prices from bids and offers gives plenty of scope for error. Work things through on paper first or, better still, use a spreadsheet.

3. The price of the butterfly should equal the last trade of the component futures and the two calendar spreads, provided all are liquid.

4. Butterflies are still directional trades. Beware of micro-curve influences such as pivot points, liquidity factors and spread activity having an undue effect on the fly.

Condor spread

Calendar spreads are known to be the difference between two delivery months in the same futures contact, and butterflies are the difference between two sequential spreads in the same futures contact. It should therefore follow that condor spreads are the difference between two butterflies? Not so; they are actually the sum of two butterflies.

Looking at condors in terms of the component futures price, they are expressed as:

$(P_1 - P_2) - (P_3 - P_4)$

where P_1 is the price of the nearest delivery month in the spread and P_n is the next dated delivery month $(P_n = P_1...P_2....P_3....P_4...)$. Note that the difference between P_2 and P_3 must be the same time period as that between P_1 and P_2, and P_3 and P_4.

An example could be H2M2U2Z2, and in terms of the prices in use for the previous examples:

H2M2U2Z2 bid =
(H2(bid) - M2(offer)) - (U2(offer) - Z2(bid)) =
(97.320 - 97.220) - (97.170 - 97.110) = 0.040

H2M2U2Z2 offer =
(H2(offer) - M2(bid)) - (U2(bid) - Z2(offer)) =
(97.325 - 97.215) - (97.165 - 97.115) = 0.060

Or, expressed as the sum of the two butterflies:

$B_1 + B_2$ = H2M2U2 + M2U2Z2 = 0.050 + 0.000 = 0.050

where B_n are the sequential component butterflies.

Or even as the constituent spreads:

$S_1 - S_3$ = H2M2 - U2Z2 = 0.1050 - 0.055 = 0.050

Condor spreads are usually more volatile than the butterfly and the calendar spread. They represent disparate views; opposite opinions on different sections of the yield curve, which are more pronounced and volatile when used with larger intervals of six or 12 months For example, a trader thinking that the yield curve might steepen at the front part of the curve but not continue this effect much beyond one year, might purchase the one-year condor, hence being long the white one-year calendar spread and short the green one-year calendar spread (+H2-H3-H3+H4). However, it requires a very particular opinion, and due to the multiple transaction fees involved, a similar objective might be achieved by use of a calendar spread only.

> ## Traders' notes
>
> It is worth keeping an eye on condor quotes. A tight 'paper' price might make it possible to trade the two butterflies, or two component spreads, against it but will require a decent payoff to justify the multiple fees incurred.

Introduction to strips, packs, bundles and stacks

Strips, packs, bundles and stacks are not strictly spreads since their overall position totals do not net out to zero. Instead, they are the sum of their totals and all legs have the same signage, meaning that all legs are long or all legs are short. They have been included in this section on intra-contract spreads because, although they are usually used to spread against other instruments and not intra-contract, all the component legs of the strategy are part of the same STIR future and quoted as a strategy. Consequently, this section will provide a description of them and the next will detail their common uses.

Strips

Strips are a generic term for any number of sequential STIR futures contracts. A strip might contain, for example, three sequential delivery months such as H2, M2 and U2 or it can contain 20 or more contracts. A strip can be the same as a pack or bundle, but differs in that it can start or finish at any point on the range of STIR futures available, provided all contained within are sequential. Strips are often used as terminology when talking about the futures price curve. They are not traded as strategies in their own right, except when they are presented as packs or bundles.

Packs and bundles can be considered as defined strips since they cover a given number of contracts at a given point on the price curve. Strips are ill-defined since they can refer to any sequence of futures contract, such as either the four quarterly months in the first year or the entire sequence of futures from year one to year ten (in the case of the CME Eurodollar). Packs and bundles provide definition in that they cover a limited number of contracts, over a specific part of the strip, and can be traded as separate strategies. They can also benefit from exchange fee concessions from being traded as a single strategy.

Stacks

Stacks are multiples of a single month. They are usually used as a proxy for a pack or bundle when those are not easily available. A stack as a proxy for a pack comprising four contracts would simply be four times the individual contract.

Packs

Packs are the simultaneous purchase or sale of four quarterly contracts, equally weighted, within the yearly colour banding system.

Reminder: This colour banding system defines the first four quarterly delivery months as being white, the next four as red, then green, blue, gold, orange, pink, silver and copper. Only CME Eurodollar goes as far as copper. The Liffe Euribor stops at gold and Sterling at blue. Generally, liquidity can become poor after the blue packs.

An example of a white pack would be:

$P_1+P_2+P_3+P_4$

where P_1 is the first quarterly delivery month and P_n are the consecutive quarterly delivery months.

A red pack would be:

$P_5+P_6+P_7+P_8$

Packs are priced and quoted on the net change between the current trading price and the previous day's settlement price.

- **Liffe** uses a quote convention of the **totals** of the net change, and

- **CME** uses the **simple average** of the net change.

By using the following fictitious net change data for a white pack, the effects of these different conventions can be observed.

Table 3.7 – Effects of different conventions

H2	M2	U2	Z2
–0.030	–0.003	–0.03	–0.02

On Liffe, the pack would be priced as of the totals of the net change:

-0.03 + -0.03 + -0.03 + -0.02 = -0.110

The CME pack would be priced as the simple average of the net change:

$$\frac{-0.03 + -0.03 + -0.03 + -0.02}{4} = -0.0275$$

- The **Liffe** methodology is known as the **total change convention** and is priced in increments of half a tick or 0.005.

- The **CME** is priced in quarter ticks or 0.0025 and is termed the **annualised convention** since it more accurately reflects price movements of bonds and swaps, which are popular products for inter-contract spreading.

Problem of half-tick prices

Although the CME method is more intuitive and easier to compare with other products, it does conceal a problem. Since the Eurodollar futures are priced in half ticks (the front month is even priced in quarter ticks), this presents an averaging problem for pack and bundles that are priced in quarter ticks. For example, all the net changes shown in the example above are tick integers (whole numbers) but if a fraction of a half tick is introduced for any contract, in this case the U6 delivery month, its effect becomes apparent.

$$(-0.03 + -0.03 + -0.03 + -0.025)/4 = -0.02875$$

The price of -0.02875 is part way between the CME-recognised quotes in quarter-tick increments of -0.0275 and -0.0300. Consequently, this price of -0.02875 is not tradable, even though the individual prices might infer it. In practice, the pack would be quoted as having traded at either -0.0275 or -0.0300, and the actual futures prices traded would be generated by the CME pack and bundle-trading algorithm. This is achieved by dealing with the integer portions first. Each component future would be initially assigned a net price of -0.025 and then each contract, starting with the furthest-dated contract, would be adjusted downwards until the trade price is achieved. In this case, if the pack had traded -0.0300, then all futures would simply be traded at -0.0300 net price change from the previous day's settlement price. If the pack had traded -0.0275, then the algorithm would adjust the prices of the individual futures in the pack. All futures would initially be assigned a -0.020 net change and then revised downwards until the traded price of -0.0275 was achieved. This would be done by assigning -0.0300 for the last three contracts.

Liffe does not have the same issue since it does not use averaging for pricing packs and bundles and its algorithm for assigning prices is slightly different. If the pack price trades at a level reflecting the current market price then those will be used as the individual strategy legs. However, if the pack trades at a price that is not easily matched by current market prices, then the algorithm will assign generated net change prices to each individual leg in equal amounts if the difference warrants it, or by a process of adjusting the most deferred leg first until the pack trade price is achieved. The benefit of this is that it keeps the individual prices of the nearer-dated, more liquid months assigned to the pack closer to the current prices trading in the market.

Since the main market for Eurodollars is on the CME and the market for Euribor is on Liffe, the differences between the two quote and allocation methodologies for packs (and bundles) are irrelevant in that each has to be used with its corresponding product. However, these differences are interesting to observe for the trading ramifications.

1. The CME generally exhibits more further-dated liquidity in its packs and bundles for the Eurodollar than Liffe does for the Euribor.

2. Liffe offers an allocation algorithm that will generate prices closer to those actually trading in the markets. The algorithm used by CME will generate prices to reflect the pack price but its use of integers only, and a deferred-first approach, means that nearer prices might diverge a little from current market prices. In reality, these differences are quite negligible. It's the price that the pack was traded at that is important, not necessarily the price levels of individual futures used.

3. Liffe's total change quote will appear larger and more volatile than the average used by CME since it is more sensitive to prices changes. For example, on Liffe, a half-tick change in each of the four individual futures of the pack will cause a two-tick change in the price quote of the pack (the sum of four half ticks). On CME, the same futures price change would only change the pack price by a matching half tick. Movements of less than a half tick for each contract, such as only one contract being bid up half a tick, would be insufficient to move the price quote but would be shown in the Liffe pack.

Pack yields

Pack yields are the returns on investing or borrowing for one year via a sequential series of quarterly STIR futures. The methodology is akin to investing \$1 (or €1) at the implied rate from the first quarterly future comprising the pack for one quarter and then reinvesting the proceeds into the implied rate from the next quarterly future for the next quarter and so on.

For example, using the following prices:

Table 3.8 – Example yields

	Price
H2	97.490
M2	97.310
U2	97.210
Z2	97.160

The pack yield can be calculated as:

$$[(1 + (100\% - H\,2\%) * 0.25) \times (1 + (100\% - M\,2\%) * 0.25) \times (1 + (100\% - U\,2\%) * 0.25) \times (1 + (100\% - Z\,2\%) * 0.25) - 1]$$

Populating the numbers gives a pack yield of 2.735%:

$$[(1 + 2.51\% * 0.25) \times (1 + 2.69\% * 0.25) \times (1 + 2.79\% * 0.25) \times (1 + 2.84\% * 0.25) - 1] = 2.735\%$$

Pack yields allow the comparison of one year's worth of cash flows derived from STIR futures with the cash flows of a one-year financial instrument such as a bond or swap or even a 12-month money market borrowing or lending. This type of comparison will be explored further in the Inter-Contract Spreading section, but the following should be noted:

- the pack yield is forward starting on the expiry of the first futures date

- each quarter is a standardised 0.25 of a year.

These two factors need to be taken into account when making comparisons with other products.

Bundles

Bundles are a variation on packs. Bundles are the simultaneous purchase or sale of a series of consecutive futures contracts starting with the first quarterly delivery month in the strip but classified by year. They are usually a minimum of two years, since a one-year bundle would consist of the first four quarterly delivery months and so is effectively a white pack. A two-year bundle is the first eight quarterly delivery months (the same as a white plus the red pack), a three-year bundle is the first 12 quarterly delivery months (the same as a white and red and green pack added together) and so on until the ten year bundle on CME Eurodollar. Liffe currently trades bundles to five years that would cover the first 20 quarterly delivery months.

Table 3.9 – Bundles

Bundle	Delivery months	Pack equivalent
Two-year	First eight quarterly delivery months	White + Red
Three-year	First 12 quarterly delivery months	White + Red + Green
Four-year	First 16 quarterly delivery months	White + Red + Green+ Blue
Five-year	First 20 quarterly delivery months	White + Red + Green+ Blue + Gold

Bundles are priced the same as packs; simple averaging on the CME and totals on Liffe. The allocation algorithms are the same as for packs for each exchange.

Intra-contract spreading with packs and bundles

There are two intra-contract trades that can be done with packs and bundles.

Bundles versus packs

Since combinations of packs are effectively bundles, the two can be spread against each other, either for arbitrage or price improvement. The tendency is for the bundles to be priced tighter than the sum of the packs and so the trade requires a liquid market which allows the spread trader to buy or sell most or all of the legs on the bid and offer. It's a trade worth watching and any pack or bundle trader should be aware of price action in one or the other. Fees will make a big impact on the profit and loss payoff, and due to the number of legs involved it is best left to those exchanges with single-fee strategy pricing.

Pack or bundle versus a stack

The second spread is the pack or bundle versus a stack. Here, one of the constituent futures of the pack or bundle is traded against the strategy itself. For example, if the red pack were to consist of H3, M3, U3 and Z3, any of these futures, but preferably one towards the middle such as M3 or U3, could be purchased or sold in a 4:1 ratio. Either the M3 or U3 is suitable, since the resulting net position would be both long and short calendar spreads, giving a better risk profile against yield curve changes, and it would tend to be more liquid than the more deferred months.

Table 3.10 – Pack versus a stack

	H3	M3	U3	Z3
Sell one red pack	-1	-1	-1	-1
Buy four H7		+4		
Net	-1	+3	-1	-1

The table shows an example of buying four M3 against selling the red pack. The net position can be regarded as two three-month spreads (one short, one long) and a six-month spread (long). Alternatively, it could be viewed as short one H3M3U3 butterfly and long a six-month spread. There would be plenty of permutations to exit the spread but really it is all about price improvement; buying a constituent future cheap to the pack or selling it dear to the pack. It is not easily done and is really only achievable when the net changes of the futures in the pack are slightly different to each other or a market participant buys or sells a pack dearly or cheaply.

Bundle yields

Bundle yields can be calculated in a similar way to pack yields but the yield should be quoted on an annualised (yearly) basis.

For example, calculating a two-year bundle yield using the following prices returns a yield of 2.901%.

Table 3.11 – Prices used in example calculation

	Price
H2	97.490
M2	97.310
U2	97.210
Z2	97.160
H3	97.100
M3	97.000
U3	96.900
Z3	96.870

$$\begin{bmatrix} (+2.51\% * 0.25) \times (1+2.69\%*0.25) \times (1+2.79\%*0.25) \times (1+2.84\%*0.25) \times \\ (+2.90\%*0.25) \times (1+3.00\%*0.25) \times (1+3.10\%*0.25) \times (1+3.13\%*0.25) \times \end{bmatrix}^{0.5} -1 = 2.901\%$$

(0.5 comes from one-year annualised convention divided by two years of data. A five-year bundle yield would be calculated as the product of 1+ future rate x 0.25 to the power of 1/5).

Summary – when to use strategies

- Calendar spreads
  These can be regarded as the bread and butter of strategy trading. Judicious buying and selling by trading yield curve movements can return small but high frequency profits for little risk.

- Butterflies and condors
  Similar to calendars, but the additional costs make them a strategy to be watched or used sparingly to convert or exit existing positions. Paper bids and offers can tighten prices beyond those implied by the outright futures or spreads and can present opportunities to the watchful.

- Packs and bundles
  More applicable to inter-contract spreading, but a useful way of buying and selling futures on or near the bids and offers if there is buying and selling in the strategy order book. Can be traded against stacks.

Spread Trading: Inter-Contract Spreads

Inter-contract spreads are the spreading of STIR futures against other interest rate products, such as bonds, with similar price sensitivities and term structures, or international STIR futures, which introduce currency implications.

Price sensitivity

So far, the intra-contract spreads detailed in the previous sections that consist of one future spread against another, or others within the same contract, have been quite simple to construct. Apart from gauging the risk associated with the spread and directional influences, the ratios of these spreads has always been 1:1 since the price sensitivities for each component future have always been the same, as have the currencies. The *price sensitivity* is defined as how the prices of all the component instruments move in relation to a change in yield or underlying interest rate. It is important to equalise this price sensitivity between products, as well as ensure that the terms of the products are similar and that currency influences are negated.

By their very nature of being different products, inter-contract spreads are bound to be more volatile and complex than intra-contract spreads. They also require multi-exchange connectivity and involve increased leg risk and higher margin requirements than intra-contract spreads. Furthermore, a degree of numerical process is required in order to work out the hedge ratios. This is the proportion in which the two contracts are spread against each other. However, in return, inter-contract spreads can offer a multitude of trading opportunities, not least being the lack of obvious competition relative to intra-contract spreads.

The main types of inter-contract spread to be covered here are:

1. swap spreads: trading bond and bond futures against STIR futures

2. swap futures against STIR futures

3. synthetic FX swaps by spreading international STIR futures.

The first involves the spreading of bonds or bond futures against strips of STIR futures; essentially a credit spread between AAA-rated and AA-rated securities. The second eliminates the credit spread and interest rate risk, leaving just a very highly correlated spread to trade. Both involve some calculation of hedge ratios and understanding of the risk factors. The third shows how STIR futures can be used in other financial products whose forward pricing depends on interest rates.

The swap spread

Swap spreads, also known as Treasury spreads, are credit spreads between AAA-rated and AA-rated securities. AAA is the highest credit rating available from the main credit rating agencies and is effectively the closest thing to an interest rate free of risk of default. Typically, AAA-rated securities are confined to government bonds of nations like Germany and the UK but will also include the USA, which was downgraded by Standard and Poor's in 2011 but it is still globally regarded as an issuer of high credit-rated bonds.

Interest rate swaps are a derivative, exchanging a fixed rate of interest for a floating rate of interest which references LIBOR or EURIBOR fixings. These fixings are based upon interbank borrowings on a representative AA credit curve.

The swap spread is the difference in yields or rates between a maturity on the swaps curve and an equivalent term on the AAA government yield curve. The government bond yield curve comprises benchmark bonds (also known as on-the-run), which are the most recently issued and therefore most liquid bonds for a given maturity. In January 2012, the most recently issued German two-year bond was a Bundesschatzanweisungen 0.25% 13 December 2013 with a yield of 0.18% (more later …).

For example on 10 January 2012, the euro two-year swap rate was 1.27% and the German two-year benchmark bond yield was 0.18%. The difference between the two of 1.09% is the swap spread. Sometimes, the swap rate can be interpolated to match the maturity of the two-year bond exactly to give a slightly more accurate version of the swap spread. This can be known as the I-spread.

The swap spread represents the upper echelon of the credit curve but still exhibits volatility over time as shown by the chart, and understanding the drivers of the swap spread is key when synthesising this spread by using bonds or bond futures and STIR futures.

Fig. 3.8 – Euro and US two-year swap spreads (1999–2012)

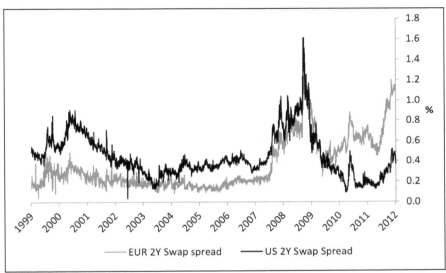

Data source: Reuters

Drivers of the swap spread

The swap spread is widely watched by market participants and its dynamics are numerous. The key to being a successful swap spread trader is knowing what is driving the spread at any one time. Easier said than done! Some of the key drivers of swap spread dynamics are as follows:

The health of the banking sector

The swap spread is essentially a credit spread between the government risk-free curve and the risky banking sector credit curve. Consequently, one of the key drivers is the perceived health of the banking sector. During the financial crisis of 2007/8, counterparty risk between banks became a key issue as market participants were highly concerned about each other's ability to honour their financial contracts and deals. This manifested itself in a widening of the swap spread both in the euro zone and the USA, as shown by the euro two-year swap spread widening out from around 0.18% in 2006 to around 120% in September 2008. In this situation investors were demanding higher swap rates to compensate for banking system fears, whilst treasury yields declined due to a flight to quality by investors seeking financial security.

During 2010/11, the euro swap spread widened sharply relative to the US swap spread due to the European sovereign debt crisis and concerns regarding the health of the European banking sector.

Corporate credit levels

The banking sector lends to corporates and is therefore exposed to default risk of these corporate entities. Default risk generally increases in times of economic turmoil or recession, leading to a widening of swap spreads.

The supply of government bonds

Government bonds are issued by national treasuries to fund public debt and expenditures, whereas swaps are derivatives that are created and not issued. This means that changes in the supply of government bonds can impact the swap spreads.

The budget deficit is a proxy for government bond supply. A higher budget deficit means a greater supply of bonds is needed to finance the deficit and this generally leads to higher government bond yields and swap spread narrowing.

The US ran a budget surplus in the early 2000s, leading to a lower supply of government bonds; this was reflected by the swap spread widening. In contrast, subsequent deficits have put narrowing pressure on the swap spread, countermanded by widening drivers during the financial crisis of 2007/8.

Availability of credit and liquidity

The availability of credit drives yields down and risk tolerance generally increases, leading to a narrowing of the swap spreads. This reached a nadir in markets during 2005/6.

US mortgage hedging

US mortgage hedging is a feature of US swap spreads and a key driver of US swap spreads due to duration matching. Duration is a measure of the interest rate sensitivity of a bond, or in this case of mortgage-backed securities. Normally, duration is fairly static for a ordinary government bond but US mortgages contain an option for the mortgagee to prepay the principal. This leads to variable durations on mortgage products, as duration lengthens as rates rise (homeowners don't refinance) and shortens as rates fall (homeowners refinance and pay back principal prematurely). Mortgage investors have to engage in duration-shortening trades like paying in swaps (or selling treasuries), which will widen the swap spread, or engage in duration-lengthening trades like receiving in swaps (or buying treasuries), which will narrow the swap spread.

In US, Freddie Mac and Fannie Mae are the largest mortgage hedgers so it is crucial to track these agencies' holdings and activities.

Corporate issuance

Banks tend to be largest issuers of corporate bonds and often swap fixed coupon bonds into floating by entering into swaps to receive fixed. This can lead to a narrowing of swap spreads.

Trading swap spreads using bonds and bond futures against STIR futures

Spreading of bonds or bond futures against STIR futures to replicate the swap spread first requires an understanding of the characteristics of bonds and bond futures. Bond futures reference cash bonds since they are physically settled by delivery of cash bonds. Consequently, bond futures are priced and gain their sensitivities from the underlying cash bonds.

Bonds and notes are different products compared to STIR futures. They are interest-paying products typically issued by a government as a process of public-sector borrowing. Notes usually refer to maturities around two years to ten years and bonds for maturities beyond that.

The most popular bonds and notes to be spread against STIR futures are:

- **US treasury notes and bond futures** spread against Eurodollar bundles and packs. They are issued by the United States Treasury Department in different maturities, ranging from two to 30 years. The most popular ones for inter-contract spreading are the two-year and five-year notes since there is limited liquidity in strips and bundles beyond this point. The treasury note futures traded on CBOT (a designated market of CME Group) are popular products to spread against Eurodollar.

- **German bonds** are considered as European benchmarks, given Germany's status as the largest European economy. The German Federal Treasury issues notes called:

  - Bundesschatzanweisungen (fortunately abbreviated to Schätz!) for maturities of two years

  - Bundesobligationen (abbreviated to Bobl) for maturities of five years

  - Bundesanleihen (Bund) for maturities of ten to 30 years

The Schatz and Bobl futures traded on Eurex are very popular products to spread against Euribor.

Introduction to basic bond pricing

A bond or note might appear like this:

```
Bundesschatzanweisungen 0.25% 13 December 2013, Price 100.13
```

This bond is a promissory note issued by the German Treasury. Germany currently has an AAA credit rating, effectively a representative risk-free interest rate for the euro zone.

The name Bundesschatzanweisungen means that this is a German two-year note. It was actually issued on 18 November 2011 maturing on 13 December 2013, so it was originally slightly longer than two years. This is common in bond markets; an *n-year* bond is an approximate term.

The price of 100.13 is expressed as a percentage of the nominal value, which can be regarded as the amount of the bond held expressed as a unit of trading. For example, to purchase €100 nominal value of this bond would cost €100 x 100.13% which is €100.13. If the bond was held to maturity, the investor would receive back from the German treasury this nominal value of €100, which also known as the redemption value.

The coupon on this bond is 0.25%. This is the amount of interest that the investor will receive (annually on 13 December). If an investor owned €100 nominal of this bond (for which they might have paid €100.13), they would receive a coupon of €100 x 0.25% each December (note that for recently issued bonds like this one, the first coupon is often skipped and the interest added on to the next. In this case, if the bond had been purchased in November 2011, the first coupon would be December 2012, not 2011 and would be slightly over one years' worth of interest).

This coupon of 0.25% represents the return on the bond. However, if it were held to maturity having been purchased at 100.13, it would offer a slightly lower return since the investor would only receive €100 redemption value at maturity versus what they had paid, leading to a small loss (100% - 100.13%). This small loss amortised over the life the bond (approximately -0.13/2 = -0.065%) would reduce the coupon return to give a yield to maturity (YTM) of around 0.18% (0.25% + -0.065%).

The YTM, in this case of 0.18%, is the return that the investor locks in when they purchase the bond and hold it to maturity (there is the issue of coupon proceeds to consider, but reinvestment risk is not really relevant outside of institutional bond portfolio management). However, if interest rates on similar bonds subsequently rise to 1%, then the return of 0.18% that the investor has locked in will be relatively unattractive. Another investor would only be willing to purchase this bond at a lower price that increases their return to the market rate of 1%. For example, the bond might now be trading at a price of 98.50 (98.50% per €100 nominal). The gain of 1.5% (100% - 98.50%) between now and maturity added to the coupon of 0.25% would return 1% yield to maturity (1.5%/2 + 0.25% = 1%).

This can be basically quantified by considering the price of a bond as the net present value of the bonds future cash flows (coupons and redemption value):

$$P = \left[\sum_{t=1}^{n} \frac{c \times N}{(1+i)^t} \right] + \frac{R}{(1+i)^n}$$

P = bond price

c = coupon

N = nominal amount

R = redemption amount

n = number of payments

t = time

i = yield to maturity

This formula basically states that a bond's price is the sum of the present value of its cash flows.

Using a yield of 0.18%, the two-year German bond can be valued as follows:

$$P = \frac{0.25\% \times 100}{(1+0.18\%)^1} + \frac{100 + (0.25\% \times 100)}{(1+0.18\%)^2} = 100.14$$

The higher the yield or interest rate that is used to discount these cash flows, the lower the sum of these discounted cash flows will be (lower bond price). Using a yield of 1% results in a bond price of 98.52:

$$P = \frac{0.25\% \times 100}{(1+1\%)^1} + \frac{100 + (0.25\% \times 100)}{(1+1\%)^2} = 98.52$$

Note that the price of 100.14 is slightly different from the 100.13 quoted earlier using a yield of 0.18% and the price of 98.52 differs from the price of 98.50 before. This is due to using a basic bond pricing methodology that assumes pricing of the bond on a coupon payment day, rather than the present day.

These examples illustrate the inverse relationship between bond prices and interest rates:

As interest rates or yield increase, bond prices will decline.

As interest rates or yield decline, bond prices will increase.

If required, the bond pricing formula can be used to solve the yield to maturity if the bond price, coupon, dates and redemption value are known.

Bond market variations

German bond markets trade in decimals, pay their coupons annually and calculate day counts (for precise bond valuation between coupon dates) with an Act/Act convention (Actual number of days in a period/Actual number of days in the year). In contrast, US bond markets are priced in imperial measures, namely 32nds and 64ths, pay coupons semi-annually and use an Act/Act convention. In reality, this does not add much complication, but traders need to be aware of these differences and conventions.

Calculating bond prices in Excel

Bond pricing between coupon dates is considerably more technical than the basic bond pricing illustrated earlier. Fortunately, Excel contains bond-pricing analytics that can be very useful to the trader.

The bond-pricing function in Excel is found in the **Formula** tab in the ribbon (Excel 2007/2010 – it's the **Insert** tab in Excel 2003). Click on **fx** (also found next to the formula bar), use **Category** to select **Financial** and then **PRICE**. This is the bond-pricing function and will require certain variables, namely:

- Settlement (start) date – this can be expressed via a DATE function (US style – see picture) or by referencing a cell in the worksheet

- Maturity (date)

- Rate (coupon)

- Yld (yield)

Note the scroll bar to the right in the picture. There is more to fill in!

- Redemption (100)

- (coupon) Frequency – use 1 for German bonds, 2 for US bonds

- Basis–Day count convention – use 1 for Government bonds

Fig. 3.9 – Microsoft Excel 2010 PRICE function, pricing Bundesschatzanweisungen 0.25% 13 December 2013 on 10 January 2012

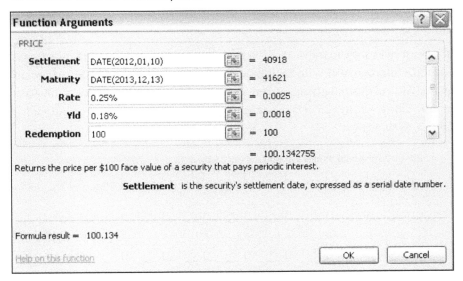

143

Clean and dirty bond prices

Bond prices are quoted on a *clean basis* in the secondary markets – that is, without including interest due from the date of the previous coupon. The investor buying a bond between coupon dates will have to compensate the seller for this interest between the trade date and the previous coupon date. The investor will purchase the bond in the market at the clean price but the total invoice price will have accrued interest added on top. This total invoice price is called the *dirty price*.

The dirty price is the actual amount the investor will pay (seller receive) and so it is a number that is often used in hedge ratio calculations.

Excel contains additional functions for calculating accrued interest, namely ACCRINT, which requires details of the previous coupon date (Excel has a function for this called COUPPCD) and the next coupon date (COUPNCD).

Note: when using ACCRINT, there is an input called ISSUE. Usually, this can be populated with the previous coupon date unless it is a recently issued bond like the 0.25% 13 December 2013 used earlier. In this case, the first coupon date has been skipped, giving an extra-long first coupon period and so ISSUE should be the issue date of the bond (18 November 2011).

Price sensitivity to interest rate movements

It has been shown that, like STIR futures prices, a bond's price will fall as interest rates or yields rise, and its price will rise as interest rates fall. They will both react the same way to movements in underlying interest rates.

The big question is: by how much?

If interest rates were to move 1% (100 basis points), how much would both bonds and STIR futures move? With STIR futures, it's easy; a movement of 100 basis points or 1% (0.01) in the underlying interest rates will move the STIR futures by 100 basis points. This is worth €25 or $25 per basis point for Euribor futures or Eurodollar futures, as shown by:

1,000,000 (notional value) x 0.0001 x 90/360 = €25

This is known as the *basis point value* (BPV) or, in the United States, as the *dollar value* of a 01 (DV01).

Modified duration

Bonds use a price-sensitivity measure called *modified duration* to calculate the price sensitivity to a 1% movement in underlying yield. It is literally a modified version of the measure of *Macaulay duration* (named after its creator, Frederick Macaulay).

Macaulay duration expresses, in years, how long it takes for the price of a bond to be repaid by its internal cash flows and as such is a reflection of the bond's risk. Generally, a bond with a higher duration figure will be riskier and more susceptible to changes in its price given movements in underlying yields or rates. Duration is determined by coupon yields and maturity and will generally increase for bonds with lower coupons and yields, and longer maturities.

Macaulay duration is derived from the weighted average term to maturity of the cash flows from a bond and this term figure doesn't easily compare as a risk measurement against other instruments. A measure of a bond's price sensitivity expressed in years cannot be directly compared with the price sensitivity of a STIR future. However, by modification, it can be adjusted to express the *percentage* change in price with respect to a change in interest rates.

Modified duration is the modified version of Macaulay duration. It is expressed mathematically as:

$$\frac{\displaystyle\sum_{t=1}^{n}\left[t \times \frac{CF_t}{\left(1+i\right)^t}\right]}{\dfrac{P}{1+\dfrac{i}{n}}}$$

P = Bond Price

CF = cash flow

n = coupon frequency

t = time

i = yield to maturity

Modified duration can be found within Excel's **Function** as **MDURATION**. It takes the same variables as **PRICE** and in the case of the 0.25% 13 December 2013 returns a value of 1.92.

Fig. 3.10 – Microsoft Excel 2010 MDURATION function, pricing Bundesschatzanweisungen 0.25% 13 December 2013 on 10 January 2012 (note scroll bar to right – additional inputs required) MDURATION(DATE(2012,1,10),DATE(2013,12,13),0.25%,0.18%,1,1)

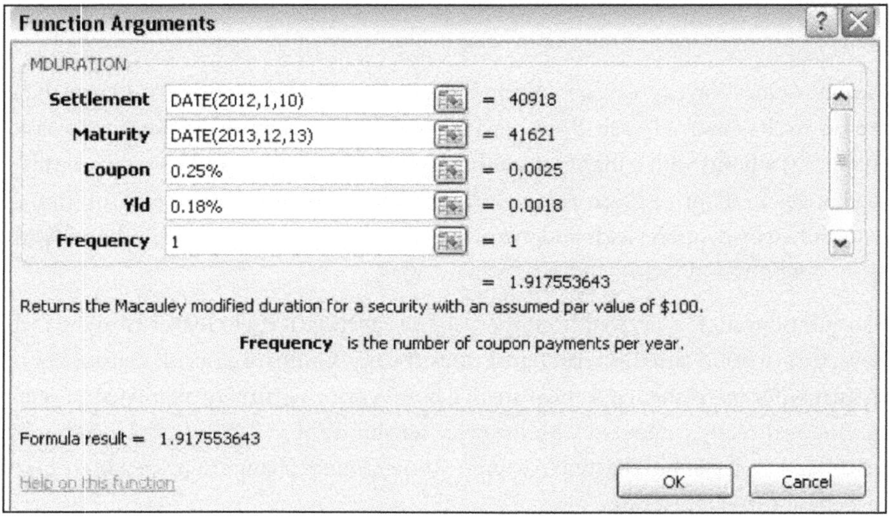

This figure of 1.92 reflects the projected percentage price change given a 1% movement in interest rates either up or down.

Therefore if yields were to increase from 0.18% by 1% to 1.18%, modified duration would predict that the bond price would fall by 1.92%.

Duration is a linear measure and can be further adjusted for *absolute* changes in the bond price for small incremental moves of one basis point. This is the *basis point value* (BPV) or DV01 of the bond and is expressed as:

BPV = dirty price x modified duration x 0.01% (1 basis point)

Where the dirty price is the clean price quoted in the market with interest accrued from the last coupon date. Accrued interest can be calculated in Excel using **ACCRINT**.

For the 0.25% 13 December 2013 on 10 January 2012, the accrued interest is 0.037.

Fig. 3.11 – Microsoft Excel 2010 ACCRINT function, pricing Bundesschatzanweisungen 0.25% 13 December 2013 on 10 January 2012 (note scroll bar to right – additional inputs required and issue date used since this is a recently issued benchmark bond – ACCRINT(DATE(2011,11,18),DATE(2012,12,13),DATE(2012,01,11),0.25%,100,1,1,TRUE))

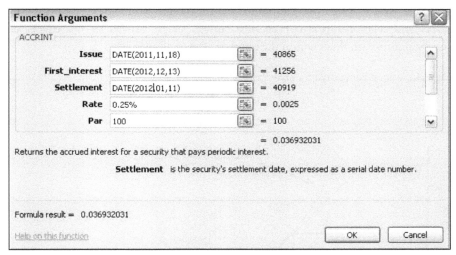

Therefore the BPV is:

$(100.13 + 0.037) \times 1.92 \times 0.01\% = 0.0192$

The BPV of the bond example, with yields at 0.18%, is 0.0192, meaning that if rates were to increase to 0.19%, the €100 of bond could be expected to drop by €0.0192, and if it fell to 0.17%, the €100 of bond would rise by €0.0192.

This can be verified by re-pricing the bond with an interest rate change of +0.50%

Using modified duration:

$100.13+0.037) \times -1.92 \times 0.50\% = -0.96$

Or by using BPV:

$50 \times -0.0192 = -0.96$

Both modified duration and BPV predict that given a 0.50% increase in yields, the bond price will fall from a dirty price of 100.167 (100.13 + 0.037) by 0.96 to 99.207.

This can be verified by using the PRICE function to calculate the actual change in price given a 0.50% increase in yield. The same data is used as before, but changing the yield from 0.18% to 0.68% results in the bond price falling to 99.217.

Convexity

The small difference of €0.01 between the actual change and the change predicted by the BPV is due to convexity. Convexity is due to the relationship between a bond's price and yield and the way duration reflects it. As shown in Figure 3.12, the bond price/yield relationship is curved in a convex shape, caused by the effects of compounding cash flows within the bond pricing methodology.

Fig. 3.12 – Bond convexity at a given price and yield point

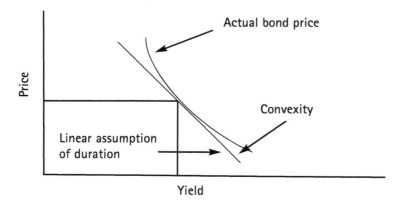

In contrast, the duration calculation presumes a linear relationship fitted at a tangent at the current bond yield and the difference between this and the curvature of the bond yield relationship when yields change is the convexity effect. Using modified duration or BPV for large changes in increases in yield changes will tend to overestimate the fall in price of the bond; it is common practice to adjust it back by the convexity value. However, convexity is a lower order risk when setting up swap spreads using bonds or bond futures against STIR futures.

Determining the hedge ratio

The calculation of BPV provides a comparable measure of price sensitivity for bonds and it is now possible to determine by how much both a bond and a STIR future will change in relation to a change in interest rates. A hedge ratio can be determined from the BPV of the STIR futures and the bond.

Earlier, the BPV of a Euribor future was shown to be €25, and the BPV of the bond described above is €0.0192 per €100. If €10,000,000 of the bond were purchased, the BPV of the position would be:

$$\frac{€10,000,000}{€100} \times 0.0192 = €1920$$

In order to determine how many Euribor futures would be need to be purchased, the BPV of the bond position is divided by the BPV of the Euribor making:

$$\frac{€1920}{€25} = 77$$

77 (rounded) Euribor futures would be required to be sold to hedge €1,000,000 of the bond used in the example. However, this is a hedge for a cash bond and since swap spreads are commonly set up entirely using derivatives it is necessary to look at bond futures.

Introduction to bond futures

Bond futures are different to cash bonds in that they are a derivative based on notional characteristics. The exchanges list bond futures for two, five and ten-year maturities in the euro zone and two, three, five, ten and 30 years in the US. They trade on a quarterly March, June, September and December cycle.

The table displays the contract specifications for the euro and US two-year bond futures. These are popular instruments for trading against STIR bundles to replicate the two-year swap spread.

Table 3.12 – Contract specifications for euro and US two-year bond futures

	2-Year Schatz	2-Year Treasury Note
Exchange	EUREX	CBOT
Deliverable bond	€100,000 6% coupon bond with remaining maturity of 1.75 to 2.25 years	$200,000 6% coupon note with a remaining maturity of one yr. Nine months to two yrs
Delivery period	The tenth calendar day of the respective quarterly month	Any business day during delivery month
Last trading day	Two exchange days prior to the delivery day of the relevant maturity month	Last business day of the calendar month
Tick size	0.005 (€5) €100,000 x 0.005/100	1/4 of 1/32 of one point ($15.625,) $200,000 x (1/128) /100

Bond futures are physically settled meaning that during the delivery period the futures seller is obliged to deliver a bond matching the contract specifications to the futures buyer. However, delivering such a bond might be problematic. Whilst the notional amounts and maturity ranges are not insurmountable, it is less likely to be able to deliver a bond with exactly a 6% coupon. Yet that is what is required.

The exchanges get around this problem by publishing a list of bonds that are eligible for delivery against the bond future. Most will not have a coupon of 6% but will have a conversion factor that compensates for the difference between the 6% coupon of the bond future and the coupon of the bond that is actually delivered against the future.

Table 3.13 – Deliverable bonds against EUREX March 2012 Schatz future

ISIN number	Coupon	Maturity	Conversion factor
DE0001137362	0.25	13.12.2013	0.906868
DE0001135242	4.25	04.01.2014	0.970555
DE0001141547	2.25	11.04.2014	0.928548

The table shows a list of eligible bonds that are deliverable by the futures seller into the March 2012 Schatz future. None of them have a 6% coupon and so the conversion factor provides compensation.

The delivery period for the March 2012 Schatz future is 10 March 2012. The futures seller might choose to deliver the 0.25% 13 December 2013 bond out of these three eligible bonds. The futures buyer is expecting to receive €100,000 of a 6% coupon bond with a remaining life between 1.75 and 2.25 years. However, the 0.25% coupon bond that is actually going to be delivered will be worth much less than the 6% coupon bond that is expected. So the futures buyer adapts the payment to the seller to compensate:

€100,000 x F x C + Acc$_t$

F = futures EDSP (expiry price)

C = conversion factor

Acc$_t$= accrued interest on bond on delivery day

If the March 2012 Schatz future expired in March at 110.405, a futures seller might choose to deliver €100,000 0.25% 13 December 2013 to settle the bond future. The futures buyer is expecting a 6% bond and so adjusts the payment via the conversion factor to compensate for receiving €100,000 0.25% 13 December 2013, which will be less valuable.

The futures buyer will pay:

€100,000 x 110.405% x 0.906868 = €100,123

Notice how F x C = 100.12, which is very close to the price of the 0.25% 13 December 2013 referred to earlier (100.13).

The cheapest-to-deliver (CTD) bond

Conversion factors are rather technical. They are calculated and published by the exchanges and do not change. The basic methodology is to re-price each deliverable bond using a 6% yield, the settlement date changed to the (first day of the) delivery period and a redemption value of 1 (rather than 100). This means that a bond with a coupon of 6% would have a price of 1 (100), and a bond with a coupon less than 6% will have a price of less than 1 (<100). These prices are the conversion factors.

However, conversion factors only provide perfect compensation for all bonds in the deliverable basket for delivery when all those bonds trade at a yield of 6%. This is highly unlikely given that German yields are currently less than 1% and each deliverable bond has different maturity and liquidity characteristics.

This means that when yields differ from 6%, one bond might be cheaper to deliver by the futures seller to the futures buyer than the others. If yields are now approximately 0.18% for all bonds, all will have increased in value but the futures seller will rationally choose the bond that has increased in value the least (because they have to buy it and deliver it to the futures buyer). When yields are lower than 6%, that bond is often, but not always, the bond with the lowest duration.

There are several processes for calculating which bond is the cheapest to deliver (CTD). The *gross* and *net* basis are used here.

Gross and net basis

The gross basis of a deliverable bond is a simplified example of a cash and carry trade where a bond is purchased (that is the cash) and financed and interest received (this is the carry) and then delivered against a short futures position. The gross basis is effectively the profit or loss (the difference between F x C and P) on the carry trade but stripped down to exclude the carry.

It is calculated by:

Bond price (P) - (F x C)

In contrast, the net basis is the fully inclusive version of the cash and carry where the financing and interest receivable is included in the net basis calculation.

The bond with the lowest gross basis will usually be the cheapest to deliver. However, this method is basic and does not take into account the effect of accrued interest or the cost of carry and might not always be accurate enough, hence the need for the net basis. The bond with the lowest net basis **will** be the CTD.

Table 3.14 – Gross and net basis for deliverable bonds against EUREX March 2012 Schatz future on 11 January 2012. H2 Schatz was 110.405

Coupon	Maturity	Conversion factor	Yield	Price	Gross basis	Carry	Net basis
0.25%	13.12.2013	0.906868	0.143	100.205	0.0822	0.1282	0.2104
4.25%	04.01.2014	0.970555	0.127	108.096	0.9419	-0.4701	0.4718
2.25%	11.04.2014	0.928548	0.096	104.806	2.2897	-0.1670	2.1227

The table shows the gross and net basis for deliverable bonds underlying the March 2012 Schatz future. The bond with the lowest gross and net basis is the 0.25% 13 December 2013, which also has the lowest duration due to its shorter maturity.

Rationally, the bond futures seller will choose to deliver this bond since it would cost less than the others.

This can be illustrated via the gross basis calculation.

The 0.25% 13 December 2013 could be purchased on 11 January at 100.205 (this is slightly different to the price of 100.13 used earlier since this is a day later and yields have fallen) and a future sold at 110.405. The proceeds to the seller at delivery would be F x C or 110.405 x 0.906868 = 100.123. This means the bond would have been purchased at 100.205 and effectively sold via the future at 100.123, giving rise to a loss of 0.0822. This loss is not great but it is better to buy this bond and deliver than buy one of the other bonds and face cash and carry losses of 0.94 or 2.28, as shown by the gross basis of the 4.25% 4 January 2014 and 2.25% 11 April 2014 respectively. Most cash and carry trades will result in a loss. This small loss on the CTD is considered to be the price of embedded optionality, reflecting the value of the choice that the bond future seller has over the selection of which bond they can deliver (and when in the delivery month in the case of US bond futures).

Calculating the net basis

The net basis is the gross basis adapted for the financing costs of buying the bond minus any interest and coupon income received (and reinvested).

For the 0.25% 13 December 2013, the financing costs are determined by:

$$P \times \left[i \times \frac{D}{B} \right]$$

P = dirty bond price

i = repo rate (secured financing rate)

D=days in carry period

B = days in year base (360 for euro money markets)

The bond is purchased at a dirty price of 100.205 + 0.0403 = 100.245

(Note that in European bond markets, settlement is on a T+3 good business days convention so purchasing the bond on Wednesday January 11 2012 would settle on Monday January 16 and it is this date that should be used in the calculation of accrued interest and the carry period.)

The repo (financing) rate is 1.07%, the number of days in the carry period is 56 (12 March minus 16 January – note the stated delivery date of 10 March falls on a Sunday in 2012). The year base is 360 days, using a European money market convention. Therefore:

$$100.245 \text{ x} \left[1.07\% \text{ x} \frac{56}{360} \right] = 0.1669$$

Over these 56 days, the bond will accrue interest (there are no coupons paid during the carry period). The accrued interest on 16 January settlement date was 0.043 and accrued interest recalculated with the settlement date at the futures delivery date of 12 March is 0.079. This means that the bond accrues 0.0387 interest during the carry period.

The cost of carry is given by:

Financing cost during carry period - interest accrued during carry period

So:

0.1669 - 0.0387 = 0.1282

This carry cost is added onto the loss made on the cash and carry via the gross basis, giving a net basis of:

0.1282 + 0.0822 = 0.2104 (as shown in the table)

The US two-year deliverable basket

The US economy is larger than Germany's and consequently the deliverable baskets are larger for US bond futures than on German bond futures.

Table 3.15 – Gross and net basis for deliverable bonds against CBOT March 2012 2 yr. bond future on 11 January 2012. H2 2Y bond future was 110.32 and the repo rate was 0.38%. All prices decimalised

Coupon	Maturity	Price	Yield	Accrued	Conv factor	Gross basis	Cost of carry	Net basis
0.125	31 Dec13	99.785	0.235	0.0041	0.90380	0.08472	0.0554	0.14009
0.750	15 Dec13	100.980	0.239	0.0574	0.91400	0.15484	-0.0766	0.07820
1.000	15 Jan14	101.512	0.245	0.4918	0.91440	0.64197	-0.1302	0.51137
1.250	15 Feb14	102.070	0.257	0.5095	0.91520	1.11231	-0.1821	0.92989
1.250	15 Mar14	102.137	0.263	0.4087	0.91170	1.56481	-0.1829	1.38185
1.500	31 Dec13	102.484	0.233	0.0495	0.92630	0.30191	-0.2370	0.06490
1.750	31 Jan14	103.059	0.254	0.7846	0.92720	0.77684	-0.2885	0.48779
1.750	31 Mar14	103.281	0.264	0.4973	0.92100	1.68344	-0.2875	1.39593
1.875	28 Feb14	103.418	0.266	0.6902	0.92630	1.23550	-0.3144	0.92081

The table shows that the CTD bond in the basket is the 1.50% 31 December 2013 with the lowest net basis of 0.06490. However, it does not have the lowest gross basis (or the lowest duration). Those go to the second CTD which is the 0.75% 15 December 2013.

However, when the coupons on the deliverable bonds are higher than the repo rate of 0.38%, the bonds exhibit positive carry (meaning you get paid to finance the bond – but still have duration risk). The coupon on the 1.50% bond is higher than the 0.75% bond, meaning that this bond receives more accrued interest, the difference in conjunction with the financing costs resulting in a slightly lower net basis. However, there is likely to be competition between these two bonds over the life of the March bond future for title of CTD and the bond future will price itself off that bond.

Traders' notes

- Be careful about holding long positions in US bond futures into the delivery month (e.g. in March for the March 2012 contracts). You might be delivered to on any day of the delivery month. Most of the open interest in the US bond futures rolls into the next contract at the end of the month prior to the delivery month (e.g. open interest in the March 2012 US bond futures will start to roll into the June 2012 contracts by late February).

- Traders need to be aware of bond auction schedules since a basket of deliverable bonds might be augmented by new stock and hence the possibility of a new CTD.

- Bond futures prices, lists of deliverable bonds, conversion factors and delivery dates are easily found on exchange websites. US cash bond prices and yields can be found at Yahoo! Finance and German bond prices on the website of Xetra, the electronic platform of Deutsche Börse. Bond prices, futures and swap rates can be found on the website of the *Financial Times* (**www.ft.com**).

Hedge ratios for bond futures

The hedge ratio for the Bundesschatzanweisungen 0.25% 13 December 2013 against STIR futures was established earlier. The hedge ratio for a bond future referencing a CTD can be calculated in a similar way but with two main differences.

1. Bond futures are standardised contracts and so are quoted in standardised quantities. These quantities are quoted as part of the futures contract specifications. They are usually in denominations of 100,000 dollars or euros, except for the US two and three-year treasury note futures, which are $200,000.

2. In order to equate the CTD bond with the future, its BPV, once calculated, must be divided by its conversion factor.

The Bundesschatzanweisungen 0.25% 13 December 2013 was the CTD for the EUREX two-year Schatz future. The BPV of the Bundesschatzanweisungen 0.25% 13 December 2013 was calculated earlier as:

BPV = dirty price x modified duration x 0.01% (1 basis point)

To calculate the hedge ratio between the EUREX 2-year Schatz future and the Liffe Euribor future requires the BPV of the CTD bond. Using the earlier values from 11 January 2012 equals:

100.245 x 1.902 x 0.01% = 0.0191

The BPV for the CTD underlying the March 2012 EUREX Schatz future can be calculated by incorporating the contract size and conversion factor.

BPV of EUREX March 2012 Schatz future = 100,000 x (0.0191/100/0.906868) = €21.02

(Note that the BPV figure of 0.0191 is per €100 nominal and so needs to be divided by 100 to represent a value per €1.)

This is divided by the BPV of a Euribor future, which is €25, to give a hedge ratio of:

21.02/25 = 0.84

This figure of 0.84 is the ratio of how many Euribor futures would be needed to offset a EUREX Schatz future. 84 short Euribor futures would hedge a position of long 100 Schatz futures.

Calculating hedge ratios by regression analysis

Regression analysis can be used as an alternative to duration-based hedge ratios. Time series data between bond or bond futures prices and STIR futures prices will indicate via regression analysis a ratio that will most reduce the difference in standard deviation between the two instruments. This ratio can be determined by using regression statistic Beta. This will measure the amount of fluctuation of one variable against another. It can be found within Excel as the function SLOPE.

The measurement of Beta needs to be verified as being statistically significant by the use of the R-squared value, found within Excel's RSQ function. This R-squared value is the proportion of the variance in one instrument that is attributable to the variance in another. The higher the R-squared number is, the greater the relationship between the performances of the instruments.

Regression is a useful way of verifying a hedge ratio or fine-tuning a ratio that does not appear to be performing as expected, perhaps due to unexpected volatility. However, regression statistics are highly susceptible to the data sets being used. Time periods, vagaries or errors will seriously affect Beta and R-squared values and the resulting hedge ratios.

The TED spread

The TED spread was originally a trade between the US treasury bill market and unsecured Eurodollar cash deposits covering a term of any period between one and 12 months. The "T" came from the treasury bill and "ED" from the Eurodollar market. It was effectively a short-term version of the swap spread. An example might be a three-month T-Bill traded against a three-month US Dollar LIBOR borrowing. However, the TED spread in its original form has largely been superseded by OIS/LIBOR spreads (more later …) and term TED spreads constructed with derivatives.

Term TED spreads involve a TED spread covering a period of two or five years and is constructed by using cash bonds hedged by strips or bundles of STIR futures. It can be a finely engineered trade, using the cash flows of the quarterly delivery cycles of STIR futures to hedge the cash flows of bonds. Bonds of certain duration are matched by a corresponding STIR futures strip of a similar term.

Term TED spreads are riskier trades than intra-contract spreads and the combinations of the different kinds of inherent risk can add up to amounts that would be unpalatable to an intra-contract trader. However, in return there can be more short-term opportunities. It is important to understand the mechanics of these spreads and where the movement in the spread is originating.

It is important to understand that term TED spreads are essentially credit spreads, akin to the swap spread. They are spreads between assets of different credit classes. Government bonds such as the US Treasuries or German Schatz and Bobls have the highest credit rating and lowest credit risk of any class of security. This is because they are issued and guaranteed by the treasuries of national governments. In contrast, STIR futures, such as Eurodollars and Euribor, are based on the inter-bank market. Whilst this market still commands a high credit rating, the deposits are unsecured, only being backed by commercial organisations and subject to the possibility of failure and default, as amply illustrated by the financial crisis of 2007/8. Stress in the banking system can also be indirect, as detailed in the section on swap spread drivers. Although the chance of bank failure is low, it is always a statistical possibility and so is reflected in the swap spread between treasury instruments and swap rates. This spread is also subject to event risk such as September 11, or systemic risk factors such as the Asian financial crisis (1997), the global financial crisis of 2007/8 or European sovereign debt crisis of 2010/11. In fact, the swap spread is vulnerable to anything that might cause a flight to quality, as investors find the safest home for their money – typically the debt of large economies such as the USA and Germany.

This credit spread that exists within the term TED spread is derived from the primary market measure of credit risk: namely, the spread between the benchmark treasury bond and the swaps market. The bond markets are supplied by new issuance from the treasury and the amount and frequency of issuance is governed by treasury funding requirements, which are driven by government policy. Typically, an auction schedule is published in advance of issuance, and an on-going process of bond auctions to primary dealers creates a turnover of bonds where one issue is replaced by a more recent issue of the same maturity. The new issue becomes the on-the-run benchmark issue whilst the previous becomes an *off-the-run*. Since the new benchmark is usually the most liquid tradable bond within its maturity, its yield is taken as being the representative for that segment of the market. By comparison, the off-the-run has usually been purchased and now held as part of the portfolio of institutional investors and its yield will generally be slightly higher than the benchmark, reflecting the difference in liquidity. The other side of the credit spread is the interest rate swap rate and this is the market representation of inter-bank risk. It is a liquid over-the-counter market with maturities between two and 50 years.

Calculating the term TED spread

Term TED spreads are calculated by constructing a notional coupon-paying bond with the same characteristics as the cash bond being used in the trade, but using the rates from the STIR futures strip to generate its price. This will effectively price an identical bond but based on the credit rating of the futures strip. The difference in yield between this notional bond and the actual bond will be the term TED spread.

Table 3.16 – Term TED spread methodology for €100M Bundesschatzanweisungen 0.25% 13 December 2013 on 20 December for settlement on 23 December 2011

Contract	Dates start	Dates end	Days	Futures Prices	100–P	Discount factors	Bond cash flows	Numbers of futures to hedge
	23/12/2011							
		21/03/2012	89		1.406	0.996535		99
H2	21/03/2012							
		19/06/2012	90	98.870	1.130	0.993728		99
M2	20/06/2012							
		18/09/2012	90	98.985	1.015	0.991213		99
U2	19/09/2012							
Coupon		13/12/2012		0.2671%		0.988922	0.264	
		18/12/2012	90	99.030	0.970	0.988815		99
Z2	19/12/2012							
		19/03/2013	90	99.015	0.985	0.986386		99
H3	20/03/2013							
		18/06/2013	90	98.985	1.015	0.983889		99
M3	19/06/2013							
		17/09/2013	90	98.920	1.080	0.981240		98
U3	18/09/2013							
Coupon + Par		13/12/2013	86	100.25%		0.978533	98.098	94
		17/12/2013	90	98.855	1.145	0.978439		

By expressing the futures strip as a coupon-paying instrument, it is more likely to respond to movements in the yield curve in a similar fashion to the cash bond (more later …). Consequently, the spread between them is more representative of the credit spread and not unduly influenced by the changing shape of the yield curve.

The table shows a spreadsheet used to construct a term TED spread for the €100M Bundesschatzanweisungen 0.25% 13 December 2013 on 20 December 2011 for settlement on 23 December 2011.

Contract column

This shows the Euribor futures contracts used to set up the TED spread against the 0.25% 13 December 2013 bond.

Dates start and Dates end column

These columns show the periods covered by the futures contracts and the stub. The stub is the period from the settlement date of the bond (23 December) to the first futures settlement (21 March). This is 89 days and so an interpolated three-month EURIBOR rate is used. The effect of this is to extend the futures strip to cover the immediate period from spot to the forward period covered by the future. Alternatives could include using serial futures.

Futures prices and 100-P columns

These are the Euribor futures prices used in the spread expressed as an implied forward rate via 100 minus the price.

Discount factors

The first discount factor is calculated as:

$$Df = \frac{1}{1 + EURIBOR\ RATE \times AccrualFactor}$$

So that:

$$\frac{1}{(1 + 1.406\% * 89 / 360)} = 0.996535$$

The next discount factor is derived by applying the forward-starting implied forward rate from the H2 future onto the previous discount factor:

$$\frac{0.996535}{(1 + 1.130\% * 90 / 360)} = 0.993728$$

This process is continued until a discount curve is derived covering the term of the cash bond. It is then linearly interpolated so that discount factors match the cash flow dates of the bond. These are 13 December 2012 for the first coupon of 0.25% (in this case the coupon is a little higher, including accrued interest from the issue date of 18 November 2011 to reflect the fact that no coupon was paid on 13 December 2011) and 13 December 2013 for the repayment of par and final coupon (100% + 0.25%).

Bond cash flows

These are the bond cash flows multiplied by the interpolated discount factor. The sum of these cash flows will give the dirty price of the bond now re-priced using Euribor futures rates.

Table 3.17 – 0.25% 2013 bond re-priced using Euribor futures.

Adj Bond Price	98.362
ACC	0.0240
Clean	98.3381
Strip yield	1.1063%
Cash bond	yield 0.2118%
TED	0.8945%

This is shown in the table as the adjusted bond price (0.264 + 98.098). The accrued interest is subtracted to give a clean price of 98.34 and this is used to calculate the yield on the bond using the YIELD function in Excel as previously demonstrated. This returns a yield of 1.11%, which is representative of the Euribor futures strip yield.

The cash bond yield on 23 December 2011 was 0.2118% (price 100.075) and the difference between these two rates of 0.895% is the two-year term TED spread for the 0.25% 13 December 2013 bond.

Number of futures to hedge

The number of futures to hedge is the number of futures needed to hedge the risk of the bond.

This is determined by observing the effects of a one-basis-point change in yield on the value of the bond over a period that is covered by a particular Euribor future, divided by the BPV of the Euribor future (€25). This can be approximated as:

$$\frac{Notional \times DP / 100 \times 0.01\% \times DF_n \times \dfrac{days}{Year}}{BPV_{STIRfuture}}$$

DP = Dirty price of the cash bond

For the first (stub) period from 23 December 2011 to 21 March 2012, this would be:

$$\frac{€100M \times 100.099 / 100 \times 0.01\% \times 0.996535 \times \dfrac{89}{360}}{€25} = 99$$

This means that 99 Euribor futures would need to be sold to hedge €100M 0.25% 13 December 2013 covering the period 23 December 2011 to 21 March 2012.

To cover the period 21 March to 19 June 2012, a further 99 futures would be need to be sold. Usually the stub period is combined with the first futures period, meaning a total of 198 H2 futures would be sold. This process is continued until all of the bond's term is covered. In total Euribor 785 futures would need to be sold.

For those traders with access to Bloomberg, there is a function (TED) to do the hard work. The following screenshot shows the output, which is very similar to the Excel calculations above.

Fig. 3.13 – Bloomberg Term TED Spread for €100M Bundesschatzanweisungen 0.25% 13 December 2013 on 23 December 2011. Used with permission of Bloomberg Finance LP

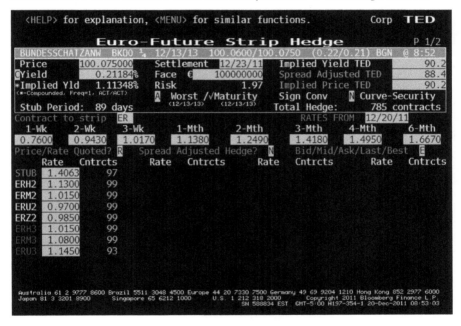

The TED spread and the swap spread

The TED spread is a good proxy for the swap spread and both are highly correlated (85%), as shown by the following chart. However, the TED spread constructed as above takes some articulation and requires execution of a futures strip comprising different numbers of quarterly futures, which precludes the use of bundles. Traders generally prefer simpler solutions, so the term TED spread is often replicated entirely in the derivatives space using bond and STIR futures, which also shows a very good correlation to the swap spread. However, it should be remembered that the TED spread from derivatives is effectively forward-starting (along with other differences discussed later ...) and so will not be as close a fit to the swap spread as the term TED spread.

Fig. 3.14 – Two-year European TED spread based on Bundesschatzanweisungen 0.25% 13 December 2013 (black broken line), two-year European TED spread using bond futures (Schatz H2) and Euribor H2 bundle (thin dotted black line) and interpolated two-year European swap spread (solid blackline). Dated 16 November 2011 to 20 December 2011.

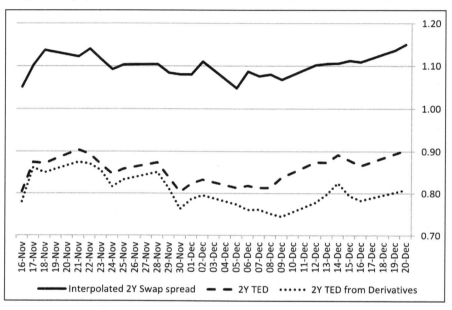

Trader's notes: Buying and selling the TED spread

In expectation of the TED spread widening, the bond/bond futures would be bought and STIR futures sold.

In expectation of the TED spread narrowing, the bond/bond futures would be sold and STIR futures bought.

Constructing the term TED spread using derivatives

The TED spread is often replicated entirely in the derivatives space and is a very popular way of trading the swap spread.

The following table shows some popular versions of the TED spread. For example, the two-year term TED spread is between a two-year bond future and two-year STIR future bundle. The bundles can be replaced by variations of packs or stacks in return for an acceptance of higher (curve) risk.

Table 3.18 – Examples of term TED spreads of US and German bonds using derivatives

Bond future	Bundle	Pack	Stacks
CBOT 2-Year Treasury note	CME Eurodollar 2-year bundle	CME Eurodollar packs	CME Eurodollar futures
CBOT 5-Year Treasury note	CME Eurodollar 5-year bundle	CME Eurodollar packs	CME Eurodollar futures
EUREX 2-Year Schatz	LIFFE Euribor 2- ear bundle	LIFFE Euribor packs	LIFFE Euribor futures
EUREX 5-Year Bobl	LIFFE Euribor 5-year bundle	LIFFE Euribor packs	LIFFE Euribor futures

The term TED spread can be replicated by trading, for example, a two-year bond future against a strip or bundle of stir futures. This will provide a reasonable proxy for the credit risk inherent in the two-year swap spread.

First of all, the strip yield from a STIR future bundle needs to be calculated for a proxy of the two-year swap rate.

Strip yields can be calculated as:

$$[(1 + IFR_1 \times accrual) \times (1 + IFR_2 \times accrual) \times (1 + IFR_3 \times accrual)...\times(1 + IFR_n \times accrual)] - 1$$

Where IFR is the implied forward rate from the futures (100% - price%) and the accrual is the year fraction covered by the future (0.25).

Using Euribor futures prices from 11 January:

Table 3.19 – Euribor prices from 11 January

Mar–12	98.985
Jun–12	99.095
Sep–12	99.135
Dec–12	99.135
Mar–13	99.135
Jun–13	99.11
Sep–13	99.065
Dec–13	98.985

The strip yield can be calculated as follows:

$$[(1+1.015\% \times 0.25) \times (1+0.905\% \times 0.25) \times (1+0.865\% \times 0.25) \times (1+0.865\% \times 0.25) \times$$
$$(1+0.865\% \times 0.25) \times (1+0.890\% \times 0.25) \times (1+0.935\% \times 0.25) \times (1+1.015\% \times 0.25)]^{0.5} - 1 = 0.92\%$$

The implied yield from the two-year Schatz future can be calculated by using a yield calculator like the YIELD function in Excel to solve for the yield to maturity of the CTD when the price is:

F x C

F= Futures price

C = Conversion price

And the settlement date is changed to match the futures delivery date.

The futures price on 11 January was 110.405 and the conversion factor for the CTD (Bundesschatzanweisungen 0.25% 13 December 2013) was 0.906868 giving:

110.405 x 0.906868 = 100.123

Putting this into the YIELD function in Excel (and changing the settlement date to the delivery date of 13 March) returns 0.18% (compared to 0.143% for the CTD).

Fig. 3.15 – Excel YIELD function returning yield of 0.18% for March 2012 Schatz future YIELD(DATE(2012,3,13),DATE(2013,12,13),0.25%,100.123,100,1,1

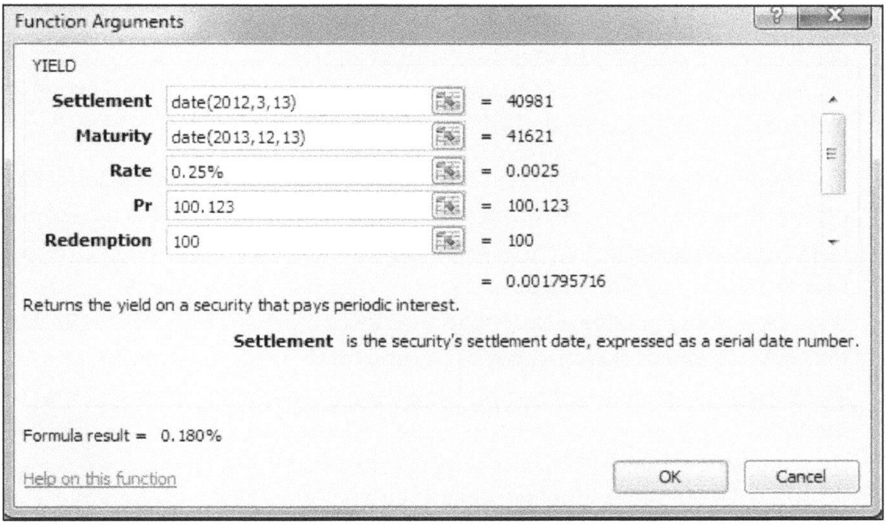

The two-year euro term TED spread is then calculated as:

0.92% - 0.18% = 0.74%

This TED spread calculated with bond and STIR futures will replicate the two-year swap spread as shown in Figure 3.14. However, there are some important provisos that should be remembered.

- The TED spread calculated from futures is derivative-based and therefore will be forward-starting (in March 2012) whereas an interpolated two-year swap spread would start on 11 January (+2) and run until the maturity of the CTD (13 December 2012).

- The TED spread calculated from futures has a maturity mismatch in that the STIR futures cover a forward period from March 2012 to March 2014, which is approximately three months more than the CTD. Seven futures, instead of eight, could be used instead – but this would preclude the use of exchange-traded bundles.

- The TED spread calculated from derivatives will include basis from both the bond and STIR futures.

- The STIR future strip yield method applies an equal weighting to each quarterly rate, as implied by the futures price. In comparison, bond cash flows are effectively weighted, since the nearer-dated cash flows benefit from the effects of reinvestment of coupons (thereby earning interest on interest). This means that the nearer-dated coupon payments of bonds are more important than further-dated ones and, in order to truly compare a strip yield to a bond yield, a method of weighting the cash flows of the futures strip is necessary. This was illustrated earlier by creating a notional bond from STIR futures.

- The bond future interest rate sensitivities and the consequent hedge ratios are derived from the CTD bond, which itself is derived from the basket of deliverable bonds. It is advisable to ensure that this deliverable basket is fully populated and that the bond auction schedule will not introduce more eligible bonds of deliverable grade into the delivery basket. If this happens, then it is possible that the CTD status can change suddenly, creating new hedge ratio characteristics. There is a stronger possibility of this happening when a greater period of time to the bond's delivery exists and the trader will need to estimate the possible consequences. It might be that a new CTD bond might not significantly change the hedge characteristics, but it can be advisable to model the characteristics of this yet-to-be auctioned bond and compare its sensitivities to the existing CTD bond. Details of forthcoming bonds are available on government auction schedules and it is realistic to price them in advance using the yields from similar issues.

The choice of bundle, pack or stack

Bundles, packs or stacks can be traded against bond futures as a proxy for the STIR futures strip.

A pack is four quarterly contracts with a total BPV per pack of €100 BPV (4 x €25) and a two-year bundle has eight quarterly contracts with a BPV of €200 (8 x €25). A stack can be used as a proxy for both of these. This is where four single contracts (for example H2) are traded with a combined BPV of €100 to match that of the pack or eight contracts to combine to make a BPV of €200 to match that of a bundle.

All three can be easily executed, the first two as exchange-traded strategies, and stacks as outright trades.

Intuitively, bundles should make the best hedge since they will most closely replicate the cash flows and duration of the bond future. However, the correlations in the table show that the red pack and any stack from H2 onwards makes an equally good proxy. However, note that using shorter-term strategies such as packs and stacks involves an acceptance of increased curve risk.

Table 3.20 – Correlations between Eurex Schatz H2 and Liffe Euribor

H2	M2	U2	Z2	H3	M3	Two-year bundle	White pack	Red pack
0.933	0.970	0.988	0.984	0.994	0.992	0.992	0.976	0.994

Indeed, it is only the white contracts and white pack that provide a lesser hedge, but at approximately 0.97 this is still a good proxy. The only contract to be avoided as a spread against the bond future is the front month, since that will tend to lock into cash LIBOR/EURIBOR fixings.

The choice between bundle, pack or stack will be mainly down to preference and acceptance of the different amounts of curve risk involved. Stacks are easily transacted and have the advantage that their number can be adjusted to provide an easy hedge ratio. However, they are a single point on the yield curve and so will have the highest curve risk. Packs and bundles have less curve risk, respectively, but can be less easy to transact, hedge and monitor.

Trading and displaying the spread

Buying the spread involves buying the bond future and selling the futures strip.

Selling the spread involves selling the bond futures and buying the futures strip.

Displaying a term spread as the difference between the strip yield and the yield of the CTD bond is useful for relative comparisons with the swap/benchmark spread, but rather meaningless when trading the spread between two instruments whose markets' prices are presented quite differently. There are several ways to display term spreads, but it is important that the contract price, trade ratio and tick values are incorporated in order for the spread to represent all the variables involved. One method is to present the spread in price format. This incorporates the prices of the relevant instruments, their quantities as determined by the hedge ratio and the respective tick values per basis point.

This is expressed as:

$$(P_{bf} \times T \times Q_{bf}) - (P_s \times T \times Q_s)$$

where:

Pbf   is the price of the bond future

T   is the tick value per basis point

Qbf   is the number of contracts used

Ps   is the price of the futures strip. This is a simple average of the prices used, whether for a bundle, pack or stack.

Qs   is the quantity of contracts used

The quantities are determined by dividing the total BPV of the futures strip by the BPV of the bond future. Given that the BPV of a single Euribor future will always be €25, the BPV of a bundle is simply the number of contracts within that strip multiplied by €25. There are eight contracts within a bundle, so the BPV will be €200 (8 x €25). This figure is divided by the BPV of the Schatz future, say €20, giving a figure of ten. Therefore, one bundle, comprising eight contracts, should be traded against ten Schatz futures.

The same methodology can be used for using packs instead of bundles. A pack will have a BPV of €100 (four contracts x €25); dividing this by the BPV of the Schatz future (€20) gives a ratio of one pack to five Schatz futures.

Stacks are slightly more flexible in that they can comprise any number of contracts, but the same methodology is used. A stack of, say, ten Euribor December futures will have a BPV of €250 (10 x €25) and dividing that by the BPV of the Schatz (€20) will result in a hedge of 12.5 Schatz futures.

Pricing examples

Given the following prices as at 28 October 2005, the average of the eight contracts of the two-year bundle is 97.2281.

Table 3.21 – Prices as at 28 October 2005

Euribor	Z5	H6	M6	U6	Z6	H7	M7	U7	Average
	97.630	97.460	97.320	97.220	97.125	97.075	97.020	96.975	97.2281

The Schatz Z5 future is 105.70 and the hedge ratio is calculated as ten Schatz futures per bundle (eight contracts). The spread is then calculated as:

(105.70 x 10 x 10) - (97.2281 x 25 x 8) = -8,875.625

Although the value of the spread is large, it has the benefit of behaving like an intra-contract spread. An increase in the value of the spread will lead to a profit for a long spread position – that is, a long position in the bond and a short position in the bundle, and vice versa. Furthermore, the difference between the purchase and sale price of the spread will indicate the overall profit or loss on the trade.

Trading example 1

28 Oct 2005

The chart shows the rising trend of the swap spread and the price spread, driven by increasing swap and bond prices against an economic outlook suggesting higher interest rate rises. However, movements in one spread are not exactly mirrored in the other. There are the known risks of credit, maturity mismatches and forward-starting considerations, as well as vagaries in the data between the instruments involved in the graphical display. Different settlement times, uses of bids, offer or mid prices and data errors can all affect the display properties of these spreads.

Fig. 3.16 – Euribor term TED spread (two- year bundle) (RH) and swap spread (LH)

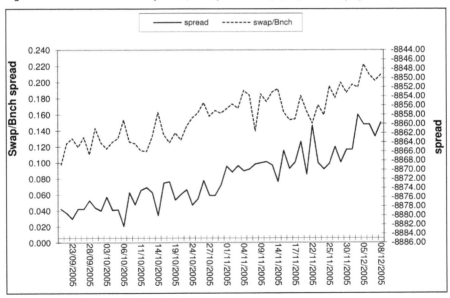

A sharp rally in the swap/benchmark spread from 24 October was partially reversed on 28 October, but with the price spread falling more sharply. This presented an opportunity to buy the spread cheaply, looking for a continuing upward trend.

The following market prices were available. The Schatz was trading down 2.5 ticks on the day and the two-year Euribor bundle was trading down ten ticks (remember that Liffe bundles and packs are quoted as the cumulative net change).

Table 3.22 – Available market prices 28 October 2005

Eurex Schatz Z5	105.70								
Euribor	Z5	H6	M6	U6	Z6	H7	M7	U7	Average
	97.630	97.460	97.320	97.220	97.125	97.075	97.020	96.975	97.2281

The CTD bond was the 2.25% 14/9/07 and its BPV for the Schatz Z5 future was calculated to be €19.99. The Liffe two-year bundle had a BPV of €200 (8 x €25) and the ratio determined to be ten Schatz futures per bundle. Ten Schatz futures were purchased and one bundle sold, effectively buying the term spread. The price was calculated to be:

$$(105.70 \times 10 \times 10) - (97.2281 \times 25 \times 8) = -8{,}875.625$$

3 November 2005

Both spreads have bounced back by 3 November and the following prices were observed.

Table 3.23 – Available market prices 3 November 2005

Eurex Schatz Z5	105.70								
Euribor	Z5	H6	M6	U6	Z6	H7	M7	U7	Average
	97.610	97.400	97.250	97.220	97.150	97.060	97.005	96.950	97.1656

Making a price spread of

$$(105.64 \times 10 \times 10) - (97.1656 \times 25 \times 8) = -8{,}869.125$$

The spread was purchased on 28 October for -8875.625 and sold on 3 November for -8869.125, a difference of 6.5. Multiplying 6.5 by 100 gives a profit of €650, verified by the individual profit and losses below.

Table 3.24 – Profit and losses

	28th Oct	3rd Nov	P/L (€)
Schatz	105.70	105.64	-600
Z5	97.630	97.610	+50
H6	97.460	97.400	+150
M6	97.320	97.250	+175
U6	97.220	97.150	+175
Z6	97.125	97.060	+162.50
H7	97.075	97.005	+175
M7	97.020	96.950	+175
U7	96.975	96.900	+187.50
		Σ	650.00

Trading example 2

22 Nov 2005

On 22 November, a sharp spike in the price spread was noticed with no observable equal reaction in the swap spread. The price of the Schatz had risen sharply from 105.465 on 21 November to 105.565 on 22 November, a rise of 10 ticks, whereas the average price of the two-year bundle had actually fallen 0.04 ticks. It was decided that the Schatz was too expensive relative to the futures strip, especially since there had been no major increase in the swap spread.

A decision was taken to sell the spread, but unfortunately no suitable prices were available in the bundles and packs (imaginary scenario!). It was decided to use a stack instead, concentrating on Euribor H7, which displayed a correlation of 0.9943 against the Schatz future. 20 contracts were bought at a price of 96.955 and the total BPV calculated to be 500 (20 x €25). The Schatz future had a BPV of 19.99 and so 25 (500/19.99 and rounded) contracts were sold at 105.565.

The spread was calculated to be:

(105.565 x 10 x 25) - (96.955 x 25 x 20) = -22,086.25

23 Nov 2005

One day later, the spread had corrected. The Schatz had fallen to 105.52 and the Euribor H7 had risen to 96.980. The spread was bought back to close and it was calculated to have fallen to -22,110.00, a change of 23.75, which, multiplied by 100, returned a profit of €2,375.

This was verified by calculating the profit on the Schatz as €1,125 (105.565 - 105.520 x 25 x €10) and the profit on the Euribor H7 as €1,250 (96.980 - 96.955 x 20 x €25).

Trader's notes

- When calculating the BPV of a CTD bond, it can be useful to recalculate it forward at the delivery date of the bond against the bond future. This will generate a forward BPV to compare with the spot version. The difference between the spot and forward BPV might not be much, but could help the decision-making process when rounding hedge ratios.

- Compare the swap/benchmark spread to the term spread, calculated from weighted strip yields to minimise yield curve effects on the spread value, to determine what is driving the spread.

- Short sellers of term spread should always be aware of the asymmetrical nature of the spread.

- When trading term spreads, go to the point of least liquidity first. Strategies such as bundles and packs will be less liquid than the bond futures. Plan to get filled on that part of the trade first, to minimise execution risk.

OIS/LIBOR Spreads

OIS/LIBOR spreads are a spread between a LIBOR fixing and an overnight index swap (OIS) of similar term (for example three months). OIS are short-term swaps exchanging a fixed rate for a floating rate which is based upon a daily overnight rate reference. This is commonly EONIA for euro-based products and Fed Funds for US based products.

European OverNight Index Average (EONIA)

EONIA is computed as a weighted average of all overnight unsecured lending transactions in the interbank market, initiated within the euro area by the Panel Banks. It is reported on an Act/360-day count convention and is displayed to three decimal places.

Federal funds rate (Fed funds)

The Federal funds rate is the interest rate at which depository institutions lend balances at the Federal Reserve to other depository institutions overnight on an uncollateralised basis.

Both EONIA and Fed Funds are overnight lending rates and these can be used as the basis for swap transactions to extend the borrowing term related to overnight rates.

OIS Swap Example

A bank pays fixed for a one-week (7-day) EONIA swap at 0.450% on €100m (Act/360).

Fig. 3.17 – Diagram of OIS swap example

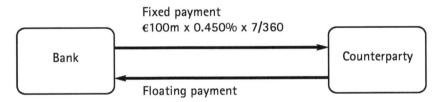

The fixed side is calculated as a simple interest calculation for the term of the swap and the floating side is calculated by compounding the notional principal and interest day by day. Unlike interest rate swaps, OIS settlement is a single net payment at maturity

If during the course of the week EONIA is fixed at:

Table 3.25 – EONIA prices

Day	EONIA
Monday	0.483
Tuesday	0.535
Wednesday	0.462
Thursday	0.458
Friday	0.390

The fixed side is calculated as a simple interest calculation for the term of the swap.

$$€100M \times 0.45\% \times \frac{7}{360} = €8750$$

The floating side is calculated by compounding notional principal and interest day by day.

$$€100M \times \left[1+0.483\% \times \frac{1}{360}\right] \times \left[1+0.535\% \times \frac{1}{360}\right] \times \left[1+0.462\% \times \frac{1}{360}\right] \times$$
$$\left[1+0.458\% \times \frac{1}{360}\right] \times \left[1+0.390\% \times \frac{3}{360}\right] - €100M = €8633$$

Note that Friday's fixing is used for Friday and the weekend.

Retrospectively, the bank will pay €8,750 and the counterparty will pay €8,633, but since OIS settlement is a single net payment at maturity, the bank will pay €117 to the counterparty.

Bearing in mind this was a one-week swap on €100M, the net exchange of €117 is tiny; and this is a feature of short maturity overnight index swaps. This means that there is often less profit or loss at risk of counterparty default on an OIS compared to an interest rate swap and this is further reduced since there are no intermediate cash flows. This, along with the swap referencing a rate that closely tracks official policy interest rates, means that OIS rates trade at levels very close to secured lending rates (general collateral repo rates) and official policy rates.

In contrast, LIBOR rates are fully funded, unsecured interbank transactions with inherent counterparty risk. Consequently, a spread between the two is an indication of counterparty risk premium and general bank creditworthiness. Most of the drivers of the swap spread detailed earlier apply to OIS/LIBOR spreads.

Fig. 3.18 – 3M OIS/LIBOR Spreads. US 3M OIS/LIBOR spread (thick grey) and euro 3M OIS/LIBOR spread (thin black). RH scale in basis points. 2007–2012

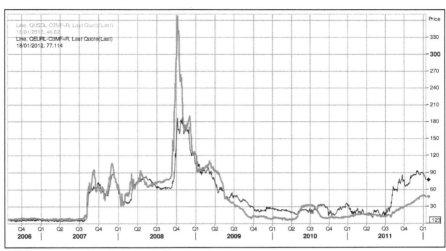

Source: Reuters

The chart shows these effects most noticeably in 2008 during the financial crisis and during the 2011 European sovereign debt crisis when the spread widened dramatically. Most of this widening was caused by LIBOR rates increasing sharply.

Overnight index futures and OIS futures

A summary of overnight index futures and OIS futures is presented in the table. OIS futures have similar characteristics to STIR futures but unfortunately are currently fledgling. The Liffe 1M EONIA overnight index future is also fledgling, leaving only the Fed Funds futures traded against the Eurodollar STIR futures as a viable proxy for an OIS/LIBOR spread.

Table 3.26 – Summary of overnight index futures and OIS futures

	1M EONIA	3M EONIA OIS	3M FED FUNDS OIS	FED FUNDS
Exchange	LIFFE	LIFFE	CME Group	CME Group
Size	€3,000,000	€1,000,000	$1,000,000	$5,000,000
Contracts	Monthly	Quarterly with serial	Quarterly	Monthly
Quote	100 - R	100 - R	100 minus R (realized rate during the quarter, with daily compounding of the effective overnight Federal Funds rate)	100 minus the average daily Fed Funds overnight rate for the delivery month
Tick size	0.00005 (€12.50) [3Mx0.00005x30/360]	0.00005 (€12.50)	0.000025 ($6.25)	0.000025 ($10.42) [5Mx0.000025x30/360]
Expiry	Last day of ECB Reserve Maintenance Period (approx. tenth of month)	Two business days prior to the third Wednesday of the delivery month	Last day of reference quarter	Last business day of delivery month

This might be rather academic given OIS futures are fledgling, but traders should be aware that the 3M Fed Funds OIS future is backwards-looking, settling to the realised rate during the quarter calculated by daily compounding of the effective overnight Fed Funds rate.

This means that to trade OIS/LIBOR spread using a June 2012 3M Fed Funds OIS future would require a March 2012 Eurodollar future to cover the same period.

Fig. 3.19 – Structure of a Fed Funds/Eurodollar spread

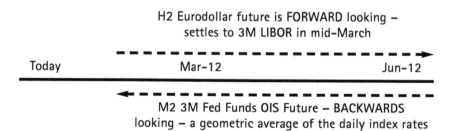

H2 Eurodollar future is FORWARD looking – settles to 3M LIBOR in mid-March

Today   Mar–12   Jun–12

M2 3M Fed Funds OIS Future – BACKWARDS looking – a geometric average of the daily index rates

The diagram shows the structure of an OIS/LIBOR spread using a June 2012 3M Fed Funds OIS future and a March 2012 Eurodollar future. The trade would be set up in a 1:1 ratio since the BPV of the 3M Fed Funds OIS future is $25, the same as the Eurodollar future.

In contrast the Liffe 3M EONIA future is forward-looking like a Euribor future and so a March 2012 3M EONIA future would be traded against a March 2012 Euribor future in a 1:1 ratio since both contracts have a BPV of €25.

US OIS/LIBOR spreads using Fed Funds/Eurodollar futures

The Fed Fund futures are liquid contracts traded on CME Group (CBOT) and are an average of the overnight Fed Funds rate over the course of the delivery month.

They appear similar to Eurodollar futures in pricing mechanism but are priced as 100 minus the average daily Fed Funds overnight rate for the delivery month. This means that as the delivery month progresses, and in the absence of a rate-setting Federal Open Market Committee meeting, the contract will become less volatile due to this averaging process. Fed Fund futures are also one-month serial contracts in contrast to the three-month Eurodollar (serial and) quarterly contracts. This means that OIS/LIBOR spreads replicated by using Fed Funds futures and Eurodollar futures need to be traded with overlapping periods.

Fig. 3.20 – Example of a Fed Funds/Eurodollar spread

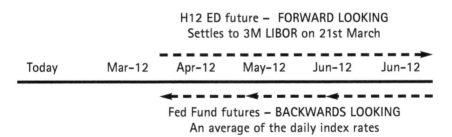

The diagram shows this process. A H2 Eurodollar future covers a period of 90 days from the delivery date of 21 March 2012. This would be hedged using a ratio of Mar-12, Apr-12, May-12 and Jun-12 Fed Funds futures. The ratio of how many Fed Fund futures to use to hedge or spread against a three-month Eurodollar future is determined by the period of time covered by the Fed Funds future with respect to the Eurodollar future.

Trading example: Fed Funds/Eurodollar spread

A position of 1,000 H2 Eurodollar futures would have a BPV of $25,000 (1000 x $25). A Fed Funds future has a BPV of $41.67 as given by:

$$\$5,000,000 \times 0.01\% \times \frac{1}{12} = \$41.67$$

Where $5M is the contract size, 0.01% is one basis point and 1/12 is a one-month contract expressed as a proportion of a year. The Fed Funds futures trade in a tick size of ¼ basis point ($10.42) for the front month (½ basis point ticks thereafter).

Therefore 600 Fed Funds futures would have to be traded against 1,000 Eurodollar futures, as given by:

$$\frac{\$25,000}{\$41.67} = 600$$

The only question now remaining is in what ratios?

The Eurodollar forward period covers 90 days from the delivery day of 21 March (to 19 June). To calculate the ratio of March Fed Fund futures needs the number of days to cover the period from the 21 March to Month end (ten days). After that, April has 30 days and May 31. In June, the number of days from month beginning to the end of the Eurodollar forward period on 19 June is 19. The total of all these days is 90 (10 + 30 + 31 + 19).

Therefore the length of overlap in March is ten days out of a total of 90 and therefore the fraction of Eurodollar exposure covered by a March Fed Funds future would be 10/90 = 0.11. Out of a total required of 600 futures, 67 March futures would be required (0.11 x 600).

In April, there are 30 days included in the 90 Eurodollar forward exposure period, meaning 200 (0.33 x 600) April futures would be required.

Table 3.27 – Hedge ratios for Fed Funds/Eurodollar spread

Fed Fund Contract	Eurodollar Start and end dates	Month end	Length of overlap of FF rate exposure with H2 ED rate exposure (days)	Fraction of ED forward period (Length of overlap/90)	No of FF contracts (Fraction x 600)
Mar–12	21/03/2012	31/03/2012	10	0.11	67
Mar–12		30/04/2012	30	0.33	200
May–12		31/05/2012	31	0.34	207
Jun–12	19/06/2012	29/06/2012	19	0.21	127

The table shows the fractions of the Eurodollar (ED) forward period for each month and the number of Fed Funds futures needed to hedge or spread against this exposure.

Alternatively, 600 stacks could be used with the acceptance of curve risk.

Buying and selling the spread

In expectation of the spread widening, the Fed Fund futures would be bought and Eurodollar futures sold.

In expectation of the spread narrowing, the Fed Fund futures would be sold and Eurodollar futures bought.

Trader's Notes

The drivers of the Fed Funds/Eurodollar spread or a 3M OIS/LIBOR spread are largely the same as those that drive the TED spread and the swap spread.

However, there are some subtle difference between Fed Fund rates and the LIBOR rates underlying the Eurodollar futures prices that can also influence the spread. Fed Funds rates comprise all brokered domestic inter-bank trades complied in a trade value weighted average and the Fed Fund futures are a forward-looking expression of the average of daily Fed Funds for the delivery month. In contrast, Eurodollar futures settle to LIBOR fixings, survey-based compilations of London inter-bank rates from a relatively small number of panellists.

Spreading STIR futures against swap futures

The swaps market is a liquid over-the-counter (bilateral agreement) derivative with maturities ranging from two years to 50 years. They are one of the most widely used over-the-counter (OTC) derivatives in terms of notional value. Futures on swap products were introduced by the exchanges shortly after the millennium, to try to capture a share of the hugely liquid swaps market by constructing standardised contracts to replicate the OTC market. Both CME Group via CBOT and Liffe have launched swap futures in similar forms, but all have remained fledgling. Indeed, all US-dollar-denominated products (both CBOT swap futures and US Dollar Liffe Swapnote) have no volume at the time of writing. However, the euro-denominated Swapnote contracts have daily volumes of several hundred or a few thousand contracts. It is not clear whether this is due to reluctance by swap traders to embrace these products as a hedging tool, or apathy and lack of understanding amongst the general trading community. However, swap futures provide an ideal spread partner for STIR futures since their yield is very similar to the equivalent term STIR futures strip yield and so they do not have the credit spread risk associated with spreading against bond futures.

Swap futures are designed like bond futures. US swap futures are specified as $100,000 notional of a five, seven, ten or 30-year bond with a 4% coupon. The Liffe Swapnote futures are euro and US-dollar-denominated 100,000 6% bonds with maturities of two, five and ten years.

Selected contract specifications for the five-year CBOT and two-year Liffe € Swapnote are shown in the table.

Table 3.28 – Selected contract specifications for five-year CBOT and two-year Liffe € Swapnote

Exchange	CBOT	LIFFE
Product	5Y interest rate swap future	2Y Swapnote
Currencies	$	€
Trading Unit	Notional price of 5Y swap with fixed rate of 4%, semi-annual payments and notional 100,000 principal versus floating side based on three-month Libor.	A bond future, with 100,000 notional principal and 6% coupon referenced to the swap market
Size & tick value	$100,000 ($15.625)	€100,000 (€5)
Settlement	Cash settled to the final settlement value, which is determined as: $100 * [4/r5 + (1 - 4/r5)*(1 + r5/200)^{-10}]$ r5 represents ISDA® Benchmark Rates for five-year US dollar interest rate swaps on the last day of trading	The EDSP is the present value, as of the delivery day, of the notional principal amount and the notional coupons of the note. The discounting of the cash flows is performed using a swap curve which is constructed, on the last trading day, from the ISDA Benchmark Euribor Swap Rate fixings

An introduction to interest rate swaps

A swap is an agreement to exchange one set of interest flows for another, with no exchange of principal.

A standard or vanilla interest rate swap is an agreement between two counterparties, where a set of cash flows from a fixed rate are exchanged for a set of floating rate cash flows. The holder of the fixed leg of the swap makes regular uniform payments to the holder of the floating leg. This party, in return, makes regular payments to the fixed leg party, but the amounts of these vary according to prevailing interest rates.

Fig. 3.21 – Diagram of an interest rate swap

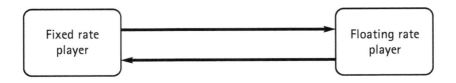

The cash flows are exchanged on different bases. For example, in a European swap the fixed side operates on an annual 30/360 convention, the same as the corporate bond market, and the floating side uses a six-month money market Act/360 convention. In a US swap, the fixed side is semi-annual 30/360 and the floating side quarterly Act/360. The actual amounts of the interest payments are calculated using a notional amount or principal that is never exchanged.

Swap rates are initially set by calculating the present values of their cash flows. At the inception of the swap, the difference between the present values of both the fixed and floating side cash flows is set to zero. This means that at inception there is no financial advantage to entering into an interest rate swap as either fixed-rate receiver (floating-rate payer) or fixed-rate payer. Effectively, the fixed side pays a rate that values the total of the fixed cash flow at the same present value as the floating-rate cash flow total. Consequently, when the swap contract commences, there will be no advantage to either the fixed or floating side of the swap and therefore no upfront payment. During the lifetime of the swap contract, the present values of the variable side of the swap, based on changing rates, will deviate from the fixed rate side, which do not change, crediting one side at the expense of the other.

The table demonstrates the process of determining the cash flows at inception of a notional two-year swap based on a notional amount of €1M starting on 1 February 2012. The fixed rate payments are based on a rate of 1.346%.

Table 3.29 – Example of a euro two-year swap, based upon a notional of €1M and a fixed rate of 1.346%

Dates		DF	Fixed side accrual	PV Fixed payments (1.346%)	Floating rates	Floating side accruals	PV Floating payments
01 February 2012							
01 August 2012		0.9962			0.75%	0.51	3777
01 February 2013		0.9912	1.00	13242	1.00%	0.51	5066
01 August 2013		0.9837			1.50%	0.50	7419
03 February 2014		0.9737	1.01	13081	2.00%	0.52	10061
				26324			26324

Columns explained:

DF

Discount factors are used to present value cash flows and are usually backed out of the swaps curve and interpolated to match the swap cash flow dates. The methodology for this was covered in 'STIR Futures Pricing' and used elsewhere for present valuing cash flows.

Accruals factor (AF)

This is the fractional part of the year expressed as a decimal based on the appropriate convention. For the fixed side, this will be 30/360 and for the floating side this will be Act/360. Since the floating side cash flows are semi-annual, it is to be expected that this value will be approximately 0.50 (180/360). However, small differences in day counts and non-business days affect the figure accordingly. In this example, the Excel function YEARFRAC was used.

PV Fixed side

This is calculated as:

    Principal x fixed rate x AF x DF

Floating rates

These are the six-month EURIBOR fixings that are used to calculate the floating side payments. Of course, only the first period can be known in advance and so the rest are six-month forward rates derived from the discount factors (using the same methodology as presented in 'STIR Futures Pricing' in Part 1).

PV floating side

The cash flows for the floating side are calculated in the same way as the fixed, except floating (forward) rates are used each period.

The totals of the fixed and floating cash flow columns are the present value of the cumulative income streams, as at the start date of 1 Feb 2012. The fixed leg amounts to 26,324 and the floating side is the same. This has been deliberately engineered by changing the fixed rate so that there is zero net present value between these two streams of payments. The difference between these two payments streams must be set to zero at the inception of the swap so that there is no advantage to either counterparty. This is achieved by changing the fixed rate on the fixed leg so that it will equalise the present value totals of both the floating and fixed legs and reduce the difference between the present values of the fixed and floating cash flows to zero. This rate is the quoted swap rate and is driven by the changing rates of the forward curve.

Liffe € Swapnote

Swapnote is a unique product, patented by UK money broker ICAP and licensed to Liffe. Swapnote is not a future on a swap but rather a bond future priced from the swap curve (instead of the benchmark curve used for bond futures based on government-issued debt). Consequently, Swapnote is more like a corporate bond having the same credit rating as the swaps market than a swap rate. It is available in two, five and ten-year maturities. It is based upon a notional €100,000 6% coupon bond, and is priced by the total of the net present values of the cash flows derived from a zero coupon yield curve comprised of a range of industry-standard financial instruments that represent the swaps curve. This makes Swapnote representative of the term structure and credit pricing of the swap market.

Swapnote is settled to ISDAFIX, which is an International Swaps and Derivatives Association (ISDA) fixing. This is considered to be the leading benchmark for rates on interest rate swaps worldwide. ISDAFIX is calculated daily. On its expiry day, Swapnote will settle to the sum of the present value of its cash flows derived from the ISDAFIX fixing rate, using a basis convention of an annual 30/360 fixed side versus six-month Euribor. The fixing is calculated from a range of rates collected from a sample of swaps dealers.

Pricing Swapnote

Swapnote is designed like a bond future but without some of the complexities. It is cash settled with no delivery option, meaning that it will be priced on a notional 6% two-year bond starting on the Swapnote expiry day.

The forward price (bond future) of this notional bond would be expressed as:

$$F = (P + Acc_0) \times \left(1 + i \times \frac{D}{B}\right) - (Acc_t + Coupons\,Re\,ceived)$$

F = Bond future value

P = clean price (for example a two-year maturity using a two-year swap rate as yield)

i = term repo financing rate

D = days in term repo (term between settlement date and delivery date)

B = year base (360)

Acc_0 = Accrued interest on settlement date

Acc_t = Accrued interest on delivery date

Coupons Received = any coupons received and reinvested during term between settlement date and delivery date

Using data from 20 December 2011, the € 2Y Swapnote H2 future is valued at 109.06 compared to the settlement price for the Swapnote of 109.19.

$$(110.13 + 4.53) \times \left(1 + 1.418\% \cdot \frac{92}{360}\right) - (0 + 6) = 109.06$$

The valuation methodology is to value a bond on 20 December 2011 (settlement date 23 December) that will have a two-year maturity on the H2 Swapnote future delivery date which is 21 March 2012. The process is as follows.

- Price a 6% bond with a settlement date of 23 December 2011 (t+3) and a maturity date of 21 March 2014. This means that on the delivery date of 21 March 2012, the bond will have a maturity of exactly two years. The yield on the bond will be an interpolated swap rate equivalent to 2.24 years. This was found to be 1.379% using a two-year swap rate of 1.36% and a three-year swap rate of 1.439% from 20 December. Using a basis of 30E/360 (number 4 in Excel PRICE function) and an annual coupon frequency (number 1 in Excel PRICE function) returns a clean bond price of 110.14.

Fig. 3.22 – PRICE Function:
PRICE(DATE(2011,12,23),DATE(2014,3,21),6%,1.3793%,100,1,4)

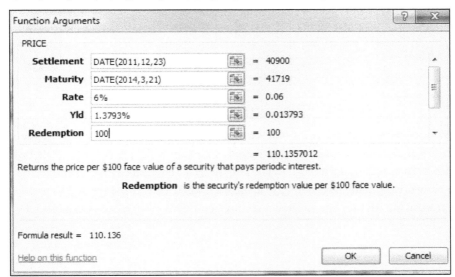

The accrued interest on 23 December 2011 for this bond was 4.53. Adding this to the clean price gives a dirty price of 114.67.

The cost of financing this dirty price for 89 days (23 December 2011 to 21 March 2012) at a three-month EURIBOR rate of 1.418% gives a total of 115.07.

On the delivery date of 21 March 2012, the accrued interest will be zero since it is a coupon day and a full annual coupon of 6 is received. This reduces the forward price to 115.07 - 6 = 109.07. This is the theoretical price of the H2 Swapnote future as at 20 December 2011.

The Swapnote can be alternatively valued by using a discount factor curve backed out of EURIBOR and swap rates. This is the same process as described in 'STIR Futures Pricing'. The EURIBOR and swaps curve on 20 December 2011 were as shown in the table from which discount factors were derived.

Table 3.30 – Euribor and euro swap rates and discount factors as at 20 December 2011

Trade date	20–Dec–11 Tue	Spot Value	2	Spot date	22–Dec–11 Thu
Depos & Swap term	Dates	Rates (%)	A/360 Deposit Accrual	30/360 Swap Accrual	Discount Factors (DF)
SN	23–Dec–11 Fri	0.5830	0.0028		0.999984
1M	23–Jan–12 Mon	1.1380	0.0889		0.998989
3M	22–Mar–12 Thu	1.4180	0.2528		0.996428
6M	22–Jun–12 Fri	1.6670	0.5083		0.991597
1Y	24–Dec–12 Mon	1.4700		0.0056	0.985434
2Y	23–Dec–13 Mon	1.3600		0.9972	0.973323
3Y	22–Dec–14 Mon	1.4390		0.9972	0.958026

A notional 6% coupon 2 year bond starting on the delivery date of the H2 Swapnote future of 21st March 2012 would be valued as the sum of the present value of its cash flows. There will be no accrued interest on the 21st March since this is a coupon day a basic bond pricing methodology can be used where each cash flow will be present valued at the relevant interpolated discount factor. This process is shown in the table:

Table 3.31 – Swapnote pricing using Euribor and euro swap-derived discount factors

2Y SWAPNOTE	100,000			
Swap Start Date	21-Mar-12 Wed	coupon	6.0000%	
Maturity Date	21-Mar-14 Fri			
Dates	DF	EUR Fixed Rate	30/360 Annual Fixed Accrual	EUR Fixed
21-Mar-12 Wed	0.996472			
21-Mar-13 Thu	0.982525	6.0000%	1.00000	5895.15
21-Mar-14 Fri	0.969603	106.0000%	1.00000	102777.89
				Price
				109.06

- The first cash flow of 6% coupon x €100,000 (Swapnote contract size) is on 21st March 2013. Using an discount factor from the discount factor curve interpolated to match this date gives a present value of €5895

- The final cash flow of 100% (par) + 6% coupon x €100,000 is on the maturity day of 21st March 2014 and returns a present valued cash flow of €102778

- Adding these cash flows together returns €108,673. Dividing this by the contract size and multiplying by 100 to express the sum of the present value of the cash flows per €100 nominal gives €108.67

- The bond price of €108.67 is the price of a 2.25 year bond starting in December 2011 but without the first coupon on 21st March 2012. To express it as a two year bond starting in March 2012, the price is divided by the discount factor for 21st March 2102 giving 108.67/0.996472=109.06. (Note this methodology gives the same results as calculating forward starting discount factors covering the bond's forward cash flows and using these to discount the bonds cash flows.)

Forward swap rates and Swapnote forward yields

The theoretical Swapnote price can be used to calculate the 2 year forward swap rate starting on 21st March 2012 valued on 20th December 2011. It simply needs the yield of the bond to be calculated. The YIELD function in Excel can be used returning a value of 1.376% with a 30E/360 basis and single coupon frequency.

Fig. 3.23 – YIELD function: YIELD(DATE(2012,3,21),DATE(2014,3,21),6%,109.06,100,1,4)

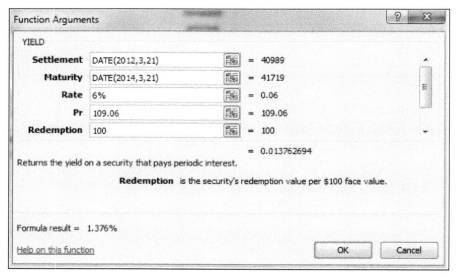

This is effectively the same as the 2 year forward starting swap rate that can be calculated from the discount factor curve presented above as:

$$\left[\frac{0.996472}{0.969605} \right]^{\frac{1}{2}} = 1.376\%$$

This can be compared with the forward yield from the H2 Swapnote future. This was trading at 109.19 on 20 December 2011. This can be inputted into the YIELD calculator with all other variables remaining unchanged. This returns 1.314%.

Fig. 3.24 – YIELD function: YIELD(DATE(2012,3,21),DATE(2014,3,21),6%,109.19,100,1,4)

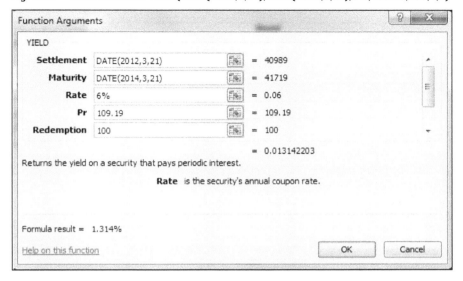

The Swapnote yield is lower than the two-year forward swap rate since Swapnote is a derivative and the forward-starting swap rate is effectively a forward-starting sequential series of Euribor forwards, and basis will exist between them (see 'STIR Futures Pricing').

For users of Bloomberg, Swapnote analytics are available (for the H2 Swapnote, this would be RWH2 Comdty FVD <go>). Liffe also provide an Excel-based Swapnote calculator free of charge on their website (search for Swapnote>Pricing).

Trading € Swapnote against Euribor bundles

Trading Swapnote against Euribor bundles is an interesting trade since there is effectively no credit spread and both instruments are forward-starting for the same term, meaning that they are essentially the same thing.

The trade can be viewed in yield terms by backing out the forward yield from Swapnote prices as above and comparing to Euribor strip yield based upon (and detailed earlier):

$$[(1+IFR_1\times accrual)\times(1+IFR_2\times accrual)\times(1+IFR_3\times accrual)...\times(1+IFR_n\times accrual)]-1$$

Where IFR is the implied forward rate from the futures (100% - Price%) and the accrual is the year fraction covered by the future (0.25)

Fig. 3.25 – H2 € 2Y Swapnote forward yield (dotted black) and H2 Euribor convexity adjusted bundle yield (solid black line) November 2011 to March 2012

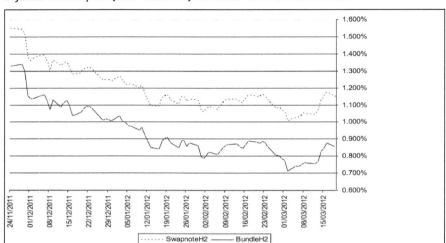

The graph shows the highly correlated relationship between the Euribor bundle yield and the Swapnote forward yield. There is a basis between the two yields since the Swapnote yield, although being a yield on a forward-starting swap derivative, ultimately has to settle to the swap curve constructed on the last trading day from the ISDA Benchmark Euribor Swap Rate fixings (see Swapnote contract specifications). The swaps curve, being a sequential series of Euribor six-month forwards, presently trades at a higher rate than the Euribor futures three-month implied forward rates due to term risk. This is the credit premium that exists for term lending versus rolling funding in shorter intervals and reflects the premium demanded by the markets to reflect the credit and liquidity perceptions between three- and six-month EURIBOR (see 'STIR Futures Pricing').

The trade would be set up to be duration (BPV) neutral. The BPV of a Euribor bundle would be the sum of eight contracts BPV (8 x 25 = 200) and the BPV of the Swapnote would be calculated in a similar way to that of a bond future.

The modified duration of the Swapnote can be calculated as the modified duration of a two-year bond starting on 21 March 2012 but with the yield set to 1.314%, which is the implied forward yield calculated earlier, based upon the Swapnote futures price trading at 109.19.

Fig. 3.26 – Modified duration function:

MDURATION(DATE(2012,3,21),DATE(2014,3,21),6%,1.314%,1,4)

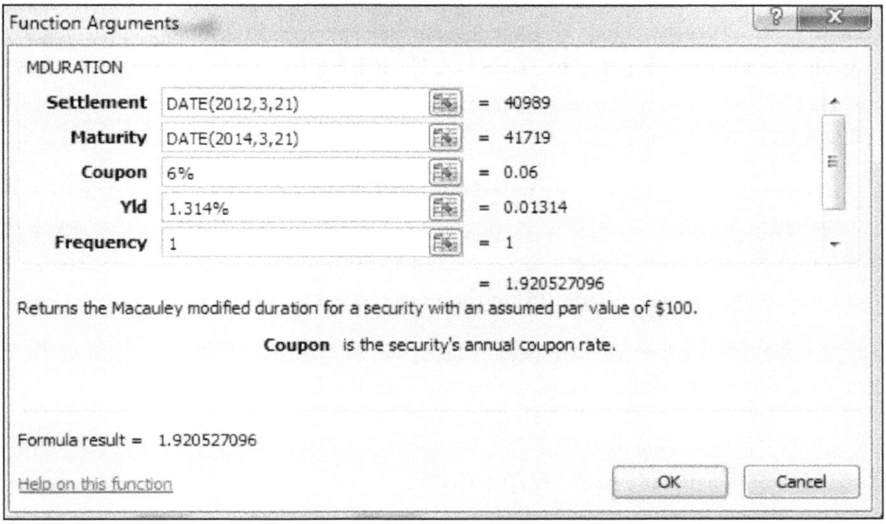

The BPV of the Swapnote can be calculated as follows:

€100,000 x 109.19/100 x 1.921 x 0.01% = €20.975

A position of long 100 H2 Swapnote futures would be hedged with 10.485 bundles (2,097/200). Of course, it is not possible to trade 10.485 bundles, only 10 or 11, in which case the Trader needs to make an informed decision as to round up or round down.

Unlike a bond future, the BPV of the Swapnote will not decline due to the passage of time between settlement (December 2011 in the example) and the Swapnote expiry (March 2012) since the contract is a two-year forward-starting bond. In contrast, a bond future references a cash bond (CTD) of finite term, which will diminish as time progresses, thus shortening its duration. Consequently, if this were a trade based on a STIR futures strip being used to hedge (or trade relatively against) a bond future, the inclination would be to round down. However, being a Swapnote future this does not apply and further analysis, such as regression analysis (detailed earlier), might be useful in order to make the choice.

CBOT interest rate swap futures

The CBOT interest rate swap futures are designed to appear similar to the CBOT Treasury note futures. They all have a notional value of $100,000, a notional 4% coupon, and are denominated in 32nds (1/32), each having a value of $31.25 per 1/32 but usually traded in minimum increments of one half of a 32nd, with a value of $15.625.

The interest rate swap futures are based on the notional price of the fixed rate side of a swap with notional $100,000 principal and semi-annual payments of 4% per annum, exchanged for floating three-month LIBOR. They trade in price terms of points ($1,000) and 32nds ($31.25) of the notional value ($100,000).

Hedge ratios for the interest rate swap futures can be calculated by determining their BPV or DV01 in the same way as illustrated with the Liffe Swapnote.

Trading CBOT interest rate swap futures

Once the BPV of the interest rate swap future has been calculated, spreads against Eurodollar packs, stacks and bundles can be calculated in the usual way. It should be noted that the BPV of the interest rate swap futures will vary as the forward start swap rate moves, whereas the Eurodollar BPV will remain static at $25.

Since interest rate swap futures are priced in 32nds and Eurodollars are decimalised, the pricing difference can make the visual monitoring of the spread between the two instruments a little difficult. The best approach is to monitor the cash flows of the trade in a spreadsheet, where both sides of the spread reflect the price, ratio and tick value in a similar way to what was demonstrated for trading term spreads. Note that the CBOT interest rate swap future should be decimalised for comparison with the Eurodollar. The decimalised tick value will be $10 (($31.25 x 32)/100).

Apart from trading against Eurodollars, these interest rate swap futures are very suitable for trading against CBOT Treasury note futures. The combination of these two allow term spread trading without the convexity bias inherent in Eurodollar forward rates, or the complexities and liquidity issues when trading bundles for five or ten years (if available or liquid).

Spreads between international STIR futures

Spreads between international STIR futures can be traded as, for example, Euribor futures against Eurodollar futures. However, the consequences can be surprising, not being merely a country spread differential. If the trade is done in a 1:1 ratio, the trader has a position that is correlated to a FX (Foreign eXchange) swap which in the derivatives space can be replicated using CME currency futures calendar spreads. This gives rise to spreading opportunities between STIR futures and currency futures.

FX forwards

FX forwards are forward exchange rates. These can be derived from the relationship between the FX spot rate and the interest rates of the base and pricing (variable currency) by:

$$F = S \left[\frac{1 + \left(i_p \times \dfrac{D}{B_p} \right)}{1 + \left(i_b \times \dfrac{D}{B_b} \right)} \right]$$

F = forward FX rate

S = spot FX rate

i_b = base currency interest rate

i_p = pricing currency rate

D = actual number of days

B_b = base currency year convention

B_p = pricing currency year convention

Example: On 23 January 2012, the €/$ spot rate was 1.2960. This means that $1.2960 (the pricing currency) will buy (or sell) one unit of the base currency which in this case is €1.

If three-month (92 days) interbank rates for the euro and dollar were 1.12% and 0.56% respectively then the three-month €/$ could be derived as €/$1.2942:

$$1.2960 \times \left[\frac{1 + \left(0.56\% \times \dfrac{92}{360} \right)}{1 + \left(1.12\% \times \dfrac{92}{360} \right)} \right] = 1.2942$$

This rate is the FX rate at which two counterparties would agree to buy or sell euros for delivery in three months' time.

FX forwards are conventionally quoted as the difference between the forward (F) and spot rates (S), expressed in *pips*. Pips are *points in percentile*, which are to FX what basis points are to interest rates. One pip is one hundredth of 1 cent, which is the fourth decimal place on the quote. To express in pips, multiply the difference by 10,000:

F-S = (1.2942 - 1.2960) x 10,000 = -18.49 pips

An approximation of this is:

$$S \times (i_p - i_b) \times (D / B)$$

Where:

$$[1.2960 \times (0.56\% - 1.12\%) \times (92 / 360)] = -18.55\,pips$$

This is merely an approximation but useful for spreaders looking to replicate this since STIR futures can be traded as a difference (minus) but not be divided (more later …).

FX swaps

FX swaps are single period currency swaps, usually used to hedge single period currency exposures and very short dated FX swaps are commonly used to roll settlements for spot FX transactions.

FX swaps involve two simultaneous transactions: a spot purchase or sale combined with a forward sale or purchase and are quoted as the difference between the spot and forward rate as with the forward quote above.

An FX swap differs from an FX forward in that the swap is two transactions together whereas a forward is a single forward-dated purchase or sale of currency.

FX swaps can be replicated in the derivatives space using futures. CME Group offers a range of currency futures with sequential quarterly expiries. The difference between expiries is tradable as calendar spreads, which are effectively exchange-traded forward-starting three-month FX swaps.

FX futures

CME Group offers a range of currency futures. Those which that are relevant to STIR futures markets are presented in the table.

Table 3.32 – Contract specifications for CME Group currency futures

	€/$	€/£	CHF/$	£/$
Contract size	€125,000	€125,000	CHF125,000	£62,500
Contract listing	6 quarterly months	6 quarterly months	6 quarterly months	6 quarterly months
Delivery	Physical	Physical	Physical	Physical
Tick size	0.0001 ($12.50) 0.00005 ($6.25) for spreads	0.00005 (£6.25) 0.000025 (£3.125) for spreads	0.0001 ($12.50) 0.00005 ($6.25) for spreads	0.0001 (£6.25)
Notes	Good liquidity, trades in further-dated contracts	Poor liquidity	Good liquidity, little trade in further-dated contracts	Good liquidity, trades in further-dated contracts

It should be noted that CME currency future calendar spreads are quoted in pips as:

$$Future_{furthestdated} - Future_{nearestdated}$$

This is the opposite way round to STIR future calendar spreads, but is to match the FX forward market convention.

Synthetic FX swaps using STIR futures

Synthetic forward FX swaps can be constructed by using the implied forward rates from STIR futures as substitutes for the base and pricing currency interest rates used in the FX forward pricing equation earlier.

The data from table 3.33 is from 23 January 2012 and includes LIBOR and EURIBOR rates, CME currency futures and spreads, currency basis swap quotes and Euribor and Eurodollar futures quotes.

Table 3.33 – Selected data from 23 January 2012 (CME spreads and currency forwards in pips, currency basis swap in basis points)

€/$	1.2960
US 3M LIBOR	0.56%
3M EURIBOR	1.12%
CME €/$ H2 future	1.3025
CME €/$ M2 future	1.3035
CME €/$ M2H2 Spread	+10
€/$ 3M forward	+6
3M €/$ CBS	-75
H2 Eurodollar	99.505 (0.495%)
H2 Euribor	99.120 (0.88%)

The three-month forward was calculated earlier to be -18.5 pips and the market quote from the data is observed to be +6 pips. The difference is due to currency basis, at the present time a key driver in euro-based FX swaps markets.

Most currency instruments are quoted against the US dollar, which as the world's reserve currency means that there is global demand among international banks dealing in dollar-based products for dollar-based funding. Usually, they can swap their own domestic currency (like euros in the case of European banks) for US dollars to term fund their dollar trading books. In the past there has been a small basis payable to reflect this demand for dollars.

For example, a bank lending dollars would receive the full rate of interest on that lending, but the bank receiving the dollars and lending the other currency would receive the rate of interest *plus* a negative basis. This basis might typically be in the region of -2 basis points. However, during the financial crisis of 2007/8 and the European sovereign debt crisis of 2010/11 this basis widened out to around -100 basis points for three-month dollar borrowing against euros. This meant that banks looking to borrow dollars were paying the full rate of interest but receiving the rate of interest plus -100 basis points on their euro lending.

Currency basis is directly tradable via currency basis swaps (CBS) but the basis will manifest itself in FX forward and swap quotes.

On 23 January, the three-month euro currency basis swap (CBS) was -75 bps, which would change the forward pricing equation by approximately:

$$1.2960 \times \left[\frac{1 + \left(0.56\% \times \dfrac{92}{360}\right)}{1 + \left((1.12\% - 0.75\%) \times \dfrac{92}{360}\right)} \right] = 1.2966$$

This difference between the forward and the spot of +6 pips [(1.2966 - 1.2960) x 10000] is the basis-adjusted market forward rate and matches the market quote of +6 pips given in the data table.

This forward could also be synthetically replicated using STIR futures by replacing the interbank rates with implied forward rates from Euribor and Eurodollar futures as given in the data. The FX forward equation using basis-adjusted implied forward rates from the STIR futures would be:

$$1.2960 \times \left[\frac{1 + \left(0.4950\% \times \dfrac{90}{360} \right)}{1 + \left((0.8800\% - 0.75\%) \times \dfrac{90}{360} \right)} \right] = 1.2972$$

The FX forward/swap would be quoted as +12 pips [(1.2972 - 1.2960) x 10000], which is comparable with the market quote of +6 pips; but remember that the STIR futures version is forward-starting in March 2012 whereas the market quote is spot (23 January +2).

The CME group €/$ M2H2 calendar spread was trading at +10 pips on 23 January, the difference between the M2 and H2 futures essentially being a forward-starting (on the March expiry of the CME €/$ H2 future) three-month FX swap. This is broadly comparable with the STIR futures FX forward being mindful of differing conventions. For instance, using the STIR futures derives a 90-day forward starting FX forward, whereas the CME €/$ calendar spread is effectively a three-month forward starting FX swap, three months being dependent on money market conventions which could be anything between 89 and 94 days.

Trading synthetic FX swaps

Unfortunately the above equations and methodologies do not lend themselves to trading. It is not possible to divide futures. However, it is possible to subtract them (by buying one and selling the other) and this is where the FX forward approximation detailed earlier comes in.

$$S \times (i_p - i_b) \times (D / B)$$

The forward starting FX swap can be approximated by the difference between the H2 Eurodollar and Euribor which it will replicate ($i_p - i_b$).

H2 Eurodollar – H2 Euribor

The interest rate differential between the two should broadly map the FX forward, particularly the comparable CME €/$ M2H2 calendar spread, being mindful that it will not reflect currency basis effects.

The following chart shows a study based in late 2011.

The differential between the Z1 Eurodollar and Euribor futures is mapped against the CME €/$ H2Z1 calendar spread. The two are correlated at 37%. This is not particularly positive, but it has to be remembered that late 2011 was a period of economic turbulence in the euro zone and this is shown by the level of the currency basis in the chart. The STIR future differential will not include basis, whereas the CME calendar spread will. The larger and more volatile the basis, the larger the discrepancy between the two will be, and the lower the correlation.

Fig. 3.27 – Z1 Eurodollar rate – Z1 Euribor rate (broken black line), CME €/$ H2Z1 calendar spread (solid black line) and 3M €/$ currency basis swap (dotted black line). RH scale in bps. 14 September 2011 to 19 December 2011.

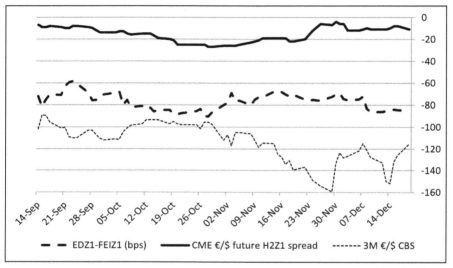

Data from Reuters

To put the effects of the basis in context, a similar study is presented in the next chart (based upon £/$).

Fig. 3.28 – Z1 Eurodollar (ED) rate – Z1 Short Sterling (FSS) rate (LH scale broken black line), CME £/$ H2Z1 calendar spread (RH scale solid black line). 14 September 2011 to 19 December 2011.

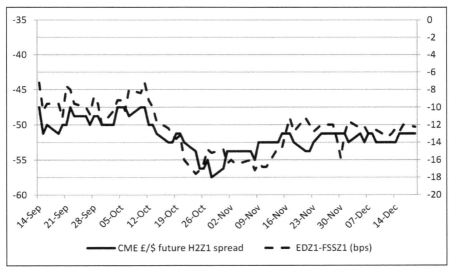

Data from Reuters

The three-month £/$ currency basis ranged between -30 to -18 bps during this period, much lower and more stable than the euro basis. This has the effect of stabilising the relationship between the STIR futures differential and CME calendar spread as reflected in a correlation between the two of 76%.

Synthesising FX swaps using STIR futures is an interesting trade and perhaps a surprising exposure for those traders who think the difference between two international STIR futures is just a country spread. It can be worth following, but liquidity in further-dated CME currency futures can be an issue, along with current high levels of basis and basis volatility.

Summary – when to use the strategies

- Term TED spread

  Trading the term TED spread by using bundles, packs or stacks is a popular trade for both short-term and long horizons. Term spreads can be position-traded by using the best match between the STIR futures and bond futures, which will tend to be bundles. Packs and stacks can be used for short-term high frequency trading, bidding and offering them against the liquidity of the bond futures. Remember that this will be a volatile spread compared to others described in this book, being driven by credit influences.

- Swap futures

  A great substitute for bond futures, virtually eliminating the credit spread risk against STIR futures, but compromised by the current lack of business in swap future products. High frequency short-term traders should look to trade the swap first and then hedge where available, with stacks perhaps being the easiest option (albeit with curve risk).

- International STIR futures

  A proxy for forward-starting FX swaps. These can be spread-traded with international STIR futures against currency future calendar spreads but are largely driven by currency basis influences.

Trading Considerations for STIR Futures

4

Zero-Sum Game – Know the Players

Futures trading is a zero-sum game: one participant's financial gain or loss is exactly balanced by the financial losses or gains of other participants. Put another way, one trader's gain is another trader's loss.

During each trading day, a very considerable sum of money changes hands as price movements translate into changing profits and losses. This monetary swing is based upon both traders' existing positions and on new money coming into the market. For each existing position in the market or for each new position taken out in the market, there has to be a trader on the other side of the deal. For buyers there has to be a seller and for sellers there has to be a buyer. But only one of them can be the winner.

The aim of the trader is to be, on-balance, a net taker from the market – a consistent winner. Surprisingly, though, not all market participants have the same objective; so it is important to know your fellow players.

Players

'Players' is a collective term for all market participants. Not all have the same objectives. They all have different sensitivities to market price movements. Some players are not overly concerned about giving away the edge to complete a transaction, but for others it is critical. Some participants might expect to give away money in order to build a position in the market. For example, a large seller selling into a rising market in order to build a larger position that would otherwise have been unachievable in a falling market. Since all trading is anonymous, it is not possible to be sure who is on the other side of a trade or what their motive is. However, being aware of the different player categories and being familiar with their characteristics can be beneficial in trying to decipher price action. These different kinds of player can be broadly divided into:

- *price takers*: someone who buys the offer or sells the bid price, since filling the transaction is of prime importance

- *price makers*: a player who works the bid and offer in order to achieve the best possible fill level.

Hedge funds

Hedge funds are a relatively new market participant of note. They have been around since the 1950s ,when Alfred Jones developed leveraged market-neutral trading, where a long position is offset with a short position – effectively *hedging* the trade from broad market risk. Hedge funds became a generic term for all types of alternative asset management, from the huge macro players such as Soros, Robertson and Steinhardt, to the sophisticated niche players in esoteric areas such as convertible bond arbitrage. In recent decades, the number of hedge funds increased exponentially as investors diversified away from the languishing post-dotcom long-only stock markets, and talented managers were enticed by the performance-based remuneration. Unsurprisingly, this large increase in the number of hedge funds all seeking to trade alternative markets led to reduced trading opportunities. Many hedge funds have therefore entered the futures markets (among others) in the search for new opportunities.

Since hedge funds have large amounts of capital upon which they need to make meaningful returns, they are normally confined to directional trades in outrights, rather than spreads or strategies. They are commonly present in STIR futures markets when building a position based on their expectations for futures interest rates. They can generally be characterised by their persistent buying or selling around certain moveable levels, and sometimes into resistance in order to facilitate business. Although they can establish positions of tens of thousands of lots, they are unlikely to spook the markets by trading abnormally large clips, but rather rely on market ebbs and flows to work multiple orders around market demand. Hedge funds are not over-concerned about small costs or slippage, preferring to get the business done. Consequently, they are more price takers than price makers.

Banks

Banks are normally the highest-volume players and this can cover both proprietary and agency trading. Their proprietary business can appear much in the same manner as hedge funds and it can be virtually impossible to distinguish between them, although this is ultimately of little consequence since their motives will be similar. Their agency business comprises telephone brokerage and electronic order routing business. Trade quantities will be variable from medium to large orders, but with high frequency. Very large orders might be transacted wholesale via block trades, where larger trades are pre-negotiated by the bank representing both counterparties. Block trades have minimum quantity criteria defined by the exchanges and are permitted a delay in reporting the transaction to market. They are characterised by a label attached to the reported trade.

Agency business is characterised by high frequency institutional-sized business and is the backbone of the markets order flow. Sometimes it appears more noticeable after events, such as economic releases, where traders immediately drive market movements, but larger institutional orders enter the market minutes later when the number has been disseminated by the banks to their clients. Banks are primarily concerned with transaction flow but price is important to them since they will often be acting on price orders or routing electronic limit orders. They are usually price makers and will often work the bids and offers. Their business is often termed *paper*.

Hedgers

Hedgers are usually corporate bank customers who are either using the STIR futures markets directly to hedge an interest rate exposure, or using a tailored over-the-counter bank product to achieve the same effect, in which case the bank will be hedging the exposure directly. Hedgers' business can be classified under bank or broker agency since they use them as an intermediary. Their business can be both price taking and making but might be more inclined towards the former because the fill can be of prime importance.

Brokers

Brokers are similar to a bank's agency business but smaller in size, perhaps specialising in retail business instead of institutional business. Their business might be based on electronic order routing, characterised by small but frequent volume flow with a mixture of price taking and making.

Independent traders/liquidity providers

Independent traders include both individual traders and proprietary groups. They are primarily price makers; actively working the bids and offers of outrights or spreads to gain a profit, although they will easily switch to price taking in volatile conditions. They are the main cause of noise in the STIR futures markets by their sheer numbers and low propensity for risk. A lot of their business is scratched (bought and sold at the same price for zero profit or loss) and reimbursed by exchange rebate schemes or clearing member volume discounts, but their collective influence on the markets should not be underestimated. They can be principal causes of congestion in markets and often position themselves in the same direction, adding to the noise surrounding a particular trade.

Flippers/predatory algorithms

A generic term for market bullies. Flippers are a variation on the independent trader, or an automated algorithm, being large, high frequency traders who try to exploit the activities of smaller traders. They are both price makers and takers but their main aim is to 'shake the tree' of smaller traders with much lower risk profiles. They act very much like market bullies, trying to identify what other traders are looking to do and then attempting to loosen their position on a trade.

High frequency and algorithmic trading

High frequency trading (HFT) and algorithmic trading are catch-all terms for a number of different computer-based trading strategies, where software programs replace the trader in the decision-making process. HFT and algorithmic trading has seen explosive growth in the last decade, fuelled mainly by banks, hedge funds and proprietary trading groups. Some market participants ascribe up to 60% of exchange volumes to these activities.

Algorithmic trading is primarily driven by automation of order execution, where buy-side traders divide large trades into several smaller trades in order to manage market impact and risk. Example algorithms include iceberg orders, where only the tip of a large order is shown at a time.

HFT is computer-based interpretation of information and order flow to generate short-term high speed trading decisions. It is highly quantitative, employing algorithms to analyse incoming market data and implement proprietary trading strategies. Trading positions are usually held only for seconds and trading turnover of these positions is huge, often generating large volumes of trade but usually resulting in no net position at the end of a trading day. HFT is mostly employed by proprietary firms and is very dependent on latency and speed to market.

The rise of algorithmic trading and HFT has resulted in a dramatic change of the market microstructure, particularly in the way liquidity is provided, the speed of market transactions and market access.

Liquidity is now very transitory, meaning that bids and offers can appear and disappear very rapidly and spreaders have to be very careful about 'leaning' on contingent orders. Releases of economic figures are now largely untradeable for human traders – machines will read embedded 'meta tags' in wire service news stories or economic releases and make conditional trading decisions in milliseconds.

Access or speed to market has also become critical. Most algorithmic and HFT programs are written directly to an exchange API by software developers but latency can have a material effect on trade-execution times. The exchanges have responded to this by building and offering co-location facilities. For example, Liffe customers can now pay to locate their trading servers beside the Connect matching engines in a data centre in Essex. This is designed for the most time-sensitive customers like algorithmic or HFT traders, who need the fastest possible access to the market, with order round-trip times of single figure milliseconds.

Whilst algorithmic trading is portrayed as being highly sophisticated, in the absence of reliable artificial intelligence most of its trading rules are very black and white, qualified by a lot of conditionality. The algorithms tend to be based on four trading premises: technical, statistical, event and predatory.

1. **Technical analysis**

   Algorithmic trading programs will try to emulate the technically-inclined trader and identify buying and selling opportunities using conventional technical analysis. More advanced mathematical refinements might be added, such as economic noise reduction filters (e.g. Kalman filters), which aim to smooth trends by stripping away confusing extraneous activity.

   The likes of Man Group and Winton Capital are large hedge funds specialising in trend-following futures strategies.

2. **Statistical arbitrage**

   Statistical arbitrage seeks to exploit pricing anomalies between different financial instruments using quantitative techniques. The earlier inter-contract spreading examples all qualify as statistical arbitrage; for example, trading bundles against swap futures.

   Statistical techniques like mean reversion (or mean regression) are commonly used for spreads and spreading strategy-type trades. Mean reversion works on the basis that prices will return to a historic mean price after deviating away due to trading factors. Price history is used to calculate trading bands around a mean, and these are used as the base for trade initiation.

3. **Event trading**

   This is the automated response and trading of events, primarily economic indicators. Economic figures and indicators can move markets substantially and it is relatively easy to link trading applications with information sources, even via simple Excel-based RTD links. Such programs tend to be refined beyond the simple "bad figure – sell" or "good figure – buy" methodology by using conditionality parameters.

4. **Predatory**

Predatory algorithms seek to mimic or disrupt other market participants. Electronic activities of other traders might be closely monitored by computer and those who are deemed to be successful are emulated. Spreaders are disrupted in their trading by an algorithm trading the other side of a spread leaving the spreader legged out.

Algorithmic trading is very prevalent at present but under regulatory scrutiny, as the effects of algorithmic and HFT trading are very debatable. Proponents argue they add liquidity and efficiency, whereas detractors believe they could be a source of systemic risk and point to the extreme volatility during the flash crash of May 2010 as a prime example of this. From the STIR futures traders' point of view, they definitely need to be taken into account in trade evaluation. There are financial barriers against competing at a similar level, but an understanding how algorithmic and HFT activity is driving the markets might extend the trading life of the human trader a little longer!

Supporting cast

There's a supporting cast of players surrounding the markets. Some are essential, providing infrastructure (such as software providers or clearing services), but some are purely peripheral and should carry a wealth warning.

'Winning' trading systems

These trading systems claim to be money makers in the futures/stock/commodities markets. They are not to be confused with information or charting packages, which provide the data and analytics upon which the trader can base their own decisions. They are normally internet-marketed systems, using a form of technical analysis to generate buy and sell signals. The methodology might be sound and some might work for some traders, but a healthy dose of scepticism and common sense is required. Systems can work in some markets for a time, but there's no one-size-fits-all solution to futures trading. Trading systems can be economical with the truth regarding drawdowns – which is the amount of loss a position might suffer before it becomes profitable. And their studies might be based upon lagging indicators, which always look better in hindsight. If a system is so great, why is it being marketed? If it sounds too good to be true, it probably is.

The pundits

The pundits are the television and newspaper commentators, analysts and economists who provide the markets with their opinions. Most are highly qualified and well regarded in their fields, but talk is cheap and, again, a measure of scepticism is required. Very few pundits are mavericks, preferring the comfort of consensus, and they are usually content gradually shifting or spinning their opinions as the consensus changes over time. Also, it's important to gauge their motive. Most pundits will not publicly air their opinions until their paying clients have been briefed, which means that if their opinion is highly regarded, then it's probably already discounted in the markets. Often, a market opinion might just serve as a public reinforcement of a company's position or outlook.

How to Play

Specialisation

Most successful traders find a niche within the markets where they become completely familiar with the contract characteristics, market drivers and the other types of participant. Niches can be a particular STIR futures contract, or a specialisation within a group of contracts, such as trading packs and bundles. The benefit of a niche speciality is that it usually provides the bread-and-butter daily earnings of trading, and can finance the more occasional macro trade. Very few traders specialise in more than one or two contracts, even with electronic trading opening up the world markets, since there is a limit to how much information can be closely monitored by one person.

The choice of niche will differ between traders according to propensity for risk. Some will prefer the action of the outrights, willing to accept losses in exchange for greater gains, whereas others will seek the stability of spread trading, looking to make steady if unspectacular returns but with little downside. Finding a niche takes time, but it is important to find it since it is this specialisation and intimate knowledge that becomes the trader's edge or advantage over other market participants.

Traders should be prepared to change specialisations according to market conditions, as some strategies might become busier than others or a period of low volatility might push traders into the outrights in search of profits. However, being a specialist in a particular area will always be key to successful STIR futures trading.

Key characteristics and considerations

There's no such thing as a blueprint for the perfect trader, but successful traders often share common traits and responses to market situations. Certain desirable characteristics should be obvious, such as expertise, common sense, a sense of proportion, emotional stability and the ability to concentrate; but other characteristics are more important by how they are applied to the markets.

Conviction versus dogma

There's a world of difference between these two, but it's not always easy to see it. Confidence and conviction are useful characteristics to have in futures markets, provided the trader doesn't allow them to become dogma, usually through intransigence. Having an opinion on a market or a trade is a reflection of confidence and conviction, but deciding what the market will do is dogma.

Sometimes, this distinction becomes blurred when the conviction necessary to support a trade verges on the dogmatic. Great traders, such as George Soros, have walked a very fine line between the two, but by doing so have been able to build the large positions that made their reputations. Traders of any repute should always frequently question their position, outlook or trade. What has changed within the last five minutes that might change the trader's view? Has there been, or will there be, any new information coming to market that might change the trader's view? Once the questioning of the validity of an open position stops, intransigence sets in and conviction turns to dogma.

Conviction can be a very useful trading tool. Whereas specialisation will normally yield the daily profit or loss, having the conviction to trade the occasional large position when it is right to do so can make the difference between traders. It is by no means necessary to make large directional trades to be a successful trader, especially if the trader is content with their lot, but specialisation can occasionally highlight opportunities where, for example, something is far oversold, overbought or out of kilter against something else. Having the conviction to recognise this and the confidence to establish and responsibly manage a position can make the difference between an average monthly performance and a spectacular one.

Variant perception

Variant perception was the phrase coined by hedge fund manager Michael Steinhardt to describe differences between his viewpoint on a market and that of the consensus. He considered a complete understanding of market expectations to be a vital part of his success and benefited enormously when the gap between his disparate perception and the market consensus closed. Variant perception is not merely taking a contrary view to that of the market. It is supporting a conviction with a high level of market knowledge and understanding.

Variant perception can be adapted for use in STIR futures markets to highlight differences between the market consensus and market prices. Such a difference exists, for example, when the market consensus indicates one possible interest rate outcome but STIR futures prices are predicting another. This gap between market consensus and prices can give rise to a potential asymmetric pay-off, where the consensus risks are almost fully recognised and incorporated into the futures price but any deviance from the consensus outcome results in sharp price readjustments.

Respect

A good trader will always be respectful of other market participants and considerate of their actions. This has nothing to do with social niceties. It concerns the trader's instinct for survival. There should always be respect for the person on the other side of a trade and the trader should always be asking why they are selling or buying. *What do they know that I don't?*

The fourth dimension

The fourth dimension is commonly defined as time, and logic dictates that because of the passage of time nothing is ever the same or can ever be repeated. In this respect, markets are always changing over time and the successful trader needs to adapt to these changes. Although markets can repeatedly trade a price range, it is unlikely that the drivers behind the market will remain exactly the same. The variant perception might have shifted or new information has become available. The markets might have attracted new types of player, adding noise or volatility, or a cross-market influence might be having an effect.

Traders, too, are subject to the fourth dimension. Even though they might continually trade the same market and the same niche, their attitude to the market will change over time. Confidence ebbs and flows with success and failure and attitudes to risk can change with personal circumstances. Even the trappings of success over time can change a trader's perspective as their hunger diminishes.

A successful trader should always be aware of the changing effects of time on both the markets and themselves. Being able to recognise how the trader is personally responding to the markets and how the markets are responding to new drivers is a key psychology of trading.

Deep play

Deep play was a concept developed by Jeremy Bentham, the father of Utilitarianism, where the stakes in an endeavour become so high that it is irrational for anyone to engage in it at all since the marginal utility of what stands to be won is grossly outweighed by the disutility of what stands to be lost.

Deep play was not specifically about financial markets, but its message is clear. At times of extreme volatility or uncertainty, the risk between what might be made against what could be lost can become so disproportional that it is futile to be involved. Fortunately, these situations are quite infrequent. But they do happen, and often outside market trading hours, which can be harmful to holders of overnight positions.

Perfect storms like the financial crisis of 2007/8 or the UK Exchange Rate Mechanism (ERM) debacle of the early nineties are prime examples of deep play. The UK's entry to the ERM was announced just after the market closed in October 1990, causing a discreet price spike the next day, but the real deep play was reserved for when the UK left the ERM on 16 September 1992. During that trading day, interest rates were increased from 10% to 12%. UK officials then threatened to increase them further to 15%. This caused unprecedented movements in Short Sterling futures markets, which were almost paralysed by the volatility and extreme reluctance of any traders to establish new positions. The swinging prices, although offering the possibility of abnormal profit, also carried the very likely risk of catastrophe, and those traders with an instinct for self-survival kept their hands firmly in their pockets.

Trader's nemesis

The trader's nemesis is the source of harm or ruin that can come from hubris. Success can easily breed the presumption that the markets owe the trader a living and can be dipped into at will to provide for the good things in life. It is uncanny how a trader can appear to lose his touch just as he's taken on a large mortgage for a new house, or the markets trough a new low in volatility just as performance is needed. The futures markets will always remain a speculative pursuit and should always be regarded as such. Markets and trading careers should never be taken for granted.

Game Play

Game play is about strategy and tactics. There are no clear answers and those that do exist are subject to individual perspective. Ideally, every trader should have a defined strategy for their trading and tactics for their methodology, but in practice these need to be moveable and adaptable. Game play tends to stem from a trader's own personality. Are you a team player, usually following the consensus, latching onto trends – or a contrarian, the devil's advocate deliberately taking the other side? What is your attitude to losses? Some traders just can't tolerate them; for others they are as arbitrary as profits. Answers usually come with experience. Traders need to learn to adjust accordingly.

Those traders with a low risk tolerance will be better suited to lower-risk activities such as spread and strategy trading. Contrarians might find success in moderation by fading yield curve moves, which tend to be limited in their range and quite elastic. Trend followers might be more suited to outright trading, looking for the macro trades. Ultimately it's about finding out what works and what doesn't.

The discovery process

Discovering what kind of trading does and doesn't work is dependent not only on a trader's profile, but also on the variables of market conditions, incentives and aptitude.

Trader profile is concerned with the type of trader and how suited he or she is to a class of trading. It will include the desirable characteristics and key considerations mentioned earlier. These will influence the trader's choice between outright trading and the relative value of intra and inter-contract spread and strategy trading.

Market conditions can vary substantially from month to month. What worked earlier might not work so well later on. Intra-contract spread trading needs a certain amount of yield curve movement in order to provide trading opportunities; in quieter times, or times of parallel yield curve shifts, it is likely that the spreads will be characterised by little movement and congestion. The trader then needs to be asking whether his time is better spent elsewhere, perhaps inter-contract spreading. Conversely, in times of volatility, the intra-contract spreads might prove a safe harbour.

The concept of incentive is the deliberate use of exchange rebate schemes as a profit centre. Exchange rebate schemes are targeted at traders specialising in back-month STIR futures trading. Those traders deciding to specialise in intra-contract spreads might be directed towards these far months, in order to maximise their revenue by judicious use of the incentives available.

The final criterion of aptitude is simply to stick at what you are good at. Some traders will have a natural affinity towards more complex types of trading whilst others will prefer the simple black-and-white trading of the outrights. Experience is really the only way of finding out for sure what fits and where a trader's talent is best deployed.

Trigger point

Every trade needs a trigger – causation at the point of trade. There are, broadly, three categories of trigger.

The first is a **reactive** response to price action, possibly driven by news or events.

The second is **proactive**. This should be the majority of a trader's activity. Proactive trades involve opening a position deemed (after due consideration) to offer a good chance of returning a profit. A proactive trade might be the deliberate legging of a spread on the bid or offer, resulting in a risk-free position, by trading one side in full expectation of a higher-than-average chance of receiving the fill on the other side. Proactive trading is considered and thought-out, maximising the balance of probability in favour of the trader.

The third trigger is **signals**. These are actions based on buy and sell signals, invariably technical in nature. Technical signals rely on technical analysis, the abstract study of price movements to predict future price movements. Technical analysis is the antipathy of fundamental analysis; it is exclusively concerned with price action rather than what might be behind market movements. Technical analysis is based on the three premises that market prices discount everything (that all available information is already included in the futures price), prices move in trends and history repeats itself.

There are a wide range of indicators based on technical analysis. Each generates buy and sell signals by attempting to identify price trends or overbought or oversold market conditions. Traders tend to either be big fans of technical indicators or dismissive. However, their use is widespread within the trading community and some familiarity is useful, even if it is solely to be aware of how other traders are using them.

Guide to technical indicators

Technical analysis is a vast field and it is beyond the scope of this book to cover every indicator in existence. However, many indicators are simply variations on existing ones. They stem from four main categories.

Trend indicators

Trend indicators include some of the simplest technical indicators. They try to give an objective measure of price direction by separating a trend from surrounding noise. Noise can be defined as excess price fluctuation or variation from a trend and is very common in futures markets.

Moving averages

Moving averages are one of the most popular and easily understood indicators. In their simplest form, they are a rolling average price over a period of time; for example, a ten-day moving average would be the average of the last ten days' prices. For each subsequent day, the latest closing price replaces the oldest value, maintaining a population of ten days at all times. Periods of five, ten, 20, 50 and 100-day moving averages are popular choices. The shorter periods will be most responsive to short-term price fluctuations; the longer period moving averages will smooth out more of the noise.

Simple moving average (SMA)

Simple moving averages are very easy to interpret since the technique smooths price series and makes trends easier to identify. Moving averages are commonly used in multiples for technical analysis, either as double or triple-moving averages. A double moving average will use two different observation periods such as a ten-day and 20-day period. A triple moving average plots three moving averages of different observation periods, such as a ten-day, 20-day and 50-day period. The use of double or triple moving averages allows the identification of crossovers. A double crossover is where the shortest moving average crosses through the longer one. This is commonly considered to be a buying signal; the longer average is viewed as price support level. A triple crossover provides stronger evidence of the buy signal when the shortest moving average passes through the two higher ones. The opposite can also be used to identify sell signals.

Moving averages are, by nature, laggard indicators because they change only after the price has already begun to follow a trend. They are most effective when the market is trending and are useful for identifying trends but will not predict them. It should be noted that any form of moving average analysis using a longer averaging period will generate fewer signals and will require a larger price move before responding. This might be seen as sacrificing potential profits in order to confirm a signal. A shorter averaging period will generate a larger number of signals as it requires less of a price move before responding; however, the risk that a signal is false will increase.

Weighted, exponential and volume-adjusted moving averages

There are further varieties of moving average which incorporate a weighting component in their structure. The weighted moving average also smooths price data by removing noise over a period. It is, however, more sensitive to recent price changes since it assigns a greater weight to the most recent prices; the simple moving average gives all prices equal emphasis.

There are several further versions of weighted moving average.

The exponential moving average analysis is a variation on the weighted version – they both assign greater weight to the most recent data. However, they differ in that instead of dropping off the oldest data point in the selected period of the moving average, the exponential moving average continues to maintain all the data. For example, a ten-day exponential moving average will contain more than ten prices. Each observation becomes progressively less significant but still includes in its calculation all the price data in the life of the instrument. The exponential moving average can be considered as another method of weighting a moving average.

The other weighted moving average type is the volume-adjusted moving average. These are weighted moving averages that use volume as a weighting mechanism. Volume-adjusted moving averages assign the majority of weight to the days with the most volume.

Average directional movement index (ADX)

The directional movement index (DMI) was developed by J. Welles Wilder. It is a technical indicator that measures the directionality of price movement over time to identify trending and non-trending periods. The DMI actually comprises two directional indicators, which are then averaged to produce the ADX. This is plotted on a scale of 0 to 100, with values below 20 indicating a trendless market and a value above 30 indicating a trending market. Crossovers can be applicable to this indicator.

It should be noted that ADX is a laggard indicator and so will not perform well as a trading signal generator. It is usually used in combination with other indicators.

Vertical horizontal filter (VHF)

The vertical horizontal filter is similar to the ADX in that it is also an indicator of trends within markets. It is calculated by analysing the difference between the highest and lowest values versus the daily fluctuations. Rising values indicate trending prices, whilst falling values can be indicative of level or congested prices. As with the ADX, the VHF is commonly used with other indicators to provide additional verification of a price movement but can be used to determine the amount that prices are trending. A higher VHF value will indicate a higher degree of trending and points to the use of trend-following indicators. The VHF can also be used as a contrarian indicator, where congestion periods might follow high VHF values and trends could follow low VHF values.

Example – SMA, ADX and VHF

The chart illustrates the Z1 Euribor history during 2011 with a 30-day and a ten-day simple moving average. The sub chart contains the VHF and ADX indicators for the same time and price sample.

Fig. 4.1 – Z1 Euribor (2011) with 30-day simple moving average (SMA) (solid thin line upper pane) and ten-day simple moving average (SMA) (dotted thin line upper pane) and sub chart featuring vertical horizontal filter (VHF) (thin line lower pane) on right axis and average directional movement index (ADX) (thick line lower pane) on the left axis

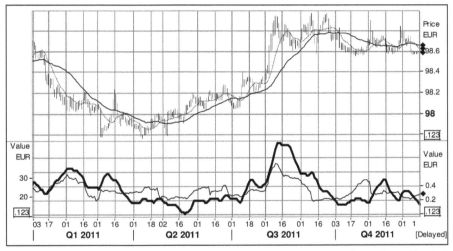

Source: Reuters Metastock

Analysis

The use of crossovers on the moving averages seems to provide indications of major trends with mixed assistance from the trend indicators.

The first crossover is in early Q2 2011, where the ten-day moving average moves above the 30-day moving average, and appears to predict the major uptrend that continues into July. Here a false downward signal (ten-day SMA moving below 30-

day SMA) is given but soon corrected by another upwards crossover (ten-day SMA moving above 30-day SMA), continuing until early October (beginning Q4), where it once again crosses down.

The ADX and VHF indicators are mostly low during the first half of the year, not confirming a rising trend, but both are more effective at identifying the end of the upward trend in late October.

Traders' notes

Moving averages are a useful indicator for major trends, but need to be qualified because of their laggard characteristics. This tends to make their charts look better in hindsight than predicting forward. The VHF and ADX indicators appear useful indicators of the validity of a trend, but need to be used cautiously.

In conclusion, trend indicators are useful for removing noise and can provide confirmation of major trends, but should not be exclusively relied upon.

Oscillator and volatility indicators

Oscillator and volatility indicators measure the periodic variation of price. They are useful in non-trending markets where prices fluctuate in horizontal bands of support and resistance. They are commonly used to predict overbought and oversold conditions.

Price oscillators

Oscillators are generally the difference between two moving averages, usually in either absolute or percentage terms. Common forms are the price oscillator (PO), with variations including volume, momentum and stochastic; they normally fluctuate around a zero line or a band, indicating overbought or oversold conditions. This is where prices have risen or fallen too far; the oscillator is commonly used as a predictor in the expectation that the prices might retrace this move. If the oscillator reaches a very high value above the zero line, the market is considered overbought, whereas if a very low value below the zero line is reached, the market is termed oversold. Overbought and oversold signals are considered most reliable in a non-trending market where prices are making a series of equal highs and lows.

Oscillators can be also be used to generate buy and sell signals when the oscillator values move above and below zero. A buy signal is given when the oscillator moves from below zero to above zero, and a sell signal is generated when the oscillator moves from above zero to below zero.

Bollinger bands

Bollinger bands are volatility indicators that visually portray the relationship between price and volatility changes. They are based upon an exponential moving average price, with two bands and a specified number of standard deviations above and below this moving average. These bands expand and contract as price action becomes volatile or quietens into a tighter trading pattern.

Like oscillators, Bollinger bands are commonly used to identify overbought and oversold markets. An overbought or oversold market is one where the prices have risen or fallen too far and are therefore likely to retrace. Prices near the lower band signal an oversold market and prices near the upper band signal an overbought market. These signals are most reliable in non-trending markets but, if the market is trending, signals in the direction of the trend are likely to be more reliable. For example, if prices are in an uptrend, a trader might prefer to wait until a temporary price pullback gives an oversold signal before entering a trade.

Bollinger bands can also be used to warn of an impending price move. The bands can often narrow just before a sharp price move. This is based upon the concept that a period of low volatility often precedes a sharp move in prices and low volatility will be reflected in narrow bands.

Average true range

This is another J. Welles Wilder indicator. The average true range (ATR) is a volatility indicator based upon the exponential moving average of the true range, which is the largest of:

1. current high less current low

2. the range between current high and previous close

3. the range between current low and previous close.

This true range captures the volatility created by an overnight gap. Positive values are required so absolute numbers are used.

Wilder found that high ATR values often occur at market bottoms, following a sharp sell-off; low ATR values are often found during extended sideways periods, such as those found at tops and after consolidation periods.

Example – Bollinger bands, ATR, price oscillator

The same Z1 Euribor data used in the previous chart is used here with a price oscillator, Bollinger bands, and average true range (ATR).

Fig. 4.2 – Z1 Euribor (2011) with 20-day period 2.0 Standard deviation Bollinger bands (upper pane), 14-day period average true range (thick black line LH scale lower pane) and price oscillator (RH scale lower pane)

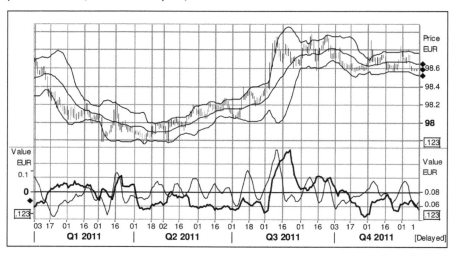

Source: Reuters Metastock

Analysis

Three quarters into Q1 2011 shows the market hitting a downside trough in sequence, with a negative oscillator and a relatively high ATR, all correctly indicating an oversold condition.

In Q2 2011 the futures price touches both upper and lower Bollinger bands but with mixed signals from the oscillator and ATR.

In late Q3 and Q4 the futures price touches the lower Bollinger band a couple of times before bouncing back, seemingly supported by a low oscillator.

The ATR appears to work well in a directional market but offers little insight beyond this. It should be remembered that Bollinger bands and oscillators are, essentially, moving averages and so will share their laggard qualities. It is highly likely, therefore, that these indicators will perform better in hindsight.

Traders' notes

The Bollinger bands and oscillator are similar but refined versions of moving averages, and suffer from the same disadvantages and advantages. Overbought and oversold indicators can give the same signal for quite extended periods of time.

The ATR appears a more sporadic tool, reflecting volatility but not necessarily direction.

Momentum and strength indicators

These types of indicator differ from the previous ones in that they can be considered leading indicators. Leading indicators are supposed to change before an actual price begins a new pattern or trend.

Relative strength index

The relative strength index (RSI) is a momentum indicator that measures price relative to past prices. It operates in a range between 0 and 100 that reflects the internal strength of a price move. Zero is the most oversold situation and 100 the most overbought one. Generally, anything over 70 is considered overbought and anything below 30 is considered oversold. It is time-period dependent, meaning that a choice of a shorter period will return more volatile results.

Overbought and oversold signals are usually most reliable in non-trending markets. In trending markets, the most reliable signal is the direction of the trend and the RSI can be used for confirmation of a signal by, for example, in an upwardly trending market, only trading buy signals after the RSI has moved back above 30 after dropping below.

The RSI is also a popular indicator for looking for failure swings. These are where the futures price might be making a new high but the RSI is failing to surpass its previous highs. This divergence is an indication of an impending reversal. Divergence between the RSI and the price can also indicate that an up or down move is weakening. However, it should be noted that although divergences indicate a weakening trend they do not in themselves indicate that the trend has reversed.

Accumulation/distribution line (ADL)

The accumulation/distribution line measures the buying and selling pressure into and out of a futures price from the difference between accumulation (buying pressure) and distribution (selling pressure). Accumulation is when the current closing price is higher than the previous close and distribution occurs when the close is lower than the previous close.

The strongest signals on ADL are when it diverges from the futures price. A buy signal is generated when there is an upward divergence and a sell signal when there is a downward divergence.

Rate of change (ROC)

Rate of change is an oscillator type of indicator that measures market momentum by comparing later prices with earlier prices. It is presented in bands around an equilibrium level, based upon the historic characteristics of the futures price. It is commonly used in ranging markets, to detect trend strengths and weaknesses, and in this respect is similar to the RSI. As with the RSI, a low value means an oversold condition and a high value means an overbought one.

Example – RSI, ADL and ROC

These indicators, particularly the RSI and ROC, should lead price movements within the same sample of Z1 Euribor as used earlier. The chart shows the three studies of RSI, ADL and ROC against the Z1 price chart.

Fig. 4.3 – Z1 Euribor (2011) (top pane) with ADL (bottom pane) 14-day ROC (second to bottom pane) and 14-day RSI (second to top pane)

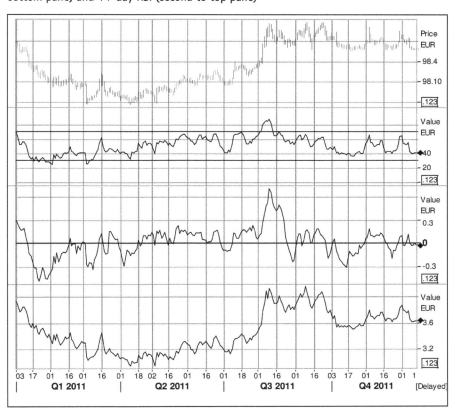

Source: Reuters Metastock

Analysis

The RSI has several points in Q1 2011 at which it has breached or touched the 70/30 boundaries. Z1 hit a low in late Q1 and is matched by an RSI below 30, indicating an oversold state. The ROC is also towards its lower trading range and the ADL shows clear distribution but is insufficiently leading to suggest that this might be slowing. In this case, the RSI and ROC seem to correctly forecast an oversold signal; a purchase at this point would have been a profitable trade.

Another signal is given by both the RSI and ROC in mid Q3 2011, indicating an overbought state. In this case the futures price slows its upward trend and trends sideways and is confirmed by a sideways ADL.

Line indicators

Line indicators include the simplest studies and also some of the most complicated. They are characterised by their use of straight lines to identify support and resistance levels.

Trend lines

A trend line is a straight line that connects two or more price points and then extends into the future to provide support and resistance levels. Trend lines can be horizontal or sloping: upwards for an uptrend and downwards for a downtrend. A trend line is considered more valid the more price points that are used.

Fig. 4.4 – Z1 Euribor (2011)

Chart by Metastock

The chart illustrates several trend lines. A rising price channel develops from April 2011 onwards and is broken to the upside in early August, resulting in a sharp upwards move. A top develops around 98.95 and heralds a gradual decline.

The effectiveness of trend lines varies from market to market but they remain one of the most popular studies since they easily illustrate trading price points. Generally, horizontal trend lines seem to provide better support and resistance levels than sloping lines.

Gann

W. D. Gann (born 1878) developed a variety of technical analysis methods based around the premises of price, time and range being the only factors to consider. He also considered markets to be cyclical in nature and geometric in design, believing that the ideal balance between time and price exists when prices rise or fall at a 45-degree angle relative to the time axis. This lead to the *Gann Angle*, where a one-unit price rise matches a one-unit time increment makes a 1x1 angle. Gann then developed these further angles:

Table 4.1 – Further angles developed by Gann

Ratio	Angle (degrees)
1 x 8	82.5
1 x 4	75
1 x 3	71.25
1 x 2	63.75
1 x 1	45
2 x 1	26.25
3 x 1	18.75
4 x 1	15
8 x 1	7.5

Gann observed that each of the angles could provide support and resistance depending on the trend. During an uptrend, the 1x1 angle could provide major support, and a reversal would only be signalled when prices fell below this angle. If this happened, prices could then be expected to fall to the next trend line, which would be the 2x1 angle. In summary, as one angle is breached, prices can be expected to move to and consolidate at the next angle.

Gann Angles are drawn between a significant bottom and top. An example of a Gann fan (a chart illustrating all the Gann angles) is given in Figure 4.5, drawn from Z1 Euribor during 2011.

Fig. 4.5 – Z1 Euribor (2011) with Gann fan study

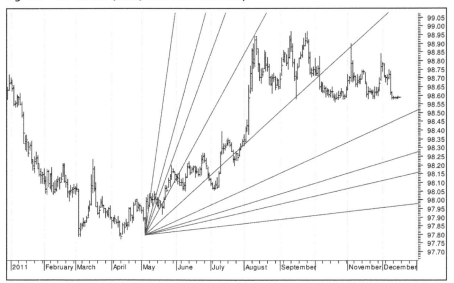

The Gann fan is based on the low in May 2011. The 1x1 angle provides broad support for the upwards trend but is broken several times. Gann would then predict that prices would gravitate downwards to the next angle, in this case the 2x1 at 26.25 degrees. However, in this study prices did not reach this level.

Gann has many supporters but his analyses can be subjective and very dependent on how they are used. It is a comprehensive study and, although relatively simple to use, it can be difficult to master.

Fibonacci

Fibonacci was an Italian mathematician born circa 1170, and put his name to Fibonacci numbers, a sequence of numbers in which each successive number is the sum of the two previous numbers. For example:

1, 1, 2, 3, 5, 8, 13, 21, 34, 55, 89, 144, 233, 377, 610, etc.

These numbers have several interrelationships. For example, any given number is approximately 1.618 times the preceding number, and any given number is approximately 0.618 times the following number. This relationship was called *phi*. Phi is considered important since almost everything with dimensional properties complies with these ratios, and many believe this includes financial markets.

When phi is applied to technical analysis, it is typically converted into three percentages: 38.2%, 50% and 61.8%. And it is used several ways, two of the most popular being **Fibonacci retracements** and **fans**.

- **Fibonacci retracements**

  These use horizontal lines to identify areas of support and resistance. They are constructed by identifying the two highs and low of a market movement, with the 100% and 0% levels being placed on the highs and lows respectively. A centre line is then drawn at the 50% level and the others at the phi ratios of 38.2% and 61.8%.

- **Fibonacci fan**

  A Fibonacci fan is displayed by drawing a trend line between two extreme points, for example, between the two highs and low of a market movement. Then an invisible vertical line is drawn through the second extreme point. Three trend lines are then drawn from the first extreme point so that they pass through the invisible vertical line at the Fibonacci levels of 38.2%, 50.0%, and 61.8%.

Fig. 4.6 – Z1 Euribor (2011) with Fibonacci retracement and fan studies

Source: Metastock Charts

Figure 4.6 illustrates the Fibonacci retracement lines and fan on the Z1 Euribor data sample. Retracement lines are used to predict potential levels of retracement following a market move and the horizontal lines of 0% and 100% reflect the relative low and high of the move. The Fibonacci levels of 61.8% and 38.2% are the set percentages of the move to which the market might be expected to adjust from its extreme points.

Analysis

The Fibonacci fan is based on the May low and the September high, with the fans intersecting the vertical line at 61.8%, 50% and 38.2%. The 61.8% phi was easily breached and the fan does not seem to yield usable results. From the lows in spring 2011, Z1 Euribor rallies with the 38.2% level acting as both resistance in late June and July respectively.

Fibonacci will always be dependent on the choice of extremities; the high and low points used and a shorter time period, instead of annual data, might yield different results.

Conclusion

None of the technical indicators described in this section can claim to be an accurate predictor of the future course of markets, neither can more complicated indicators be shown to be more reliable than simpler ones. Each trader needs to find from experience which technical indicators or combinations of indicators work best for them. The successful use of technical analysis seems to be about this process of discovering which combinations of indicators work best and when. Combinations of technical indicators do not need to be confined to a single category of indicator. Trend line indicators might easily be used with momentum studies, which can be used with oscillators.

The use of technical analysis can play an important part in the decision-making process of trading, either as a stand-alone trade-generation system or by substantiating (or undermining) existing views. Some traders will apply more weight to technical indicators than others; it is necessary for each to find their own balance. Technical analysis will always be subjective, but can be an asset when used in a considered manner – as decision-support rather than a dependency.

Endgame

A Day in the Life of a STIR Futures Trader

A fictional account of a day in the life of a STIR futures trader with most of the trading techniques presented earlier playing a starring role. Many trading days can be quite slow, so a little artistic licence has been employed. Dates have shifted, events been fabricated and names changed to protect the guilty!

06:30

I switch the computer on. The screen flickers and bursts into life with prices, news, graphs and spreadsheets.

Game on.

I'm fully wired now: nothing that really matters in the world can happen without me knowing about it. It might be on the wires or TV but the prices will break it first. The prices are everything. Fact and fiction distilled.

Storm clouds have been gathering overnight. The Dow is down 300 points and bonds have shed 20 ticks. The Fed's chairman has voiced concern at the recent "elevated diachrony in asset prices", alluding to the inflationary effects of the recent oil price spike which topped $100 in New York trade overnight. The situation in the Middle East is tense. The papers have been full of a leaked US intelligence report suggesting that Iran has achieved uranium enrichment and might now have weapons-grade plutonium. The UN Security Council has convened a meeting later this week to discuss extending sanctions and the US Seventh Fleet has entered the Straits of Hormuz, ostensibly on manoeuvres, but no one's buying that.

I'm a little nervous today. I'm short spreads across the Euribor strip and the risk is that the yield curve might steepen. I'm hoping that the inflationary talk will bring rate rise expectations closer down the strip and that the front months will fall more relative to the backs. But we'll see. I've also got a few butterflies on. OK, they're a little off-market – the result of a few trades gone wrong, but at least they balance things out a little.

The red light on my voicemail is blinking. It's David from the risk department reminding me that I'm touching my net liquidating balance. I download yesterday's trading statements. I see what he means. I'm building positions but adding little to the P&L. Maybe I'll shed a little weight. Bunds are about 30 ticks lower so Euribor will be down a few ticks. I'm hoping that might bring some spread selling as the outright sellers go for the liquidity in the fronts, causing the backs to lag. I'm short the one-year calendars – they'll move the most. I enter buy orders in the spreads a tick lower than last night's close.

I have a quick root around the news service to see what's going on. The economic diary tells me that it's going to be a busy day, UK CPI at 09:30 and US Non-Farm Payrolls at 13:30, the mother of all figures. There's a couple of A-list central bankers due to speak after a big lunch. I'll keep an eye out for them; sometimes the port loosens the rhetoric a little.

06:58

The markets have already been open for hours, covering the Far Eastern slot, but business and liquidity really starts from now on. Traders in London, Frankfurt, some early birds in the States and a few insomniac Australians and Japanese make up the global spider web, all looking for the angle, seeking the edge.

07:00

A sea of red as prices continue falling. My workstation 'dings' as fills report in. Within two minutes I've covered my entire spread position for a small profit. David in risk will be pleased.

Prices start to stabilise after an initial rush. Bunds are down 50 ticks from yesterday's close and Euribor is down seven ticks in the whites and six ticks in the reds. Looking at the ticker, I can see front month is down five ticks and then fell to a low of down eight ticks, maybe as the overnight longs panicked out ahead of the short sellers before bouncing back a tick.

It's a good start but I've still got those dodgy short back month butterflies on. They're yesterday's legacy from a long outright position that felt wrong the moment I put it on. Sometimes you get a gut feeling when it's just not going to happen, so I sold out the wings of the outright to leave a short butterfly spread. They're not too offside; they should be a scratch and there'll be a back month fee rebate. It usually pays to leave such positions to work out in the spread book, especially when it's on the market, but today it's much better bid than offered and that'll take forever. They always say 'never leg a closing spread', but it's very tempting sometimes, especially when the outright prices make it look very do-able.

'Ding', reports the computer as I sell out the body. I quickly put two bids into the market for the wings of the butterfly and now it's just a case of waiting for a bit more selling to come in. There's good quantity on the offers for both months but quite a lot of it is implied prices only. The back months are always thinner than the fronts, especially so early in the day, and I begin to regret my impetuousness. There's nothing like the initial flush of success to breed a bit of hubris.

07:30

The Bund starts to pick up a little, the selling looks to be over and the bargain hunters are moving in. The Bund is at the ten-year part of the yield curve but it'll have a knock-on effect at the front end. Already the bid quantities in two-year Schatz are increasing along with the front month Euribors. Suddenly my leg doesn't look so good. Others join my bids and the offers start melting away. It's a familiar scenario, one that I've played many times before. The choice is stark – buy now and take the loss or brazen it out? 'Ding ding'. I double click twice without further thought. 'The first cut is always the cheapest' and I'm not one for enduring pain. It's irksome, though; the butterfly looks OK as a trade now but I've managed to leg out of it above the offer price – any more trading like that and I'll be on the other side of the Starbucks counter.

08:30

Short Sterling and Gilts are trading but there's not much going on there, just a mirroring of the downtrend. The volumes are OK, though, meaning that there's plenty of open interest out there readjusting. I have a quick look through the sterling spreads to see if there's anything obvious – like a spread slightly out of kilter versus the others or some butterfly action stressing the futures strip. Everything should be in equilibrium, but sometimes when the tree has been shaken overnight things can get a little out of balance. I can't see much and there's little implied action, like where an implied-in price is pushing against a large spread bid or offer. Usually it's a large bid or offer because it's a good technical level or a good trade relative to something else, reflecting the market's enthusiasm to trade at that price.

My phone beeps. "Breakfast?" texts Tim, a friend sitting all of 20 feet away. I take another quick look around the market. There's CPI at 09.30 and so its breakfast now or go hungry. I'm flat now and with no positions and there's no point in loading up before the number, after which everything can change. I grab my coat.

09:28

'Beep', the screen alarm clock with its two-minute warning. There's UK CPI at 09:30 and it's going to be choppy. Inflation has been on the rise globally and it's the number in focus these days. The markets are looking for a high number, in the region of +0.3% month-on-month and +2.2% year-on-year, well above the Bank of England's mandate to keep it below 2% on a two-year horizon. Market reaction will be swift and there's never time to fully read and digest the number. You've got to eyeball the number, have a buy or sell order already loaded and be just one click away. Since the markets are gunning for a high number, I'm going the other way and hovering over the buy button. I'm not just being contrarian, there's usually more chance of a bigger move if the market is wrong-footed. I load up a buy order in the market depth, a tick above the offer. There's rarely much available in the best bid and offer just before a number and so you've got to pay up to trade. The seconds tick towards the half hour …

"09:30 UK CPI -0.1% MM +2.0% YY (CONSENSUS +2.2%)"

I see the minus sign and click without reading the rest. That's all I need to know and … 'ding' reports the computer as the fill comes back. The market spikes three ticks as offers are snapped up and bids ratchet upwards. I'm sitting tight for the moment, waiting for the big guns to turn up. The first movement is always the guys like me, nimble and fast, looking for the quick trade. We're in and out within a few seconds. Often the biggest move comes after the market has fully digested the news – the economists brief the bank traders who telephone the fund traders. When these elephants move, the trend will be confirmed. I look at the clock willing myself to hold on for five minutes. That'll be enough time. But the profits are burning a hole in my pocket so I sell half, locking in the gain. The pressure is off now; it's easier to hold on. A few large clips go through the market as the fund boys show up. I offer out my remaining lots and trade out of the position. A great return for three minutes' work!

Things quieten down now. Short Sterling has stabilised and locked into its new trading range. It'll be slow for a while now. It's easy to get sucked into over-trading after a successful figure trade, but often prices establish themselves and the extra transaction fees just dilute the profit. I move back to Euribor, which is calm. It's moved up a tick in sympathy with Short Sterling, which it shouldn't do really. After all, what's a small monthly move in UK CPI got to do with European interest rates? That's just the way of electronic trading these days. Correlations are sometimes enforced by the ease by which one contract can be traded against another. I'm sure that in my trading floor days the two never moved so much in unison.

I take a close look at the Euribor matrix, looking for longer-dated spreads that I can roll down into other, move attractive spreads. The plan is to find a three-month spread that I'd like to either buy or sell on the bid or offer and see if there was an easy way in by trading a 12-month calendar against the nine-month, or a nine-month against a six-month. It becomes quite easy with practice. A quick scan reveals nothing outstanding, but there's a reasonable trade in the back reds. I could bid the H2H3 12-month calendar spread and sell the H2Z2 spread against it, leaving me long the three-month Z2H3 spread. This spread is equally bid and offered but I think it might be OK as an overnighter. I place my bid in the H2H3 and kick back my chair and pick up the paper. Time for a bit of R&R.

11:00

Around the room, everyone is relaxing. The business is done for the morning and it's unlikely that there will be much going on until lunchtime, when a few early birds in the US might start moving the Treasuries around. Everyone looks upbeat. Either they've done all right or they know they'll get it back in the afternoon session. You can't beat the optimism of a futures trader in a busy market!

'Ding'. I'm partially filled on my H2H3 spread, but the H2Z2 bid has gone – taken by an Algo! I offer the spread but I'm not worried. There's no real movement in the market now and I'm sure I'll sell the offer. Even if I don't and have to sell H2Z2 down half a tick, thus buying Z2H3 on the offer rather than the bid, I reckon I'll be able to sell it out for a scratch in the next few days. I'll just have to remember to not leg it like the butterfly!

Suddenly prices begin to move.

The last trade column on my screen blinks rapidly. Large clips are passing through.

"What's going on?" someone shouts. Everyone's seen it but nobody knows.

"Israeli fighter jets over Tehran," shouts John. "It's on TV."

The TV is hurriedly switched from MTV to CNBC where the story is breaking news.

"11.45 BREAKING NEWS – FIGHTERS REPORTED OVER IRAN – SOURCE"

Bunds bounce 40 ticks and Euribor seven ticks. The wires have it now and everyone's scrambling for cover. Buyers hack into the offers, buying at almost any price in their flight to quality. It's war!

I've missed the boat but I'm just glad I wasn't short at the time. I'm not sure what my H2H3 is doing but there's no time for spreading at the moment – all the action's in the outrights. I watch the price action closely. Suddenly I see a few clips selling the bid. Someone's either taking profits or knows something. More selling. Something's not quite right. In the corner of my eye, I notice movement on the wires on the other screen.

"11:55 ISRAELI DEFENCE MINISTRY DENY JETS IN IRAN"

I click trade and sell small, joining the bandwagon but with half my usual size in markets like these. Prices stop and then surge again. On CNBC I hear the reporter now saying they're American jets and I'm in flames. I'm several ticks offside now and I can feel the sweat break out on my forehead. This could really run if panic sets in. I sit rigid, eyes glued to the screen, willing the prices not to go up further. It's the nightmare scenario every trader fears – *short and caught*! But wait, there's selling coming in again, and it's getting heavier. Prices start to fall back and soon they are back to where I sold. I cover my shorts, grateful to get out of jail free.

"12:05 'JETS ARE OURS' – IRANIAN DEFENCE MINSTER"

So says the wire. Prices plunge downwards as traders scramble to get out. Within moments the market is lower. It's just a huge flash in the pan; rumour quashed by fact.

I lean back in my chair, exhausted as the adrenalin ebbs.

13:00

My calendar spreads got filled during the maelstrom without me really noticing. The surge upward caused the fronts to outperform the backs and my order to sell Short Sterling H2Z2 is filled. In fact, it traded a full tick better. But I'm in the Z3H3 on the bid and that's looking good. I sit back and eat my sandwich and look forward to Non-Farm Payrolls. The market is looking for a good number with the TV pundits gunning for +250,000 new jobs. Yet the wide range of expectations between +150,000 to +300,000 reflect the potential volatility. Non-Farm Payrolls is a tricky one. You've got to watch for the revision to last month's figure. Last month's number was +240,000 and the market's looking for something not too dissimilar. You can trade anything over this number; Eurodollars, Euribor, Short Sterling even Swissy. They are all the same over this benchmark figure of the health of the world's biggest economy. I call up two tickets, one buy and one sell, both two ticks into the market depth. And sit waiting, the mouse tip twitching from buy to sell to buy …

"13:30 US NON-FARM PAYROLLS +64,000 VS LAST MONTH +210,000"

'Ding'. +64,000! An unbelievably low number. The global debt markets soar as the world tries to buy and the stock markets tank on recessionary worries. The TV pundits are frantic – hastily spinning their erroneous forecasts. David in risk breaks out in a cold sweat. The IT guys fan the overheating servers, muttering darkly about network traffic.

It's a bad number, and it's turning the market on its head. Bonds and Bunds bounce 60 ticks without touching the sides. Euribor spikes nine ticks before pausing and then continues upwards. I look at my fill, aghast. I only got a third of my order, the balance still being worked ten ticks lower. I delete it and offer out my position where it's snapped up voraciously. The markets are seesawing now but it's starting to stabilise. There's a sea change going on. The rogue payrolls number and its recessionary implications are replacing the former inflationary concerns as the key driver of the market. The yield curve is steepening as rate hike expectations are scaled back in the futures strip. The yields of the front STIR futures fall more quickly relative to the back months and the spread prices are moving upwards. It's a good time to be spreading now. I keenly buy calendars in Euribor and Short Sterling, but stick to the highly liquid front three and six-month calendars, knowing that I can always turn them round quickly, if necessary. They've been falling for the last few days as inflation worries pointed to higher rates but started to look sold out on the charts, almost as if they were looking for a catalyst to turn them around.

14:30

All the bond and STIR markets are up on the day now. Treasury officials come and go on the wires and TV, trying to explain the sudden weakness in the payroll number. The pundits reckon it's a one-off. The markets aren't buying that. The US economy has been holed beneath the water line and all hands are on deck.

"Have you seen that two-year bundle seller?" calls John, his eyes not leaving his screen.

The bid/offer spread can be wide on bundles, but I see this one is being offered down just a tick above the bid. That means that a buyer would be purchasing six out of the eight contracts on the bid price and paying the offer on the other two, assuming that all are trading on a half tick bid and offer. I scroll back up to the outrights and examine the white and red strips, carefully looking at the bid/offer spreads and particularly at the implied bid amounts in the back months. Sometimes, these can make the bundle look more attractive than it actually is, and what might look like an attractive purchase doesn't look so good when the implied support is removed by trades elsewhere. This looks good, though, particularly in such a firm market.

"What do you reckon?" I ask John.

"I think he's buying the credit spread on the back of all this event risk. He's selling out the bundles and buying Schatz, looking for the credit spread to widen." John replies.

I flick over to the news service and page their analytics. A hastily called-up chart shows the spread between the two-year European swaps over benchmark two-year bonds. It is clearly widening, reflecting the demand for quality.

"Well, I'm not taking the other side of that on," I say. Buying a bundle, however cheap, is a significant trade since it involves simultaneously buying all eight months. That's a lot of futures and traders like us need to spread it off somewhere, usually against the Schatz. But that would make us short the credit spread. Not a good place to be at the moment!

"I'm buying bundles against selling Swapnote," he replies. "Just wait for a decent bid in Swapnote to come in."

Good idea, I think to myself. There's virtually no credit difference between Swapnote and Euribor so it's the perfect contract to spread off against. Thanking John, I click and trade, buying bundles and selling Swapnote. I'll unwind it when the seller is finished.

16:00

The newswire flashes:

> " 'INCREASING PROBABILITY OF SECOND ROUND INFLATIONARY EFFECTS DUE TO HIGHER ENERGY PRICES' SAYS FEDERAL RESERVE CHAIRMAN AT INSTITUTE OF BANKERS LUNCHEON ADDRESS."

Prices fall. The rally is over. I've got positions and everything is spread off. But I'm nervous. Bunds give back ten ticks and STIRs three. The front months sell off more heavily than the backs and my spreads are looking wobbly. I've got my finger on the sell button but there are signs that the fall in prices is slowing. I didn't see that much selling going through the market, just a readjustment of prices to reflect the news and outright traders flattening their positions. The markets are caught between a rock and a hard place. On the one hand, inflation is raising its head, putting upward pressure on interest rates but, on the other hand, the payroll number has inflicted serious wounds. What does the market fear most: inflation or recession?

The answer seems to be the latter and the added effect of event risk from the Middle East seems to swing the balance. Prices start recovering and my positions look better. Prices continue to nudge a little higher and I start trimming my long spread holdings. There's still indecision in the market but our trading day is drawing to a close. Not in the US, though, source of the latest newswire comments. There's not much point in being over-exposed when markets can be influenced outside our trading hours, it will only lead to a sleepless night.

17:10

The markets are still twitching but I feel like I've fought my battle today. Looking around the room I can see traders packing up and logging off. Some of the guys are staying. They'll be here until late, chasing the futures around the world, addicted to the buzz.

I'm pleased with the day. It's been good and I'm leaving with more than I came in with. They say it's only ever borrowed from the market and I suppose the key to trading success is holding on to it and not giving it back.

I switch the screen off and head for the door. In a little over 12 hours I'll be back at the desk and it starts all over again …

Ten Rules for Trading STIR Futures

1. Understand what is driving the markets and causing the price action.

2. Be aware of the different risk-reward characteristics of STIR futures. Generally, spreads and strategies will always be lower risk than outrights. Spreads will become more volatile the greater the time between component expiries. Inter-contract spreads will be more volatile than intra-contract spreads.

3. Remember that inter-contract spreads can be multi-dimensional, being affected by credit, curve, interest rate and stub factors.

4. Fully understand the effects of implied pricing.

5. Remember that spreads, butterflies, condors, packs and bundles will usually be priced tighter by the market than by implied pricing. In faster moving markets, opportunities can exist in strategies, particularly those that are not subject to implied pricing (e.g. Liffe butterflies, condors, packs and bundles).

6. Use the spread matrix and butterflies as alternative ways to enter or exit trades.

7. Be aware of the effects of incentive schemes and rebates on total commissions.

8. Try to find a trading niche in the markets which balances the trader's propensity for risk against expectations of profit.

9. Maintain a healthy scepticism toward technical analysis and systems. Technical studies invariably look better in hindsight, due to their laggard nature; and predictors can often give the same signal for considerable periods of time. The simpler analyses, such as support and resistance, seem to be the most widely used and traders should be aware of their levels.

10. If the markets are tough to trade, just sit them out. Likewise with extremely volatile markets. Opportunities will always come around again.

Appendices

The Appendices contain the following data:

- A list of **STIR futures contracts** listed around the world

- **Contract specifications** for Eurodollar, Euribor, Short Sterling and Euroswiss STIR futures

- Links to the main **futures exchanges**

- Links to selected **clearing members**

- A list and links directive of **independent software vendors** (ISV)

- Links to **trading arcades**

- Graphs of **policy rate changes** (EUR, USD).

Data for the above can be also found at **www.stirfutures.co.uk**.

STIR Futures Contracts

A list of futures on short-term interest rates.

Table A.1 – Futures on short-term interest rates

Contract	Exchange	Country	Currency	Notional value	Notes
Eurodollar	CME LIFFE SGX	US	US Dollar	1,000,000	
1 Month LIBOR	CME	US	US Dollar	3,000,000	12 sequential months
Euribor	LIFFE EUREX	Europe	euro	1,000,000	
Short Sterling	LIFFE	UK	Pounds	500,000	
Euroswiss	LIFFE	Switzerland	Swiss Franc	1,000,000	
Euroyen	TFE LIFFE SGX CME	Japan	Yen	100,000,000	
BAX	Montreal exchange	Canada	Canadian Dollar	1,000,000	Three-month Canadian Bankers Acceptance futures
30 Day Interbank Cash	SFE	Australia	Australian Dollar	3,000,000	Out to 12 months only
90 Day Bank bills	SFE	Australia	Australian Dollar	1,000,000	Out to five years
3 month BUBOR	Budapest Stock exchange	Hungary	Forint	10,000,000	
91 day notional T Bills	NSE	India	Rupee	200,000	
KLIBOR	BURSA MALAYSIA	Malaysia	Ringgit	1,000,000	
NZ 90 day bank bills	SFE	New Zealand		1,000,000	
JIBAR	SAFEX	South Africa	Rand	1,000,000	
SEK STIBOR	OMX	Sweden	SEK	1,000,000	
Long ID	BM&F	Brazil	Real		Underlying asset is the 1 Day Interbank Deposit future expiring six months after expiry of this contract
1 Day Interbank Deposit	BM&F	Brazil	Real	100,000 (discounted)	Priced as an interest rate

Contract Specifications for Eurodollar, Euribor, Short Sterling and Euroswiss

Table A.2 – Contract specifications

Contract	Eurodollar	Euribor	Short Sterling	Euroswiss
Exchange	CME	Liffe	Liffe	Liffe
Notional Value/Unit of trading	$1,000,000	€1,000,000	£500,000	SFr 1,000,000
Delivery months	March, June, Sept, Dec, four serial, making a total of 40 delivery months	March, June, Sept, Dec + four serial months to a total of 24 delivery months	March, June, Sept, Dec + two serial months to a total of 22 delivery months	March, June, Sept, Dec, to a total of eight quarterly delivery months
Price quotation	100.00 minus rate of interest	100.00 minus rate of interest	100.00 minus rate of interest	100.00 minus rate of interest
Minimum price movement	0.005	0.005	0.01	0.01
Tick value	$12.50	€12.50	£12.50	SFr25
Last trading day	Second business day preceding the third Wednesday of the contract month	10.00 – Two business days prior to the third Wednesday of the delivery month	11:00 – Third Wednesday of the delivery month	11:00 – Two business days prior to the third Wednesday of the delivery month
Delivery day	Two business days after the last trading day	First business day after the last trading day	First business day after the last trading day	First business day after the last trading day

Exchanges

Liffe
globalderivatives.nyx.com or search 'NYSE Liffe'

CME Group
www.cmegroup.com

Eurex
www.eurexchange.com

Some Clearing Members

ADM Investor Services International Ltd
www.admisi.com

ABN AMRO Clearing N. V.
www.abnamroclearing.com

GH Financials Ltd
www.ghf.co.uk

The Kyte Group Ltd
www.kytegroup.com

Marex Spectron Services
www.marexspectron.com

TRX Futures
www.trxfutures.com

Independent Software Vendors (ISV)

Visit **www.stirfutures.co.uk** for links or search for:

Actant Ltd	Object Trading
BLOOMBERG L.P.	Onixs
Broadway Technology	ORC Software
Charm B.V.	Patsystems
Communicating Ltd	Rithmic LLC
Comunytek Consultores	Riverrun Systems Ltd.
CQG, Inc.	Rolfe & Nolan
Cunningham Trading Systems	RTS Realtime Systems Group
Deriva B.V.	Sol-3
Digit Base A.G.	Spread Intelligence
EasyScreen Ltd.	Stellar Trading Systems
Eccoware	SunGard Front Arena
FFastFill	SunGard Global Trading
Fidessa	Super Derivatives
FMR Computers & Software Ltd.	Syntel Financial Software
iCubic A.G.	Tradesense
Ingalys	Trading Screen
ION Trading	Trading Technologies International, Inc.
JJ Informatica Financiera S.L.	Ullink

Trading Arcades

Visit www.stirfutures.co.uk for links or
www.trade2win.com/traderpedia/Trading_Arcade_Index

Key Policy Rate Changes (EUR, USD)

EUR

Fig. A.1 – European Central Bank (ECB) euro zone interest rate changes (Main Refinancing Rate) since 2000

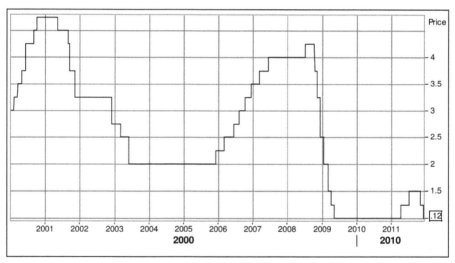

Source: Reuters

USD

Federal Reserve (FED) US interest rate changes (Federal Funds Target rate) since 2000

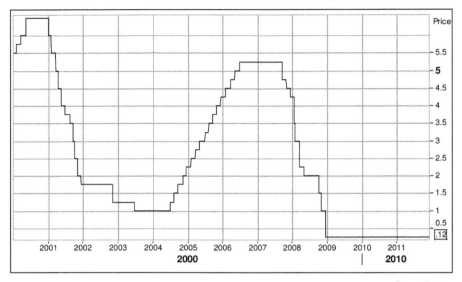

Source: Reuters

Bibliography

Available discounted at books.global-investor.com

The Eurodollar Futures and Options Handbook
Galen Burghardt (McGraw-Hill)

Excellent but technical book, specifically aimed at the US markets. Seminal text for term spreads.

The Treasury Bond Basis
Galen Burghardt and Terry Belton (McGraw-Hill)

Seminal text for bond basis trading. Good sections on bond futures but aimed solely at US market.

The Futures Bond Basis
Moorad Choudhry (Securities Institute)

Good bond basis book geared towards UK market.

Mastering Financial Calculations
Bob Steiner (*Financial Times* Series)

Easy to understand and nicely presented equations.

No Bull
Michael Steinhardt (Wiley)

A lighter read, about the trading times of top hedge fund manager Michael Steinhardt.

Market Wizards
Jack Schwager (Marketplace Books)

Entertaining collection of interviews with top traders – see also *New Market Wizards* by same author.

Interest Rate Markets
Siddhartha Jha (Wiley)

Good, current overview of interest rate markets.

Trading the Fixed Income, Inflation and Credit Markets
Neil C. Schofield, Troy Bowler (Wiley)

Excellent book on fixed income relative value trading.

Index

C

D

W

Y

Z

Milton Keynes UK
Ingram Content Group UK Ltd.
UKHW032142061224
451964UK00003B/45

9 780857 192196